Adaptation in the Age of Media Convergence

Adaptation in the Age of Media Convergence

Edited by Johannes Fehrle and Werner Schäfke-Zell

Routledge
Taylor & Francis Group
LONDON AND NEW YORK

The publication of this book resulted from a conference funded by the Freiburg Institute of Advanced Studies (FRIAS) at the Albert-Ludwigs-Universität, Freiburg.

First published in 2019 by Amsterdam University Press Ltd.

Published 2025 by Routledge
4 Park Square, Milton Park, Abingdon, Oxon OX14 4RN
605 Third Avenue, New York, NY 10158

Routledge is an imprint of the Taylor & Francis Group, an informa business

ISBN: 9789462983663 (hbk)
ISBN: 9781041175254 (pbk)
ISBN: 9781003690436 (ebk)
NUR 670

Cover illustration: Street art "Girl with a Pearl Earring" by blub #Lartesanuotarre. Photo by Johannes Fehrle (www.fehrle-photography.com)

Cover design: Coördesign, Leiden

DOI 10.5117/9789462983663

For Product Safety Concerns and Information please contact our EU representative:
GPSR@taylorandfrancis.com
Taylor & Francis Verlag GmbH, Kaufingerstraße 24, 80331 München, Germany

Table of Contents

1. Introduction: Adaptation in a Convergence Environment

Johannes Fehrle

An increased interest in adaptation studies in the early 21st century has generated countless discussions about rethinking adaptations as well as the field of adaptation studies as a whole. The impression has often been voiced, for instance by Thomas Leitch in his essay for the inaugural issue of the journal *Adaptation*, that adaptation studies is "at a crossroads," in which its methodology and material are in transition from the discipline's humble novel-to-film-studies beginnings to a broader, if somewhat unclear, future.[1] As part of a moment in the field's history, in which scholars repeatedly state ambitious research agendas, Linda Hutcheon has likewise described adaptation studies as moving "well beyond [its] familiar film/performance focus" and on to readings that highlight the politics of our time, the "indigenization" of adaptations, and approaches that question notions of priority and anteriority in unprecedented ways.[2]

There is, however, another major change – the elephant in the room of adaptation studies, so to speak: since adaptation, at least in its most common understanding, describes the transposition of a story or its elements from one medium to another, it is necessarily bound to questions of mediality and remediation.[3] Therefore, one of the most important new developments in adaptation studies is constituted by the shift in the global mediascape in light of the rise of digital media since the 1980s and the spread of the internet

1 Thomas Leitch, "Review Article. Adaptation Studies at a Crossroads," *Adaptation* 1, no. 1 (2008): 63–77.

2 Linda Hutcheon, "Moving Forward: The Next Step in Adaptation Studies." In *Adaptation and American Studies: Perspectives on Research and Teaching, With an Afterword by Linda Hutcheon*, ed. Nassim Winnie Balestrini (Heidelberg: Winter, 2011), 213, 217.

3 For my example of a "traditional" or narrow understanding of adaptation, I use Irina Rajewsky's definition of adaptation as "medial transposition." Irina Rajewsky, "Intermediality, Intertextuality, and Remediation: A Literary Perspective on Intermediality." In*termédialités* 6 (2005): 51.

Fehrle, J. and W. Schäfke, *Adaptation in the Age of Media Convergence*,
Taylor & Francis Group, 2019
DOI 10.5117/9789462983663_CH01

since the 1990s. This transformation amounts to nothing less than a shift from a largely analog, localized, image- and text-based "Gutenberg Galaxy"[4] to a more rapidly disseminating mixed analog-digital environment. It is a moment that forces us, once again, to re-examine notions of authorship, control, audiences, sources and adaptations, as well as interactions between medium and consumer, or between consumers and producers.[5] This volume sets out to explore how these shifts relate to adaptation studies and what they mean for the field. It does so by examining new forms of adaptations and their cultural embeddedness both theoretically and analytically, with the help of a range of texts constituting some of the major new forms of adaptations and adaptation environments that have arisen in the wake of the rise of digital media. In doing so, the contributions examine not only new texts and new media themselves, but the political, technological, social, legal, and economic structures that have shaped them and their being in the cultural world.

The contributions in this collection make clear that this scholarly perspective needs to do more than take into account the shifts in the media studied: it must also examine the ways in which the complex relations always involved in adaptation processes (e.g. the unstable relation between "author," producer, adapter, rights holders, text(s), and audiences, to name just a few) have become further complicated in convergence culture. As part of this complication, new questions that were often relegated to the margins in the analysis of more traditional adaptations have come to the fore. This is why convergence culture, an environment in which "old and new media collide,"[6] is of particular interest to adaptation scholars: it highlights in new ways the complex interrelations around texts as well as their critical reception and interpretation that have been raised in adaptation studies since its formation into a more cohesive, more independent field in the last decade. A convergence environment, for instance, further destabilizes received notions of anteriority, authorship, and reception by opening the object of inquiry to texts that differ from older ones that were less physically mutable.[7]

4 Marshall McLuhan, *The Gutenberg Galaxy: The Making of Typographic Man* (Toronto: University of Toronto Press, 1968).

5 Axel Bruns has coined the terms "produser" and "produsage" to highlight the blurring of the boundaries between passive consumption and active participation in a digital environment in which non-commercial actors can relatively easily create and share content online. Axel Bruns, *Blogs, Wikipedia, Second Life, and Beyond: From Production to Produsage* (New York: Lang, 2008).

6 Henry Jenkins, *Convergence Culture: Where Old and New Media Collide* (New York: New York University Press, 2006).

7 Observations about the instability of "source" text and "adaptation" have become a critical commonplace in adaptation studies over the past decade with authors drawing on intertextuality studies, Derridean deconstruction, or Bakhtinian heteroglossia to complicate notions of

With approaches that are geared towards analyzing such phenomena, adaptation studies can shed a new light on the material and the dynamics studied in convergence or transmedia studies, as it applies its comparative mode of analysis to different media. One of the strengths of adaptation studies is its eclectic mix of methods, from intertextuality and poststructuralist literary and media theory to cultural studies. These are applied to ask questions about textual relations, mediality, authorship, authority, and authenticity, to name only a few key concerns of pre-digital adaptation studies. However, as the various contributors to this volume show, a perspective that looks at texts through the dual lens of transmedia and adaptation studies does not end at rephrasing questions that have been conceptualized in poststructuralist and intertextual approaches to adaptation studies. Rather, the introduction of a wide range of new media, production, and reception contexts results not only in a significant change in the material under examination, but must – if we take media, mediality, and their different relations to production, authorship, and audiences seriously – also alter the way in which we study such adaptations and transmedia texts. Some new media, for instance, are at least potentially less narratively linear, e.g. web-based adaptations or recent video games. Other forms of adaptation, such as fanfiction, shift the center of creation away from rights holders and professional creators (however that term is defined and whichever gray areas it encompasses). These agents were once the main providers and facilitators of content and, seemingly by definition, were seen to hold the authority over which adaptations were produced and what they looked like. To be sure, such professionals still retain a central position, but today's increasingly dynamic network of production, reception, and distribution of digital or digitalized media are transforming the playing field. This process is taking place not in the sense of the straightforward democratization hailed in the early stages of the internet, however, but in more complex and often more contradictory ways. Moreover, shifts in the global economy on the one hand and the easier connectability between media, on the other, facilitate the rise of new connected textual corpuses on the side of rights holders and licensors and, on the side of consumers, different relations to these texts become possible that open up the potential for new (creative) interactions.

By the same token, remixes and mashups, new forms of parodies and rewritings, and many other offshoots of this digitally networked dynamic can productively be conceptualized as adaptations. Many of these are

textual stability, fidelity, and authorial control even in the case of comparatively straightforward adaptations from, say, novel to film.

produced for and within fan cultures that are themselves in processes of transformation, with some becoming bigger and more accepted in the cultural mainstream (as suggested by major newspapers like *The Guardian* devoting articles to fan theories about the newest developments in *Game of Thrones*), others increasingly diversifying, and still others forming niche groups that stand not only in relation to one another but have been integrated into commercial processes through media content that follows an intensified "narrowcasting" logic.[8] Fan-based and largely fan-targeted adaptations, which were still somewhat hermetic when Camille Bacon-Smith and others produced their early work in fan studies, are now shared in communities that have become much more accessible.[9] *In toto*, the rise of digital media and the effect it has had on patterns of production, reception, and interaction in a convergence environment, in which new and older media coexist and interact, quite possibly constitutes the single most important development in the material we study as adaptation and (trans)media scholars since the advent of film and photography in the 19th century.

The Blurring of Practices... and Definitions

Looking at texts in a convergence environment from an adaptation studies angle (or at adaptations from a transmedia perspective) raises questions of how the concepts of adaptation and convergence culture are connected, where they can be productively brought into contact, how far they might overlap, and where they should best be kept separate to retain their respective analytical strengths. Such questions are not only difficult (some would say impossible) to answer but also decidedly unpopular in an academic environment and a field like adaptation studies that remains deeply committed to a poststructuralist deconstruction of categories.

To be sure, neither this introduction not the collection offer final answers to the question of definitions, differences, and overlaps, in part due to its contributors' diverse materials and perspectives. One position that all contributions share, however, is the conviction that the more fluid and dynamic ways in which texts are being appropriated and re-appropriated in a convergent environment necessitate an expansion of the concept of

8 Cf. Derek Johnson, *Media Franchising: Creative License and Collaboration in the Culture Industries* (New York: New York University Press, 2013), 5.

9 Camille Bacon-Smith, *Enterprising Women: Television Fandom and the Creation of Popular Myth* (Philadelphia: University of Pennsylvania Press, 1991).

adaptation beyond the original notion of a more or less unidirectional transposition from one medium to another. This conceptualization, which was always problematic, promises finally to be laid to rest by the more dynamic media environment of convergence culture, as the simultaneous shifts in the mediascape and in the field of adaptation studies have led to a marked increase in the type of processes and texts that many scholars (including the contributors to this volume) are willing to regard as adaptations. These scholars point to shifts in the media environment and new textual (inter)relations that call into question what seemed a relatively intuitive and clear-cut process of "translation" between neatly separated media and practices.

To exemplify the blurring of conceptual boundaries that undermines all sharp distinctions, including those between the three analytical categories I will propose below, we can turn to transmedia franchises and how their worlds are constituted. There is today a greater tendency than in a predigital environment by both intellectual property holders and fans to form interconnected clusters of texts that explore what Matt Hills has called the "hyperdiegesis" of a fictional creation, i.e. a "vast and detailed narrative space, only a fraction of which is ever directly seen or encountered."[10] With an eye to official materials being created for and distributed across multiple media platforms, critics have labeled this phenomenon variously as "transmedia storytelling" (Jenkins), "transmedia worlds" (Lisbeth Klastrup and Susanna Tosca), "world-building" (Mark J.P. Wolf), "franchise storytelling" (Clare Parody), or – closing the circle between convergence, franchise practices, and adaptation studies – "transmedia adaptations" (Siobhan O'Flynn).[11]

10 Matt Hills, *Fan Cultures* (London: Routledge, 2002), 137, cited in Dan Hassler-Forest, *Science Fiction, Fantasy, and Politics: Transmedia World-Building beyond Capitalism* (London: Rowman & Littlefield, 2016), 3. On the prevalence of transmedia narratives, cf. Dan Hassler-Forest's observation that "we've seen how transmedia franchising and world-building has really surged over the past two decades, to the point where fantastic fiction seems to dominate the media industries and our cultural landscape more and more." In Henry Jenkins, "Science Fiction World Building in a Capitalist Society: An Interview with Dan Hassler-Forest (Part One)," *Confessions of an Aca-Fan. The Official Weblog of Henry Jenkins*, March 22, 2007, accessed February 15, 2019, http://henryjenkins.org/2016/09/science-fiction-world-building-in-a-capitalist-society-an-interview-with-dan-hassler-forest-part-one.html.

11 Jenkins, *Convergence Culture*. Lisbeth Klastrup and Susana Tosca, "Transmedial Worlds – Rethinking Cyberworld Design." In *Proceedings International Conference on Cyberworlds 2004*, ed. Masayuki Nakajima, Yoshinori Hatori, and Alexei Sourin (Los Alamitos: IEEE Computer Society, 2004), 409–416. Mark J.P. Wolf, *Building Imaginary Worlds: The Theory and History of Sub-Creation* (New York: Routledge, 2012). Clare Parody, "Adaptation Essay Prize Winner: Franchising/Adaptation," *Adaptation* 4, no. 2 (2011): 210–218. Siobhan O'Flynn, "Designing for the Interactant: How Interactivity Impacts on Adaptation." In *Adaptation and American Studies: Perspectives on Research*

Many instances of what these critics have labeled as transmedia storytelling, world-building, or transmedia worlds, are not adaptations in the narrow sense of an attempt to recreate existing stories in a new medium. Rather, they expand on the original instantiation of a storyworld, expanding its hyperdiegesis as they adapt, transform, and add to what Klastrup and Tosca call the "core elements" of a fictional world.[12] In most cases of transmedia storytelling, "a process where integral elements of a fiction get dispersed systematically across multiple delivery channels for the purpose of creating a unified and coordinated entertainment experience" and even more clearly in less tightly orchestrated transmedia expansions, we have texts which relate to each other, in some cases depend on each other, and often mark this relation very clearly and explicitly.[13] Despite the linked feature of intertextuality, Jenkins has nevertheless excluded adaptations from his concept of transmedia storytelling, insisting on a distinction "between 'extensions' to the core narrative or the fictional universe and adaptations which simply move content from one medium to another."[14]

In contrast to Jenkins, the contributions in this volume suggest that there are benefits to conceptualizing transmedia franchising and the related

and Teaching, With an Afterword by Linda Hutcheon, ed. Nassim Winnie Balestrini (Heidelberg: Winter, 2011), 83.
It is worth considering to what extent the separation between official products and ancillary fan productions, which at least implicitly underlies most critics' focus on official (i.e. commercial) creation, is helpful and where it is either unnecessary or even hinders our understanding of texts and practices. I discuss this question below with regard to fanfictions, but it seems worth pointing out here that one of the effects of concepts such as "transmedia storytelling" is a championing of commercial productions. Mark Wolf, for instance, only mentions fan creations towards the end of *Building Imaginary Worlds*. While he acknowledges the long history of "unauthorized sequels" and muses that such "fan productions can be seen as an extension of what audiences do all the time while experiencing a world; filling in gaps as world gestalten occur," Wolf nevertheless ultimately relegates them to the margins. Brushing fan creations, engagement, and interpretation off, he proclaims that such "theories and gap-filling ideas" are thought by "many fans" to be "canon, when they actually [!?] are not" (Wolf, *Building*, 279). What is clear from Wolf's wording is that he grants commercial culture a primacy that de-authorizes fan work and seems to allow fan creations to become canon only when it is officially recognized and even then it "is usually only accepted at a lower level of canon" (Ibid., 280).

12 Klastrup and Tosca, "Transmedial Worlds," 413.

13 Henry Jenkins, "Transmedia Storytelling 101," *Confessions of an Aca-Fan. The Official Weblog of Henry Jenkins*, March 22, 2007, accessed February 15, 2019, http://henryjenkins.org/2007/03/transmedia_storytelling_101.html. The concept of transmedia storytelling has been contentious from the beginning, cf. from a narratological perspective: Marie Laure-Ryan, "Transmedia Storytelling: Industry Buzzword of New Narrative Experience?" *Storyworlds: A Journal of Narrative Studies* 7.2 (2015): 1–19.

14 Henry Jenkins, "The Aesthetics of Transmedia: In Response to David Bordwell (Part One)," *Confessions of an Aca-Fan. The Official Weblog of Henry Jenkins*, September 10, 2009, accessed February 15, 2019, http://henryjenkins.org/2009/09/the_aesthetics_of_transmedia_i.html.

building of transmedia worlds from an adaptation studies perspective. Perhaps the main benefit of such an approach is that we do not need to draw a line between transmedial clusters of connected texts that expand and adaptations that retell, a line that risks becoming pedantic and counter-intuitive in light of current production practices. To take only one example: should we treat the various versions of the *LEGO Star Wars* video games as adaptations because they allow us to reenact the plot of the various movies somewhat "faithfully" (to use that loaded term), while disregarding that they do so in a manner modified by their action-adventure genre, the fact that the characters are now LEGO figures in an environment made of LEGO blocks, and that they poke fun at the movies through slapstick elements? These alterations essentially transform the genre of a movie like *Star Wars* from epic adventure to comic farce. If we focus exclusively on the medial transposition of plot, character, and setting, we would have to include the *LEGO Star Wars* games as adaptations on the basis of their rather direct transfer of main points of the story and characters – and this certainly makes sense. However, following the same narrow definition, we would have to exclude the older video games *Dark Forces* (1995) or *Jedi Knight: Dark Forces II* (1997), which are much closer to the original trilogy in terms of atmosphere, genre, and representation of the fictional universe, because their plot and characters are not part of any of the films. If we turn to Linda Hutcheon's definition of adaptation (or Julie Sanders' rather similar one), we can also find the basis for a wider definition: both games transpose "a recognizable other work," they involve "a creative *and* an interpretive act of appropriating/salvaging," and "an extended intertextual engagement with the adapted work."[15] They therefore qualify as adaptations, as do many fan works which similarly expand the hyperdiegesis.

As this example shows, boundaries between adaptations and franchise expansions are blurry and bound to become artificial or even counterintuitive and counterproductive in cases in which different instantiations of a fictional franchise draw on the same storyworld. They furthermore, at least implicitly, exclude most fan creations, thereby reintroducing a cultural hierarchy through the back door. Rather than stick to a preconceived notion of transposition versus expansion (which, moreover, ignores that every adaptation necessarily expands the story it adapts), we should instead ask ourselves why we look at text A, which directly identifies a novel or film as a primary source text, but not at text B, which is as clearly connected to that film, novel, or comic, being linked textually and paratextually to

15 Hutcheon, *Theory*, 8. Julie Sanders, *Adaptation and Appropriation* (London: Routledge, 2006).

the same franchise and fictional universe. As the contributions in this collection suggest, there is, in fact, much to be gained by widening both our area of inquiry to include convergence texts and our understanding of what constitutes an adaptation. As I want to suggest, a way to avoid niggling discussions such as the one outlined above and to catch all contributions collected in this volume is to reconceptualize adaptation in a convergence environment in a way that the elements that can be adapted include not only plot, character, and other traditional story elements, but also *storyworlds*.

Media Convergence: The Transformation of Texts, Contexts, and Audiences

Before going into how new media and the new convergence environment impact on adaptations and transmedia texts, it seems appropriate to re-examine Henry Jenkins' concept of convergence culture and how it relates to adaptations. Whereas convergence culture results from the rise of new media, Jenkins' discussion already indicates that its impact transcends mere technological innovation. To begin with, he defines convergence culture not in terms of new media fully replacing older media, but as the coexistence and mutual influencing of old and new media. This in turn creates new forms of texts and interactions between participants in the creation, consumption, and interpretation of these texts. But technology is only one aspect of this transitory moment. As Jenkins writes, a convergence environment is one in which "old and new media collide, where grassroots and corporate media intersect, where the power of the media producer and the power of the media consumer interact in unpredictable ways."[16] While convergence thus originates from a shift towards digital media, for Jenkins research should include the actors, particularly recipients and their interactions with texts, with each other, and with professional creators. After all, "[c]onvergence occurs within the brains of individual consumers and through their social interactions with others."[17]

This focus on consumer reception and interaction to complement questions of mediality is crucial. It serves as a reminder of the more openly participatory nature of cultural production and reception in a convergence environment that understands new media as not only part of a new text base with new medial allowances and ontologies but part of a new *praxis*: what people do with texts and how they do it is at least as important as what the texts

16 Jenkins, *Convergence Culture*, 2.
17 Ibid., 3.

themselves do. This approach can serve as an important corrective for adaptation studies, which has too often remained at the level of comparative textual analysis. Jenkins' concept thus challenges adaptation studies to approach not only texts but the contexts of their creation, distribution, and reception.

It is in this vein that the contributors to this volume situate their theoretical models and approach their case studies. They avoid the temptation of reading the texts as traditional adaptations that simply add new media into the mix and situate them instead in their cultural framework while also taking into account the dynamic interactions of their environments, be that YouTube cover culture (Constandinides), showrunners interacting with fans (Poore), fanfiction and mashup writers who turn towards commercial publishing (Soller; Voigts), or the cultural and legal frameworks in which the media industry operates (Schäfke).

Considering new trends in convergence culture and connecting them to previous research positions, this collection suggests that the transformations of media and the media industries most relevant for adaptation studies can be described as falling into three main developments:

1. the rise of new media as containers for adapted stories (e.g. computer games, networked text bodies such as wikis, online versions of older media like video or text formats, etc.) and the novel potentialities they bring with them (e.g. a greater interactivity between user and text, an ability to connect texts more closely across different media, means of expression that converge across new and old media, and so forth);
2. the transformation of audiences, regarding both their willingness and their ability to participate, and their self-conception as empowered, contributing consumers vis-à-vis media producers;
3. the transformation of production, distribution, and marketing structures under globalized neoliberal capitalism, including the rise of a franchising logic impacting (adaptive) text clusters in their form, content, production, marketing, and reception. The spread of franchised expansions that connect text corpora can take the form that Jenkins has called "transmedia storytelling," but a looser connection is much more common. Following Derek Johnson, Claire Parody, and others, I will call this "franchising" or "media franchising."[18]

18 Ibid., 95–134. Jenkins, "Transmedia Storytelling 101;" Johnson, *Media Franchising*; Parody, "Franchising/Adaptation," 210–218.

Going through these developments one by one, the most obvious and basic novelty is without doubt constituted by new (digital) media. Various internet platforms or digital entertainment formats such as video games offer new outlets into which texts from older media can be adapted. This can happen in more or less traditional ways, e.g. by retelling a plot in a different medium – with all the complications and dimensions adaptation theory continues to spell out for such seemingly simple "retellings" even in more stable, "old" media – or it can take new forms that build more strongly on these media's affordances. Whereas older media likewise depend on reader or viewer interaction in the form of interpretation as well as more material, embodied interaction with a text, digital media "do not simply place us in front of a static text; they situate us inside a system that continually produces a dynamic object."[19] Therefore, one thing that is new about many of these new media forms is that they offer ways of interaction between consumer and "text" that transcend those of older media. This can take the form of interaction with the work in its narrow sense, as is the case in video games in which users are allowed to impact on the ways in which they experience the story (at least to the extent that games' rule-based structure allows for), or on a broader textual level, as in the case of platforms which allow participation or immediate feedback (as, for instance, in the YouTube covers, which Costas Constandinides examines in his contribution).[20] In many of these media, the consumer's influence on the unfolding of the text goes beyond the insistence of poststructuralist and reader-response inspired adaptation theory that recipients are always and by necessity co-creators, even in media which allegedly put them in the role of "passive" recipients (the classic examples being television or film, particularly as conceptualized by apparatus theory). As such, new media facilitate new ways of engagement and new forms of storytelling, and this is one direction in which adaptation theory in a convergence environment can orient itself.

In one early attempt to integrate the increasingly prominent modes of interactivity into an adaptation framework, Linda Hutcheon proposed the concept of "modes of engagement" to address the various ways in which users interact with a variety of media. She suggests three modes of engagement:

19 Marie-Laure Ryan, "Digital Media." In *Narrative across Media: The Languages of Storytelling*, ed. Marie-Laure Ryan (Lincoln, NE: University of Nebraska Press, 2004), 329–330.

20 Here I invoke, and somewhat bastardizing, the distinction of work and text introduced by Roland Barthes in "From Work to Text." In *Image-Music-Text* (London: Fontana, 1977), 155–164. Whereas Barthes is interested in the role of the reader of traditional printed works and their intertextual involvement with it, participatory culture adds to this possibilities of actual textual environments and ways of interaction, such as recombining, commenting etc.

telling, showing, and the interactive mode, which she finds among other media in novels (telling), film and TV (showing), and video games and theme parks (interactive). Hutcheon argues that while "no one mode is inherently good at doing one thing and not another [...], each has at its disposal different means of expression – media and genres – and so can aim to achieve certain things better than others."[21] This fruitful area of research is one in which adaptation studies can build on related fields such as transmedial narratology, for just as new media call for a new narrative theory, so too do more interactive media necessitate a rethinking of adaptation studies. This new direction in adaptation studies will, however, also require critical perspectives from other disciplines, such as game studies, which have developed alongside these media and can therefore shed light on their particularities. In order to fully grasp what such new media adaptations do, newer approaches have to challenge and complement categories and ways of thinking developed in the more traditional, hermeneutically oriented, narratological, literary or film studies approaches that still dominate adaptation studies.[22]

Secondly, the networked digital media environment of convergence culture facilitates fan creations in unprecedented forms and numbers that range from fanfiction and videos to machinima (videos or films created using computer

21 Linda Hutcheon with Siobhan O'Flynn, *A Theory of Adaptation*, 2nd ed. (New York: Routledge, 2013), 22, 24.

22 In 2004, Marie-Laure Ryan attempted to answer the question "Will New Media Produce New Narratives?". She highlighted three shifts in narrative that follow the rise of new media: "new models of user involvement and new things to do with narrative," "new ways to present stories," as well as the challenge of finding the best fit between a medium and the "form and substance of the narrative content" best suited for that medium (Marie-Laure Ryan, "Will New Media Produce New Narratives?" in *Narrative across Media: The Languages of Storytelling*, ed. Marie-Laure Ryan (Lincoln, NE: University of Nebraska Press, 2004), 354–356). Ten years later, Ryan and Jan-Noël Thon collected attempts to formulate a "media-conscious narratology" to meet these demands (Marie-Laure Ryan and Jan-Noël Thon, eds., *Storyworlds across Media: Toward a Media-Conscious Narratology* (Lincoln: University of Nebraska Press, 2014)), a project which Thon has since extended into a monograph (Jan-Noël Thon, *Transmedial Narratology and Contemporary Media Culture* (Lincoln: University of Nebraska Press, 2016)). While such attempts at developing a transmedial or media conscious narratology are, without doubt, productive, an approach that focuses primarily or even exclusively on narrative may produce its own blind spots for an analysis of media that work not only, and sometimes not even primarily, through narrative. This is a point I explore in my attempt to take seriously the media potentiality of video games and their ludic quality and to caution adaptation scholars against reading the medium from a perspective that looks only at representations (Johannes Fehrle, "Gaming into the *Heart of Darkness*: Adapting Conrad/Coppola," *South Atlantic Review* 80, no. 3–4 (2016): 234–253). Taking a different approach, Werner Schäfke-Zell has highlighted the challenges and chances of examining video games as texts from a philological perspective in Werner Schäfke, "Videospiele als Text aus der Perspektive der Editionswissenschaft," *Zeitschrift für Semiotik* 32 (2010): 343–353.

graphics engines, usually of video games), mashups, and countless other forms of user engagement with commercial and non-commercial fictional creations, an engagement that, in turn, also influences the logics and aesthetics of commercial creations. This kind of participation is not a new phenomenon, but rather, as Martin Butler argues, "has been an integral part, if not a defining characteristic of popular culture."[23] Nevertheless, it has become more widespread, visible, and accepted in recent years. For this reason, fan culture needs to be taken into account to gain a full perspective on the range of texts and adaptations in convergence environments, as well as what people do with them.

Looking at transmedia phenomena from an adaptation studies perspective raises the question of where it is helpful to treat texts as adaptations and where applying a different framework may be more productive. The transformations of audiences and audience positions force us to think through how to reformulate our understanding of adaptation in order to do justice to this new cultural and medial environment while maintaining a certain sharpness of our critical focus and tools of analysis. One crucial difference in examining fan-created vis-à-vis commercial adaptations is that the goal of fan adaptations is usually not the monetary one of industrial productions. Fan creation instead participates in an alternative economy that traditionally defines itself as a "gift economy." This makes fan culture a social space that functions according to a different symbolic economy. While fans welcome corporate recognition to an extent, many are suspicious of attempts to monetize their creative force in ways that are too openly commercial or that enforce restrictions violating the field's rules.[24] The reflection on various motivations behind the production of texts, as well as the unwritten rules by which they are made, shared, and consumed, are only some aspects in relation to which fan creations are different. They nevertheless point both to productive new questions for adaptation studies and to the questions raised above: which texts generate productive new questions and insights when they are conceptualized as adaptations (and hence approached from an adaptation studies' angle), and where are texts more usefully conceptualized under a different concept, such as "appropriation,"[25] or a separate part of convergence culture that does not benefit from an adaptation studies perspective?

23 Martin Butler, "Net-Works: Collaborative Models of Cultural Production in Web 2.0 Contexts." In *Precarious Alliances: Cultures of Participation in Print and Other Media*, ed. Martin Butler, Albrecht Hausmann, and Anton Kirchhofer (Bielefeld: transcript, 2016), 19.

24 Cf. Roberta Pearson, "Fandom in the Digital Era," *Popular Communication* 8, no. 1 (2010): 84–95.

25 Sanders, *Adaptation and Appropriation*.

As Julie Sanders has argued, adaptation "signals a relationship with an informing source text or original," whereas appropriation "frequently affects a more decisive journey away from the informing source into a wholly new cultural product and domain." In this sense, one could ask what lies behind the classification of fanfictions as adaptation or appropriation. Such texts, while they announce their relationship with a source text paratextually, could, in some cases, be argued to move the characters, settings, and so forth "into a wholly new cultural product and domain." Far from reinstating preconceived boundaries between official and unofficial (and by implication more or less valid) adaptations, we should rather ask what is gained and what is overlooked by regarding e.g. Watson/Holmes slash fiction, i.e. fanfiction that depicts a homosexual relationship between Sherlock Holmes and Dr Watson, as adaptation as opposed to appropriation (or vice versa)? Such fan works establish a clear relationship to an original – often the BBC show *Sherlock* (2010–) – but transform it according to the rules of their community. But does this mean that their rewriting no longer "remains ostensibly" *Sherlock* and therefore falls out of Sanders' definition of adaptation?[26] If not, where do they move into the territory of appropriation or beyond it? Should we even care? What critical benefit and analytical sharpness can we draw from such a distinction? And finally, where does our question come from: are economic interests, the authorial or corporate control over a text, central for our question or do we simply perpetuate a certain cultural hierarchy surrounding "official" texts? Why should we accept Bollywood adaptations of Jane Austen, which transform the text to fit generic patterns and audience expectations, but not fan adaptations, which likewise transform a fiction according to dominant genre conventions, merely subcultural and less recognized ones like the slash or hurt/comfort genre?[27] Rather than trying to (re-)establish a boundary between official texts that remain "faithful" and unofficial (and by implication less valuable) fan works, a distinction that has haunted mainstream discussions of fandom for too long, the goal needs to be to see what is gained from discussing different fan works as acts of adaptation.

26 Ibid., 26.

27 On the point of pornographic (fan) adaptations and the generic questions of locating them, see Kyle Meikle, "Pornographic Adaptation: Parody, Fan Fiction, and the Limits of Genre," *Journal of Adaptation in Film & Performance* 8, no. 2 (2015): 123–140. On slash fiction and its relation to official products more broadly, as well as the different questions fan studies raises when studying media franchises, see e.g. Vera Cuntz-Leng, *Harry Potter que(e)r: Eine Filmsaga im Spannungsfeld von Queer Reading, Slash-Fandom und Fantasyfilmgenre* (Bielefeld: transcript, 2015).

One instance where adaptation studies can clearly benefit from fan studies are cases in which audience participation generates new forms and means of expression, which can then re-enter commercial culture, as the very different examples of E.L. James and Cassandra Clare, mashup novels, and *The LEGO Movie* discussed by Soller, Voigts, and Goggin make clear. Yet again, context is essential. Whereas participatory culture introduces new modes and forms of interaction, their integration into commercial culture sometimes reduces them merely to a simulation of a participatory ethos, gestures of participation ironically broken, decontextualized, and fed into a marketing machine that makes them fall short of the more flexible and processual aspects of fan creations. Such examinations hint at an aesthetic and economic entanglement of commercial and fan culture that is also the focus of some recent work in fan studies.

Fan studies has significantly complicated the view of fans as a resistant community operating against those in power or a wholly independent field operating according to its own subcultural capital. Instead, scholars now examine fandoms as intricately, and often contradictorily, interwoven with economies of production and distribution that partly question and partly contribute to major media companies' economic mechanisms. Moreover, fan communities uphold the social status quo in some areas while questioning it elsewhere.[28] A perspective that treats as its subject matter fannish or "audience-driven adaptations"[29] therefore needs to take into account the multiple and sometimes contradictory layers of legal, technological, economic, and cultural dynamics that order and regulate the dialogue and exchanges between fan culture and the media industries.

Finally, the third major direction for adaptation studies in a convergent environment is related to and overlaps with the two tendencies already outlined. Over the last few years, a number of what Siobhan O'Flynn calls "multiple, transmedia adaptations" have emerged. She refers to texts that have been adapted into multiple media in rapid succession. O'Flynn uses Philip Pullman's *The Golden Compass* as an example, but the list can easily be expanded to include the countless products in the *Star Wars*, *The Lord of*

28 Sophie Einwächter's insightful dissertation follows this process of regarding fans as economic actors, Sophie G. Einwächter, *Transformationen von Fankultur: Organisatorische und ökonomische Konsequenzen globaler Vernetzung*, PhD, Goethe-Universität Frankfurt am Main, 2014. Other examples can be found in Vol. 15 (2014) of the journal *Transformative Works and Cultures* that examines "Fandom and/as Labor" and specifically raises questions of free labor and the exploitation of fan work, cf. Mel Stanfield and Megan Condis, "Fandom and/as Labor," *Transformative Works and Cultures* 15 (2014).

29 Meikle, "Pornographic Adaptation," 130. Cf. also Simone Murray, *The Adaptation Industry: The Cultural Economy of Contemporary Literary Adaptation* (New York: Routledge, 2011), 189.

the Rings, *Game of Thrones*, *Tomb Raider*, or *Alien* franchises. In these cases, novels, films, and video games coexist with commercial radio and stage play adaptations, board games, and so forth, as well as countless unofficial fan adaptations/appropriations. These interconnected text clusters as much as the phenomena of new narrative media and fan creations demonstrate "that the definition and practices of adaptation are changing with the evolution of new forms."[30] Just as adaptation studies approaches can draw on newer forms of television or video game studies in studying the first, and on fan studies' approaches in coming to terms with the second development, here, too, adaptation scholars come into contact with those working under the labels of transmediality or convergence culture, transmedial narratology, and other fields. The clustered adaptations produced within a franchise logic of excess and multiplicity challenge concepts of narrative cohesion, sequence, and so forth; a phenomenon which, as Rüdiger Heinze demonstrates in his contribution, benefits from a narratologically informed adaptation studies perspective.

As this discussion makes clear, adaptation studies needs to build on a variety of disciplines to view convergent adaptations and franchise media not only in their intertextual, but also in their societal framework. Factors that come to the fore are related to social changes, changes in the structures of production and distribution, and so forth. Literary and film studies, the disciplines that have traditionally informed adaptation studies methodolgy, only offer limited tools to describe and conceptualize these. To the extent that adaptation and transmedia studies ground themselves on a cultural materialist approach, the historical and industry transformations that production studies focuses on need to influence the direction from which we approach adaptations in a convergent environment.[31] Approaches that already incorporate such elements as how Hollywood industry structures impact the shape of certain film adaptations suggests that the field can easily do so.

This Volume

The contributors to *Adaptation in the Age of Media Convergence* both individually and collectively expand the horizon of the fields of adaptation and

30 O'Flynn, "Designing for the Interactant," 83.

31 Johnson, *Media Franchising*. Derek Johnson, "Battleworlds: The Management of Multiplicity in the Media Industries." In *World Building: Transmedia, Fans, Industries*, ed. Marta Boni (Amsterdam: Amsterdam University Press, 2017), 129–142.

transmedia studies to come to terms with those changes laid out above. The contributions make clear that a project of rethinking adaptation in a convergent environment means that not only old and new media, but also old and new questions and research methods need to "collide" and be brought together in new ways.[32] To come to terms with the rise of digital media as media with new affordances, the transformation of the dynamics of contribution, control, and brand management, as well as the transformation of economic and legal structures of production, profit, and exploitation, contributions therefore draw on a wide variety of fields and approaches, and adapt their methodology to the material studied. As the contributions show, such methods can range from 19th-century theories such as pragmatist philosophy or the theory of evolution (Schober), via 20th-century narratology (Heinze), film studies (Goggin), and legal studies (Schäfke), to 21st-century theories developed in media and fan studies (Poore; Soller; Constandinides). They can also include re-evaluations of previously marginal concepts from literary studies such as Gérard Genette's notion of paratexts, which scholars such as Jonathan Gray and Dorothee Birke and Birte Christ have in recent years brought to bear on non-print media (Voigts).[33]

As the authors engage with the sometimes new, sometimes seemingly novel but merely transformed phenomena that emerge in a convergent environment around adaptive phenomena, they map the challenges of new media, fan engagement, and content and rights management by franchise holders, as well as the creation of interconnected transmedial texts and franchises. In this fashion, they offer remappings of adaptational practices within new media and the field as a whole.

Regina Schober proposes a model that regards adaptations not as a unidirectional process from "original" to derivative text, but instead as a set of dualisms between "source medium" and "adaptation" on one side, and "producer" and "recipient" on the other. To make her point, Schober draws on evolutionary theory and pragmatism. She combines this with recent network theory to develop a model that accounts for the inherently complex, non-linear, and decentralized dynamics of cultural processes, including adaptations. Adopting Bruno Latour's Actor-Network Theory, she highlights shifting connections between human and non-human actors. Adding biological conceptions of adaptation to this Latourian network

32 Jenkins, *Convergence Culture*, 2.

33 Jonathan Gray, *Show Sold Separately: Promos, Spoilers, and Other Media Paratexts* (New York: New York University Press, 2010). Dorothee Birke and Birte Christ, "Paratext and Digitized Narrative: Mapping the Field," *Narrative* 21, no. 1 (2013): 65–87.

perspective, Schober proposes to reconceptualize success in adaptations as a process of survival in a new cultural environment through (evolutionary) adaptation.

The following contributions by Bettina Soller, Eckart Voigts, and Costas Constandinides examine texts whose production and aesthetics either emerged in fan circles and then became commercialized or are positioned, commercially or aesthetically, between the professional and non-professional sphere. In her chapter, Bettina Soller analyzes what she calls "layered adaptation," a process through which texts that began their lives as (erotic) fanfiction of successful novels can be transformed first into books that stand on their own, then adaptations that finally launch their own separate franchises. Both of her primary examples, *Fifty Shades of Grey* (originally a piece of *Twilight* fanfiction) and *The Mortal Instruments* (originally *Harry Potter* fanfiction) were shared in the online fanfiction community before being rewritten for commercial publication as independent works. In her article, Soller discusses a range of topics, from issues of intellectual property to questions of collective versus individual authorship that become even more complicated in fanfiction with its processes of beta-readers and community feedback. In this fashion, Soller traces the networks of actors involved in adaptations, as well as the evolutionary/commercial flourishing of their products that Schober theorized in her contribution, by analyzing concrete examples. Instead of dwelling on these theoretical issues, Soller therefore traces how fans can "change sides" and turn into authorial and authoritative figures by shaping their own franchises. Her examination of the ways in which E.L. James, in particular, tries to stage her persona as a writer by strategically managing her past as a fanfiction writer, points to a re-emergence of the role of the author as a figure whose presence organizes a text. It is no coincidence then that similar issues of an uneasy transition from fan to writer reappear in Benjamin Poore's discussion of Steven Moffat and Mark Gatiss, creators of BBC's *Sherlock*, who likewise alternate between building on their credentials as fans and setting themselves apart from their audience.

Eckart Voigts sheds a different light on fannish ways of production that make their way into the commercial mainstream. He examines a genre peculiar to an age of media convergence: the (quirky) mashup novel. He sees these books as adaptations of techniques deriving from fan production, particularly mashing and remixing, that depend to a large degree on the paratextual management of authors and publishers. Novels such as *William Shakespeare's Star Wars®*, *Pride and Prejudice and Zombies*, or *Two Gentlemen of Lebowski* combine high culture with popular texts and phenomena.

As Voigts notes, while these texts paratextually revel in their supposed quirkiness and subversiveness, their practices of textually upholding both the cult status of the texts they "sample," as well as their adherence to intellectual property laws, make them much less subversive than their authors and their participatory aesthetic suggest.

Costas Constandinides discusses a form likewise peculiar to convergence culture: YouTube cover songs. He conceptualizes these as new forms of adaptation that have already developed their own generic patterns. Building on his older concept of para-adaptation,[34] Constandinides describes these videos as "user-generated creative contributions that, on the one hand, are associated with a specific industry-created product and, on the other, wish to feature creative talents or responses in a way that is not limited to paratextual or fan video functions." In order to highlight the stylistic distinctiveness of YouTube cover songs as a form of convergence culture adaptation (or para-adaptation), Constandinides explores the covers and distinctiveness the videos of cover songs from a media studies perspective. In doing so, he highlights their oscillation between a Do-It-Yourself (DIY) aesthetic that resonates with other forms of online communication, such as vlogs, and attempts to professionalize the recording and video quality. Blurring the boundary between amateur consumers and professional producers, his case studies show how the aesthetics of music videos by both professionals and non-professionals range between appropriating the style of fan-produced content on sharing platforms such as YouTube and the aesthetics of commercial productions, such as aspects of the studio setting popularized by professional music videos. Constandinides' chapter thus adds a different facet to Soller's analysis of the "professionalization" of fan-produced content via publishing works that try to erase fannish elements (partly for legal reasons). Instead, cover song videos strategically highlight aspects of their DIY status as a sign of the para-adaptation aesthetics he identifies in YouTube cover songs. This fannish marker, in some ways, brings these videos closer to those texts that Voigts examines, which likewise depend on a fannish gesture to succeed commercially and comedically, rather than to the polished novels deriving from Clare's and James' cleaned up, stand-alone work.

Bringing in yet another critical perspective on the tensions between official and non-official culture, Benjamin Poore examines how Mark Gatiss and Steven Moffat, the co-creators and lead writers of BBC's

34 Costas Constandinides, "Para-adaptation: Or How I Learned to Stop Worrying and Love Convergence Culture," *Adaptation* 6, no. 2 (2013): 143–157.

contemporaneous Sherlock Holmes adaptation *Sherlock*, stage themselves as *auteurs*. His interest lies particularly in how this self-staging impacts upon their interactions with certain parts of the show's fan base and how this strained relationship is, in turn, reflected in the main narrative of the TV show. As Poore argues, the various tactics through which Gatiss and Moffat try to maintain full control over the popular show and its interpretations take place both within the show's narrative and in public appearances in which Moffat in particular tries to set a legitimate range of engagement and interpretation. This negotiation is caught up in contradiction, because the show at once depends on fan investment, which – like most truly successful contemporary television shows – it caters to with added value hidden in a "drillable" text,[35] while at the same time, having its showrunners adamantly delimit the fans' range of authorial/adaptive and interpretative involvement. As Poore writes, "[t]o take fandom any further than one-way consumption is to risk the lead writers' mockery." According to Poore, this keep-your-hands-off-our-show approach geared at both fans and journalists encapsulates the show's true politics.

While complex television's lead writers can exact strong control over their work, as Poore's discussion of *Sherlock*'s lead writers shows, the expansion of the fuzzier and more diversified *Alien* franchise that Rüdiger Heinze examines opens up multiple "gaps" which – from a primarily narratological perspective – result in the continuity between individual works becoming much looser. As Heinze shows, each contribution to a franchise, no matter how closely its makers try to fit it into a preexisting canon, also includes contradictions. Even as they fill narrative gaps, these franchise contributions create new loose ends, and thus new spaces for further elaboration, facilitating both further franchise production and spaces for fan interpretation and participation. As Heinze contends in his conclusion, which Steven Moffat and Mark Gatiss would do well to heed, it is impossible to fully control a fictional universe and its commercial and cognitive receptions.

Focusing on *The LEGO Movie*, Joyce Goggin examines the toy-turned-transmedia franchise to argue that LEGO in general and *The LEGO Movie* in particular project a master builder trope that at once encourages creativity and at the same time closely regulates this creativity. Goggin sees this trope as germane to the greater context of political and economic neoliberalism, in which employees are encouraged to build their careers and lives in a brick-like manner to fit the ever-greater pressures of deregulated labor

35 The notion of drillable media goes back to Jason Mittell, "Forensic Fandom and the Drillable Text," accessed February 09, 2017, http://spreadablemedia.org/essays/mittell/.

markets. What is particularly remarkable is how the film, in a case of what Fredric Jameson would call postmodern "blank parody" or pastiche,[36] self-consciously parodies its own rhetoric, while ultimately endorsing as inevitable the very notions of corporate control it both evokes and pokes fun at. From an economic perspective, the film functions to boost sales for all products in the LEGO franchise and other franchises incorporated into it, while it displays a cultural self-awareness that works to cushion LEGO's moneymaking machinery in an aura of self-aware irony that is not unlike a magnified version of the pseudo-subversive stance taken by the mashup novels examined earlier by Voigts.

In the collection's final chapter, Werner Schäfke-Zell brings yet another layer into the examination of adaptations and franchises in an increasingly globalized environment. Schäfke examines how legal frameworks limit and influence storyworlds in different national media cultures.[37] Looking at the popular *Wolfenstein* video game franchise, he shows how the makers of the various *Wolfenstein* games manage the content to facilitate its international distribution. Schäfke describes legal limitations in the German market that influence depictions of National Socialism and the Holocaust, as well as marketing limitations linked to the self-inscribed "family-friendliness" of the Nintendo Entertainment System. Turning to the games themselves, Schäfke argues that the process of "narrative filtering," which removes or recodes references to the games' Nazi antagonists to avoid complications with German laws, actually amplifies a mythologization of Germany's Nazi past that is already embedded in the original game's *Verfremdung* (transformation) of historical reality. Ironically, this mythologization becomes much stronger through some of the filtered, superficially de-Nazified alterations released on the German market. As such, a legal framework established to prevent a positive depiction of National Socialism could, in the case of the *Wolfenstein* franchise's adaptation to legal limitations, actually work to strengthen the games' "appeal of the forbidden."

36 Fredric Jameson, *Postmodernism, or, The Cultural Logic of Late Capitalism* (Durham: Duke University Press, 1991), 17.

37 Recently Roberta Pearson has pointed to the function of laws as foundational for the material we study in adaptation and transmedia studies. As Pearson writes, "the beloved fictional worlds we study rest upon the legal and business practices that create, sustain, and protect them" (Roberta Pearson, "World-Building Logics and Copyright: The Dark Knight and the Great Detective." In *World Building: Transmedia, Fans, Industries*, ed. Marta Boni (Amsterdam: Amsterdam University Press, 2017), 110).

Taken together, the chapters highlight the diversity of issues around adaptation that arise in a convergence environment. As the contributions individually and collectively make clear, the breadth of disciplinary approaches that are necessary to grasp what happens to adapted texts and franchises in convergence culture transcends even the already broad scope of more traditional adaptation studies. The range of material in convergence culture that can be described as adaptive in some form therefore points to a need for new, sophisticated questions and models that allow us to conceptualize the flows of production, marketing, authorial self-stylization, reception, interaction, participation, and interpretation – to name only some of the most important aspects – which a new media environment raises, restructures, or more clearly lays open. The various branches of the interdisciplinary field of adaptation studies have developed a broad range of powerful approaches and theories to analyze some of these aspects. Given the often openly derivative nature of many convergence cultural products, adaptation studies is well advised to further widen its approaches to continue to be a productive focal point through which a mapping of interrelated texts can be undertaken in a 21st-century media environment.

Works Cited

Bacon-Smith, Camille. *Enterprising Women: Television Fandom and the Creation of Popular Myth*. Philadelphia: University of Pennsylvania Press, 1991.

Barthes, Roland. "From Work to Text." In *Image-Music-Text*, 155–164. London: Fontana, 1977.

Birke, Dorothee, and Birte Christ. "Paratext and Digitized Narrative: Mapping the Field." *Narrative* 21, no. 1 (2013): 65–87.

Bruns, Axel. *Blogs, Wikipedia, Second Life, and Beyond: From Production to Produsage*. New York: Lang, 2008.

Butler, Martin. "Net-Works: Collaborative Models of Cultural Production in Web 2.0 Contexts." In *Precarious Alliances: Cultures of Participation in Print and Other Media*, edited by Martin Butler, Albrecht Hausmann, and Anton Kirchhofer, 19–31. Bielefeld: transcript, 2016.

Constandinides, Costas. "Para-adaptation: Or How I Learned to Stop Worrying and Love Convergence Culture." *Adaptation* 6, no. 2 (2013): 143–157.

Cuntz-Leng, Vera. *Harry Potter que(e)r: Eine Filmsaga im Spannungsfeld von Queer Reading, Slash-Fandom und Fantasyfilmgenre*. Bielefeld: transcript, 2015.

Einwächter, Sophie G. Transformationen von Fankultur: Organisatorische und ökonomische Konsequenzen globaler Vernetzung. Phil. Diss., Goethe-Universität Frankfurt am Main, 2014.

Fehrle, Johannes. "Gaming into the *Heart of Darkness*: Adapting Conrad/Coppola." *South Atlantic Review* 80, no. 3–4 (2016): 234–253.

Gray, Jonathan. *Show Sold Separately: Promos, Spoilers, and Other Media Paratexts.* New York: New York University Press, 2010.

Hassler-Forest, Dan. *Science Fiction, Fantasy, and Politics: Transmedia World-Building beyond Capitalism.* London: Rowman & Littlefield, 2016.

Hills, Matt. *Fan Cultures.* London: Routledge, 2002.

Hutcheon, Linda, with Siobhan O'Flynn. *A Theory of Adaptation.* 2nd ed. New York: Routledge, 2013.

Hutcheon, Linda. "Moving Forward: The Next Step in Adaptation Studies." In *Adaptation and American Studies: Perspectives on Research and Teaching, With an Afterword by Linda Hutcheon,* edited by Nassim Winnie Balestrini, 213–217. Heidelberg: Winter, 2011.

Jameson, Fredric. *Postmodernism, or, The Cultural Logic of Late Capitalism.* Durham: Duke University Press, 1991.

Jenkins, Henry. "The Aesthetics of Transmedia: In Response to David Bordwell (Part One)." *Confessions of an Aca Fan. The Official Weblog of Henry Jenkins.* 10 September 2009. Accessed February 15, 2019. http://henryjenkins.org/2009/09/the_aesthetics_of_transmedia_i.html.

—. *Convergence Culture: Where Old and New Media Collide.* New York University Press, 2006.

—. "Transmedia Storytelling 101." *Confessions of an Aca Fan. The Official Weblog of Henry Jenkins.* 22 March 2007. Accessed February 15, 2019. http://henryjenkins.org/2007/03/transmedia_storytelling_101.html.

—. "Science Fiction World Building in a Capitalist Society: An Interview with Dan Hassler-Forest (Part One)" *Confessions of an Aca Fan. The Official Weblog of Henry Jenkins.* 22 March 2007. Accessed February 15, 2019. http://henryjenkins.org/2016/09/science-fiction-world-building-in-a-capitalist-society-an-interview-with-dan-hassler-forest-part-one.html.

Johnson, Derek. "Battleworlds: The Management of Multiplicity in the Media Industries." In *World Building: Transmedia, Fans, Industries,* edited by Marta Boni, 129–142. Amsterdam: Amsterdam University Press, 2017.

—. *Media Franchising: Creative License and Collaboration in the Culture Industries.* New York: New York University Press, 2013.

Leitch, Thomas. "Review Article. Adaptation Studies at a Crossroads." *Adaptation* 1, no. 1 (2008): 63–77.

McLuhan, Marshall. *The Gutenberg Galaxy: The Making of Typographic Man*. Toronto: University of Toronto Press, 1968.

Meikle, Kyle. “Pornographic Adaptation: Parody, Fan Fiction, and the Limits of Genre.” *Journal of Adaptation in Film & Performance* 8, no. 2 (2015): 123–140.

Mittell, Jason. “Forensic Fandom and the Drillable Text.” Accessed February 9, 2017. http://spreadablemedia.org/essays/mittell/.

Murray, Simone. *The Adaptation Industry: The Cultural Economy of Contemporary Literary Adaptation*. New York: Routledge, 2011.

O’Flynn, Siobhan. “Designing for the Interactant: How Interactivity Impacts on Adaptation.” In *Adaptation and American Studies: Perspectives on Research and Teaching, With an Afterword by Linda Hutcheon*, edited by Nassim Winnie Balestrini, 83–102. Heidelberg: Winter, 2011.

Parody, Clare. “Adaptation Essay Prize Winner: Franchising/Adaptation.” *Adaptation* 4, no. 2 (2011): 210–218.

Pearson, Roberta. “Fandom in the Digital Era.” *Popular Communication* 8, no. 1 (2010): 84–95.

—. “World-Building Logics and Copyright: The Dark Knight and the Great Detective.” In *World Building: Transmedia, Fans, Industries*, edited by Marta Boni, 109–128. Amsterdam: Amsterdam University Press, 2017.

Rajewsky, Irina. “Intermediality, Intertextuality, and Remediation: A Literary Perspective on Intermediality.” *Intermédialités* 6 (2005): 43–64.

Ryan, Marie-Laure. “Digital Media.” in *Narrative across Media: The Languages of Storytelling*, edited by Marie-Laure Ryan, 329–335. Lincoln, NE: University of Nebraska Press, 2004.

—. “Transmedia Storytelling: Industry Buzzword of New Narrative Experience?” *Storyworlds: A Journal of Narrative Studies* 7.2 (2015): 1–19.

—. “Will New Media Produce New Narratives?” In *Narrative across Media: The Languages of Storytelling*, edited by Marie-Laure Ryan, 337–359. Lincoln, NE: University of Nebraska Press, 2004.

Ryan, Marie-Laure, and Jan-Noël Thon, eds. *Storyworlds across Media: Toward a Media-Conscious Narratology*. Lincoln: University of Nebraska Press, 2014.

Sanders, Julie. *Adaptation and Appropriation*. London: Routledge, 2006.

Schäfke, Werner. “Videospiele als Text aus der Perspektive der Editionswissenschaft.” *Zeitschrift für Semiotik* 32 (2010): 343–353.

Stanfield, Mel, and Megan Condis. “Fandom and/as Labor.” *Transformative Works and Cultures* 15 (2014).

Thon, Jan-Noël. *Transmedial Narratology and Contemporary Media Culture*. Lincoln: University of Nebraska Press, 2016.

Wolf, Mark J.P. *Building Imaginary Worlds: The Theory and History of Sub-Creation*. New York: Routledge, 2012.

About the author

Johannes Fehrle is Associate Professor (Universitätsassistent) at the University of Graz, Austria. His monograph *Postmodern Gunslingers in a Transnational West* is forthcoming with the University of Nebraska Press. Recently he co-edited an issue on adaptation as translation (*Komparatistik Online*) and is working on a second book proposing a cultural materialist model for adaptations studies.

2. Adaptation as Connection: A Network Theoretical Approach to Convergence, Participation, and Co-Production

Regina Schober

Abstract
Cultural production is increasingly understood along the lines of self-organizing network dynamics instead of as linear and more or less stable (translation) processes with clear-cut creator-recipient dualisms. Participation and remediation, however, have always been a constitutive factor in cultural production. I propose to treat adaptations as embedded in and shaping the complex, non-linear, and decentralized networks of culture that operate along the lines of shifting and contingent connections between human and non-human actors. In doing so, I will show why it can be helpful for critical adaptation studies to take seriously the notion of cultural "function." Making productive insights into biological adaptation for cultural adaptation studies, I aim to shed light on the connotation of adaptation as temporary and contingent "knowledge."

Key words: Network theory; cultural functions of adaptation; biological vs. cultural adaptation; adaptation as a form of contingent knowledge

Adaptation as processual knowledge

Contrary to some public discourse, adaptation studies is far from thinking of adaptations as "poor" derivatives of original source texts. The so-called "fidelity discourse" has been successfully deconstructed or, as Kamilla Elliott and Simone Murray suggest, has never played as big a role in adaptation

Fehrle, J. and W. Schäfke, *Adaptation in the Age of Media Convergence*, Taylor & Francis Group, 2019
DOI 10.5117/9789462983663_CH02

studies as scholars have repeatedly claimed.[1] While the tendency to make value judgments based on how "truthful" an adaptation is to its original persists in fan communities, adaptation studies have long deconstructed unidirectional and hierarchical models of adaptation practices.[2] Furthermore, the field of adaptation studies has opened up to a variety of media and multidirectional adaptation processes beyond the field of novel-to-film adaptations. The theoretical reconceptualization of adaptation studies has been spurred on, among other things, by an increasing cultural development towards what Henry Jenkins calls "convergence culture," coinciding with a scholarly interest in the participatory nature of popular culture and of a supposedly democratic "grassroots" creativity.[3] In the Information Age, adaptation is no longer regarded as the exception but represents instead the rule as to how media products and stories emerge, proliferate, and interact with each other. Cultural production is increasingly understood along the lines of self-organizing network dynamics instead of as linear and more or less stable (translation) processes with clear-cut creator-recipient dualisms.

As people are more willing to interact with, share, and engage in a culture of circulating media content, aesthetic, legal, economic, and social questions have arisen that require new ways of thinking about culture through an array of disciplinary perspectives to explore new models of interdisciplinary collaboration. What has become visible with regard to a so-called Web 2.0 culture with its heightened focus on participation and remediation, however, has always been a constitutive factor in cultural production. I therefore suggest conceptualizing adaptation more distinctly in terms of the network model in order to account for the relational, processual, and recursive nature of adaptation. As an alternative to unidirectional analytical models which assume binary dualisms of "source medium" and adaptation or of producer and recipient, the network accounts for the inherently complex, non-linear, and decentralized dynamics of culture that operate along the lines of shifting and contingent connections between human and non-human actors.

1 Kamilla Elliott, "Theorizing Adaptation/Adapting Theories." In Bruhn, Jørgen, Anne Gjelsvik, and Eirik Frisvold Hanssen, eds. *Adaptation Studies: New Challenges, New Directions* (London, New York: Bloomsbury, 2013), 19-45; Simone Murray, *The Adaptation Industry: The Cultural Economy of Contemporary Literary Adaptation* (New York: Routledge, 2011), 8.

2 Cf. Linda Hutcheon, *A Theory of Adaptation* (New York: Routledge, 2006); Thomas Leitch, *Film Adaptation and Its Discontents: From Gone with the Wind to The Passion of Christ* (Baltimore: The Johns Hopkins University Press, 2007); Thomas Leitch, "Review Article. Adaptation Studies at a Crossroads," *Adaptation* 1.1 (2008): 65–68; Robert Stam, *Literature through Film: Realism, Magic, and the Art of Adaptation* (Malden, MA: Blackwell, 2005).

3 Henry Jenkins, *Convergence Culture: Where Old and New Media Collide* (New York University Press, 2006).

While a lot of attention has been directed towards the critical analyses of creative processes at work in a variety of case studies and even more theoretical thought has been invested in remapping the field itself,[4] adaptation theory has so far paid little attention to the question of what function adaptations have in the overall "ecosystem" of cultural production and reception. In this essay, I do not want to repeat the truism that cultural texts have cultural functions, nor do I want to list possible functions adaptations can have. Rather, I want to begin one step earlier and show why it can be helpful for critical adaptation studies to take seriously the notion of "function" and how it can contribute to and add a historical perspective to current adaptation discourses that think beyond the long obsolete category of "fidelity" as well as the problematic binaries of "original" vs. "derivative" and "author" vs. "audience." I will deliberately stick to the notion of "adaptation" for the purpose of this essay, since it is the connotation of adaptation as temporary and contingent "knowledge" that informs my theoretical argument. In doing so, I do not intend to neglect the editors' programmatic shift from traditional notions of "adaptation" towards "convergence." Quite the contrary, by turning to an early definition of "adaptation" I wish to liberate the concept from its constraining value judgments and make it productive for contemporary discourses on convergence culture.

In cultural and media studies, the term "adaptation" is mostly used in the context of intermedial transposition processes, of stories and storyworlds shifted from one medium to another. Broader definitions encompass any semiotic transposition processes, even within the same medium. What is rarely mentioned, however, is that "adaptation" is originally a term borrowed from biology, describing the evolutionary transformation processes according to which species are fitted to their environment. Although I do not want to suggest that cultural and biological adaptation are necessarily compatible concepts, I propose to shed light on some links between Darwin's theory of evolution and discourses on creativity and knowledge which emerged in the context of American Pragmatism in the late 19th/early 20th century. In reading these texts as relevant for adaptation discourses both in the natural sciences and philosophy/literary studies, I aim to make productive insights into biological adaptation for cultural adaptation studies. I thus want to bring a historical perspective to adaptation discourses in order to

4 Thomas Leitch, *Film Adaptation and Its Discontents*; Bruhn, Jørgen, Anne Gjelsvik, and Eirik Frisvold Hanssen, eds. *Adaptation Studies: New Challenges, New Directions* (London, New York: Bloomsbury, 2013); Kamilla Elliott, *Rethinking the Novel/Film Debate* (Cambridge University Press, 2003).

emphasize the importance of thinking about the category of "function." I will then connect both biological and cultural adaptation discourses by referring to recent complexity and network theory, both of which build on Pragmatist models of transitional, processual, and emergent notions of knowledge and creativity. A functional approach to adaptation can help understand and describe some of the yet uncharted terrains of adaptation, convergence, and the creative flux of narratives across media, culture(s), and history. It foregrounds the intrinsic value of adaptations as such, while drawing attention to the relational quality of adaptations in a larger system of signification, knowledge production, and interaction throughout cultural history.

Adapting adaptation: Biological versus cultural "adaptation"

One of the few attempts to bring together a biological and a cultural notion of adaptation is Gary R. Bortolotti and Linda Hutcheon's essay entitled "On the Origin of Adaptations: Rethinking Fidelity Discourse and 'Success' – Biologically." Taking their cue from Hutcheon's deconstruction of the fidelity discourse in *A Theory of Adaptation*, the authors convincingly show the benefits of proposing what they consider "a homology between biological and cultural adaptation" to redefine what the notion of a "successful adaptation" can mean.[5] Rather than judging the level of truthfulness between adaptation and original, the authors suggest that we look at how adaptations reveal "lineages of descent, not similarities of form alone," thus taking into consideration "how a specific narrative changes over time" and ultimately evaluating not (only) the adaptations but "the success of the narrative itself."[6] A biologically informed view on adaptation fundamentally destabilizes fidelity judgments, since "biology does not judge adaptations in terms of fidelity to the 'original'; indeed, that is not the point at all. Biology can celebrate the diversity of life forms, yet at the same time recognize that they come from a common origin."[7] Considering a growing distrust in value judgments in recent adaptation studies, Bortolotti and Hutcheon's concept of "successful adaptation" may seem problematic. Yet, in the biological sense, "success" does not mean that an adaptation is better in "essence" but only in

5 Gary R. Bortolotti and Linda Hutcheon, "On the Origin of Adaptations: Rethinking Fidelity Discourse and "Success" – Biologically," *New Literary History* 38.3 (Summer 2007): 444.

6 Bortolotti and Hutcheon, "On the Origin of Adaptations," 445.

7 Ibid., 445.

terms of its specific "function" in a new set of circumstances. A successful adaptation, according to evolutionary biology, is one that implies survivability, one based on what Charles Darwin calls "natural selection." Over time, Darwin holds, all species "undergo modification to some extent. The extinction of old forms is the almost inevitable consequence of the production of new forms."[8] Adaptation, in the evolutionary sense, constitutes a necessary part of the species' survival, since it is an expression of its fitness to a continuously changing environment. The very fact that an adaptation exists is a proof of its validity, since the only determining factors are time and an adaptation's evolving nature.

Bortolotti and Hutcheon hold that in following a descriptive rather than an evaluative approach towards the diversity of species and life forms, biology serves as a potential model for cultural adaptation studies. Stories, just like genes and organisms, "'evolve' – that is, replicate and change," so cultural adaptations, just like biological adaptations, should "have equal cultural validity."[9] What current adaptation studies can learn from biology, accordingly, is the ability to simultaneously think about process and origin, to maintain some sense of "core narrative" (however rudimentary it seems) and to appreciate divergence and variation. Following Richard Dawkins' meme theory, the authors argue that just like biological organisms, narratives contain a "replicator," some sort of "core idea" and a narrative "vehicle" that changes over time. While "organisms act as vehicles for genes; the literary text or the stage performance we call *adaptations* are the vehicles of narrative ideas."[10] Since a replicator's success does not necessarily equal the vehicle's success, the authors suggest that different questions need to be asked about the success of an adaptation, taking into account categories such as "persistence, abundance, and diversity," as for example, "how many people saw the musical or played the videogame and therefore know the videogame?"[11]

Although offering inspiring new perspectives on the way we regard adaptations, Bortolotti and Hutcheon's natural/biological adaptation homology is based on a variety of problematic premises. Firstly, the distinction between "replicator" and "vehicle," however valuable for biological species, bears the danger of aligning itself with a problematic form/content division. Although the notion of some sense of "core idea" that is inherent to adaptations is widely discussed in adaptation studies, Bortolotti and Hutcheon

8 Charles Darwin, *The Origin of Species* (Dent: London, 1971), 344.

9 Bortolotti and Hutcheon, "On the Origin of Adaptations," 446.

10 Ibid., 447, emphasis in original.

11 Ibid., 452.

run the risk of presuming the existence of an essentialist narrative which can easily be separated from its form or transmitting medium.[12] As I have argued elsewhere, however, every adaptation fundamentally changes the set of relations between ideas, modal configurations, and other human and non-human participants, thus affecting the ways in which the "original story" is transmitted and perceived.[13] What emerges from the process of adaptation, therefore, is not just the same story told differently but a new story based on an older one. As Darwin notes, "when a species has once disappeared it never reappears,"[14] since "the process of modification is necessarily slow, and depends on many complex contingencies."[15] One cannot go back in time: once a story is being told, it is out there to interact with all sorts of events, other media, contexts, stories, etc. Stories, and therefore adaptations necessarily change since they unfold in time and space. Even though the analogy is partly inappropriate since we can always go back to an earlier version of the story while this is not necessarily the case in biological adaptation, our perception of the actual text is inevitably influenced by its later adaptations, so a return to the "pure original" is – at least conceptually – impossible.

An approach to adaptation that takes into account the situatedness of adaptations in contingent networks of intertexts, objects, humans, and institutions challenges Bortolotti and Hutcheon's distinction between chance-based modifications in biology and "intention-based" modifications in culture.[16] Cultural adaptations too are highly based on contingency and unpredictable outcomes resulting from recursive interactions between different "actors" to employ a concept from Bruno Latour's Actor-Network Theory.[17] The category of "intention" is just as deceptive in biological as it is in cultural adaptation, since neither follows a strictly teleological program. The fact that there are always human objectives and motives involved in cultural adaptation does not substantially distinguish the one from the other. The nature-culture divide has long been deconstructed as a

12 As Johannes Fehrle argues in this collection, adaptations do not necessarily challenge but produce the existence of a "core" narrative since we always identify the core by looking for it through the adaptations.

13 Regina Schober, "Adaptation as Connection: Transmediality Reconsidered." In *Adaptation Studies: New Challenges, New Directions*, ed. by Jørgen Bruhn, Anne Gjelsvik, and Eirik Frisvold Hanssen (London, New York: Bloomsbury, 2013), 89–112.

14 Darwin, *The Origin of Species*, 343.

15 Ibid., 344.

16 Bortolotti and Hutcheon, "On the Origin of Adaptations," 453.

17 Bruno Latour, *Reassembling the Social: An Introduction to Actor-Network-Theory* (Oxford UP, 2007).

myth that assumes that biological systems work completely independent of human agency (think of evolutionary processes from bioengineering or the role of the human observer in the construction of biological "laws," for example). So, rather than asking, as Bortolotti and Hutcheon do, how a successful adaptation can be rethought in terms of looking at the narrative in general and its diverse replication, I suggest leaving behind the notion of "success" altogether because, taking the evolutionary model literally, every adaptation is successful, if only for a limited amount of time or only in a limited context. Especially in the age of the Web 2.0, with proliferating ecosystems of creative user-generated retellings, it seems that not only "every important story gets told,"[18] but also that for every re-telling of a story there is a niche audience for which this particular adaptation is an "important," and therefore "successful" adaptation.

Cultural functions of adaptation

In order to avoid falling into the trap of discussing adaptation in terms of problematic categories of "success" or "origin," it proves helpful to draw on theoretical models that focus on adaptation as a necessary constituent involved in any process of culture and knowledge formation. American Pragmatism and recent complexity theory, in particular, offer such theoretical perspectives that foreground the specific functions of adaptation as an effect and a condition of cultural evolution. Function is not meant teleologically, as in a pre-Darwinian notion of "natural" purpose. Rather, in a cultural sense, it refers to the (shifting) functions of adaptations within a particular cultural context. In the context of a "cultural turn" in intermediality studies, cultural functions have recently begun to be discussed in relation to adaptation.[19]

The main question of a functional analysis of adaptation, according to Werner Wolf, is not whether intermediality is successful or not, but how to account for it and its effects.[20] Wolf explicitly replaces "success" with "function." According to this view, the self-reflexive functions of a text's specific allusions, aesthetic contexts, and ideological implications become the focus

18 Jenkins, *Convergence Culture*, 3.

19 Cf. Werner Wolf, "Towards a Functional Analysis of Intermediality: The Case of Twentieth-Century Musicalized Fiction." In *Cultural Functions of Intermedial Exploration*, ed. by Erik Hedling and Ulla Britta Lagerroth (Amsterdam: Rodopi, 2002), 15–34.; Lars Eckstein and Christoph Reinfandt, "On Dancing about Architecture: Words and Music between Cultural Practice and Transcendence," *Zeitschrift für Anglistik und Amerikanistik* 54.1 (2006), 1–8.

20 Wolf, "Towards a Functional Analysis of Intermediality," 18.

of examination. Function, in this sense, does not (necessarily) imply a causal relationship between "original" and "adaptation." It cannot be evaluated on the grounds of empirical results. Rather, in the sense of Winfried Fluck's *Funktionsgeschichte*, statements on literary functions remain speculative in that they postulate possible references to social practices.[21] Since social function is inextricably coupled with literary "effect," novels create "implicit functional models" on which basis they want to realize their effect.[22] The function of literature is understood as the "specific condition under which literature creates meaning and effect."[23]

What makes Fluck's functional model so valuable for adaptation studies is its focus on the variability and contingency of cultural functions. Fluck presumes that although cultural functions differ depending on perspective and context, fiction always functions to exemplarily structure the world.[24] As "communicative acts," literary texts (or adaptations, for that matter) are in a "process of continuous negotiation and readjustment, necessitated by the instable reference of the literary text, which urges it to constantly renewed mediation of the real and the imaginary."[25] Fluck thus implicitly states that fictional discourses inherently extrapolate themselves in recursive communication processes, which are at work while reading one text. However, such signification processes can also be distributed to different "versions" of one text, as in adaptation. If, as Stephen Greenblatt has suggested, "collective beliefs and experiences [are] shaped, moved from one medium to another, concentrated in manageable aesthetic form" through social energy that is transformed into aesthetic and cultural objects by means of "a structured negotiation and exchange,"[26] a cultural text is "no longer only a product of an individual creator subject, able to universally fix all cultural energies at play in the seclusion of a work. Instead, it is itself regarded as an expressive field of these genuinely collective cultural energies, which facilitate the text and lend its impact to the audience."[27] Having entered the cultural field, stories are subject to modification, interaction, and development. Alternatively, to

21 Winfried Fluck, *Das kulturelle Imaginäre. Eine Funktionsgeschichte des amerikanischen Romans 1790–1900* (Frankfurt am Main: Suhrkamp, 1997), 12.

22 Ibid., 10, 14, my translation.

23 Ibid., 15, my translation.

24 Ibid., 16, my translation.

25 Ibid., 16, my translation.

26 Stephen Greenblatt, "The Circulation of Social Energy" [1988], in *Modern Criticism and Theory: A Reader*. 2nd ed., ed. by David Lodge and Nigel Wood (Harlow: Longman, 2000), 499.

27 Hubert Zapf, *Kurze Geschichte der anglo-amerikanischen Literaturtheorie*, 2nd ed. (München: Fink, 1996), 232, my translation.

approach this from another angle, stories only emerge through the combined efforts of sharing knowledge in discursive interaction and negotiation. From such a collaborative notion of knowledge, it is only a small step towards concepts of collective intelligence or participatory culture. Jenkins' claim that "none of us can know everything," and that instead "each of us knows something; and we can put the pieces together if we pool our resources and combine our skills," applies not only to collective intelligence and crowdsourcing in the age of the Web 2.0 but may render adaptation as the default position of cultural production in which "collective meaning making"[28] through the construction and reconstruction of narratives keeps stories alive but also facilitates creativity and the proliferation of knowledge.

Adaptation and pragmatism

Creativity, as a core ingredient for both knowledge and culture, is largely dependent on adaptation, since every "new" element has to be connected to something that already exists, thus making it "fit" in with both what is already there and a changing environment. If "making is connecting," as David Gauntlett rephrases the poststructuralist claim in relation to Web 2.0 culture, creativity necessarily requires an association between previously separate things in which the two are made to fit together.[29] To consider anything "new" as a combination or a re-adaptation of something old is a fundamentally Pragmatist idea. "The junction of the new and old," Dewey states in *Art as Experience*, "is not a mere composition of forces, but a re-creation in which the present impulsion gets form and solidity while the old, the 'stored,' material is literally revived, given new life and soul through having to meet a new situation."[30] Dewey's emphasis on creation as "re-creation" challenges the notion of "origin" by highlighting that cultural expression and knowledge are never finished but always in the process of *becoming*. The function of adaptation is thus not only, as Bortolotti and Hutcheon claim, to ensure survival but also to "operate" effectively in a specific context, thus to establish a meaningful connection and thereby dissolve the barrier between text and con-text, between text and recipient, between subject and object. According to William James, ideas "become

28 Jenkins, *Convergence Culture*, 5.

29 David Gauntlett, *Making is Connecting: The Social Meaning of Creativity from DIY and Knitting to YouTube and Web 2.0.* (Cambridge: Polity Press, 2011).

30 John Dewey, *Art as Experience* [1934] (New York: Penguin, 2005), 63.

true just in so far as they help us to get into satisfactory relation with other parts of our experience."[31] Such a functional understanding of culture as interlocking networks of adaptations challenges hierarchical conceptions of "original" thought and authorship, instead offering a view that presumes the horizontal coexistence of multiple "truths" negotiated in the shared process of creating meaning, depending on whether they succeed in establishing a connection.

At the same time, what "works" in a particular context cannot be fully controlled or planned, since "truth *happens* to an idea. It *becomes* true, is *made* true by an event."[32] The question why Jeff Buckley's cover version of Leonard Cohen's ballad "Hallelujah" is by far more popular than the original or the numerous other cover versions cannot be explained by simple cause and effect models. However, the song's popularity is not the whole "truth" either. The momentary (and relative) "success" of Buckley's adaptation does not mean it will be the most popular forever, nor for every listener. Just as Buckley's "Hallelujah" fulfills a certain function for a certain group of listeners or for a music industry that for various reasons promotes exactly this version, John Cale's or Justin Timberlake's versions perfectly fulfill their functions at another time and for another audience. Which version is "valid" at a particular moment depends exclusively on this moment, on what James calls "the event," the combination of contingent factors.[33]

It follows that adaptational pluralism, most explicit in convergence culture and franchise adaptations, becomes a desired concept, since, following a Pragmatist notion of truth, there exists no ultimate authority in the process of value making.[34] Therefore, if cultural production is a way of experiencing the world and of creating knowledge and meaning, it necessarily becomes a process of constant adaptation. Collective experience, to extend James' tenets to a global scale, can be perceived as "a member of diverse processes that can be followed away from it along entirely different lines."[35] James implicitly uses the concept of the network to emphasize the interconnectedness of processes involved in the act of experience. This view implies that through

31 William James, "What Pragmatism Means." In *Pragmatism: A New Name for Some Old Ways of Thinking* (Rockville, MD: Arc Manor, 2008), 32.

32 William James, "Pragmatism's Conception of Truth" [1907], in *The Pragmatism Reader: From Peirce Through the Present*, ed. by Robert B. Talisse and Scott F. Aikin (Princeton University Press, 2011), 80.

33 James, "Pragmatism's Conception of Truth," 87.

34 Cf. Michael Bacon, *Pragmatism: An Introduction* (Cambridge: Polity, 2012), 38.

35 William James, "Does 'Consciousness' Exist?" *The Journal of Philosophy, Psychology and Scientific Methods* 1.18 (1904), 481.

co-adaptation and evolution culture constantly redefines itself while allowing for and negotiating multiple viewpoints. Not only do experience and production have to be considered as actions rather than as reactions, the Pragmatist ideal of "democratic art" also understands action as interaction and reception as coproduction.

Assuming a Pragmatist concept of processual truth as continuous social practice, any adaptation can be seen as producing its specific truth within a larger network of agencies. HBO's TV series *True Blood* may serve as an example to illustrate this idea, since, as the title suggests, it self-reflexively addresses the contingent processes involved in defining what constitutes reality. So, what is "true" in *True Blood*? The vampire story focused around Sookie Stackhouse, Charlaine Harris' *Southern Vampire Mystery* novels of which this show is a serial adaptation, the additional HBO material, or the fanfiction and computer games that extrapolate the transmedial narrative around the core text of the TV series? A Pragmatist reading of these interacting narratives would argue that they are all "true," creating a more or less coherent fictional storyworld aimed at enhancing the illusion of reality. Interestingly, *True Blood*, on a different, more metaphorical level, openly commits to aligning with what Flannery O'Connor has called "grotesque realism."[36] It explores the "real" or transgressive side of human behavior to address a truth that is beyond what has been shown on TV before (after all, it's HBO, not television) and stretches the limits of reality in order to show the extreme probabilities of our ordinary lives. This truth claim may seem to be a paradox in view of the highly fictional makeup of the entire narrative. The coexistence of different levels of realism, however, is one of the self-reflexive programs of convergence culture, allowing for multiple possibilities of reception, enjoyment, and participatory engagement.

Two implications of a Pragmatist notion of adaptation are especially interesting. First, a processual notion of truth means that, as William James holds, "there can be no difference which doesn't make a difference."[37] Apart from undermining an essentialist assumption of a "core narrative," James makes an explicit statement on the recursive nature of adaptation processes. Not only do environmental differences trigger adaptational differences, but this mechanism also works the other way round. Differences that occur in

36 Flannery O'Connor, "Some Aspects of the Grotesque in Southern Fiction." In *Collected Works*, ed. by Sally Fitzgerald (New York: Library of America, 1988), 813–821.

37 William James, "Philosophical Conceptions and Practical Results" [1898], in *The Pragmatism Reader: From Peirce Through the Present*, ed. by Robert B. Talisse and Scott F. Aikin (Princeton University Press, 2011), 67.

an adaptation have an effect on the way we perceive the "original," on the relationship between original and adaptation, and on future adaptations. Any change that results from the interaction between the complex forces at hand in adaptation changes the overall picture, no matter how small. Another major implication of looking at adaptation through a Pragmatist lens is that even though every difference matters, not all differences matter to the same degree. Pragmatism clearly differentiates between the chaos of "pure experience" and the need to create some sort of structure, what James calls "superstructure," for a text to be able to communicate. Applied to adaptation, this suggests that during the course of time, there may emerge certain patterns of dominance. For reasons that are historically contingent, certain stories and versions of stories travel across time and cultures while others get lost; certain media proliferate and certain images become iconic, while others turn out to be mere fads. Mediated knowledge, to use James' words again, is "like a snowball's growth";[38] it is a proliferating, self-regulating system which is in a constant process of validation, change, and adaptation.

The use of network studies for adaptation studies

While a Pragmatist view on adaptation highlights the processual nature of culture as/and knowledge, a discussion of the functions of adaptation requires another perspective, one which focuses even more on the vertical dimension of adaptations as part of a larger system of culture and knowledge. Network studies can be regarded as a continuation of an epistemological tradition that goes back to Pragmatist and even Transcendentalist thinking.[39] Drawing on systems theory, cybernetics, and complexity theory, network studies offer a theoretical framework that allows us to locate the functions of adaptation not (only) within the recursive interactions between adaptation processes but within the complex systems of interconnections and abstract mappings.

To conceptualize cultural production in terms of networks is not new. Poststructuralist theories of intertextuality assume that texts form complex webs of cross-references and interdependencies. Julie Sanders has therefore rightfully called adaptation "a subsection of the over-arching practice of

38 James, "Pragmatism's Conception of Truth," 96.

39 Cf. Regina Schober, "'Partial Members of a Vast Natural Network": Notions of Interconnectedness in American Transcendentalism and Pragmatism." In *Network Theory and American Studies*, special issue of *Amerikastudien/American Studies*, ed. by Ulfried Reichardt, Heike Schäfer, and Regina Schober, 60.1 (2015), 97–119.

intertextuality,"[40] while Robert Stam goes so far as to call adaptations a metonymy for cultural production in general: "Virtually all films, not only adaptations, remakes, and sequels, are mediated through intertextuality and writing."[41] Such a view radicalizes the poststructuralist claim that meaning is understood as lying not exclusively within a single text but, following Mikhail Bakhtin's notions of heteroglossia and chronotope, in their contextual relations, and more specifically, in their intertextual interactions, cross-dependencies and interrelations. Recent adaptation theorists have revitalized such notions of intertextuality for the field of adaptation, arguing that adaptation has to be regarded as a complex assemblage of cross-influences rather than a unidirectional procedure between two media within an implicitly hierarchical relationship. Most explicitly, perhaps, Stam's concept of adaptation as "intertextual dialogism" directs attention to "the infinite and open-ended possibilities generated by all the discursive practices of a culture, the entire matrix of communicative utterances within which the artistic text is situated" and which, importantly, "reach the text not only through recognizable influences, but also through a subtle process of dissemination."[42] The notion of intertextuality as interconnected assemblage of cross-references is effectively expressed by Gilles Deleuze and Félix Guattari's image of the rhizome. This non-linear, horizontal, and deterritorialized formation presupposes a structure in which multiple "lines of segmentarity and stratification" form an "acentered, nonhierarchical, non-signifying system [...] defined solely by a circulation of states."[43] The rhizome can be understood as a radical network formation, which has become one of the leading metaphors for the dynamics of complex systems and phenomena in the Information Age, an age increasingly being described as "network society,"[44] "connected age"[45] or "moment of complexity."[46]

40 Julie Sanders, *Adaptation and Appropriation* (London: Routledge, 2006), 17.

41 Robert Stam, "Introduction: The Theory and Practice of Adaptation." In *Literature and Film: A Guide to the Theory and Practice of Film Adaptation*, ed. by Robert Stam and Alessandra Raengo (Oxford: Blackwell, 2004), 45.

42 Robert Stam, "Beyond Fidelity: The Dialogics of Adaptation." In *Film Adaptation*, ed. by James Naremore (New Brunswick, NJ: Rutgers University Press, 2000), 64.

43 Gilles Deleuze and Félix Guattari [1980], *A Thousand Plateaus. Capitalism and Schizophrenia*, transl. by Brian Massumi (London, New York: Continuum, 2010), 23.

44 Manuel Castells, "Informationalism, Networks, and the Network Society. A Theoretical Blueprint." In *The Network Society. A Cross-Cultural Perspective*, ed. by Manuel Castells (Cheltenham: Edward Elgar, 2004), 3–45.

45 Duncan Watts, *Six Degrees: The Science of a Connected Age* (New York: Norton, 2003).

46 Mark Taylor, *The Moment of Complexity. Emerging Network Culture* (Univ. of Chicago Press, 2001).

Jenkins likewise explicates the notion of convergence culture in terms of complexity or network theory, without explicitly using these terms. Convergence is considered a dynamic process of interaction between different agents in the (co)production of media, determined by shifting flows, which emerge through distributed agencies and reciprocal feedback loops. It is this particular focus on contingency which determines what he calls a move "toward the increased interdependence of communications systems, toward multiple ways of accessing media content, and toward ever more complex relations between top-down corporate media and bottom-up participatory culture."[47]

Networks have both an ontological and epistemological dimension. They are present in our material reality, for example in transportation, economic, cultural, or social configurations of exchange, but they also constitute heuristic models of understanding, visualizing, and ultimately reducing complexity.[48] According to Mark Taylor, complex systems are "comprised of many different parts which are connected in multiple ways." These components can "interact both serially and in parallel to generate sequential as well as simultaneous effects and events," they "display spontaneous self-organization" which results in emergent structures that are "not necessarily reducible to the interactivity of the components or elements in the system." Furthermore, complex systems are "neither fixed nor static but develop or evolve. Such evolution presupposes that complex systems are both open and adaptive." Finally, because of their emergent properties, complex systems are situated in a space between order and chaos, at "the edge of chaos."[49]

Although networks can be understood as examples of complex figurations, they are primarily models, metaphors, and abstract mappings of complexity. Networks suggest a sense of coherence and consistency in relation to the ungraspable complexity of such diverse phenomena as globalization, cognition, communication, climate change, or media convergence. Or, as Wendy Chun puts it, "networks allow us to trace if not see – to spatialize – unvisualizable interactions as flows" and "they enable of a form of cognitive mapping that links the local to the global." The "force of networks," says

47 Jenkins, *Convergence Culture*, 254.

48 Cf. Hartmut Böhme, "Einführung: Netzwerke. Zur Theorie und Geschichte einer Konstruktion." In *Netzwerke: Eine Kulturtechnik der Moderne, ed. by Jürgen Barkhoff, Hartmut* Böhme, and Jeanne Riou (Köln: Böhlau, 2004), 17–36.; Ulfried Reichardt, "The Network as a Category in Cultural Studies and as a Model for Conceptualizing America." In *Network Theory and American Studies*, special issue of *Amerikastudien/American Studies*, ed. by Ulfried Reichardt, Heike Schäfer, and Regina Schober, 60.1 (2015), 17–35.

49 Taylor, *The Moment of Complexity*, 142–143.

Chun, "stems from how they are imaged and what they are imagined to do."[50] Networks, I would continue this line of thought, are cultural patterns imbued with an ideological function, oscillating, as Alexander Galloway notes, between "the chain of triumph" and "the web of ruin."[51]

On a basic level, adaptations are processes in which multilayered connections are established between different modes of representation, authors, audiences, media, and/or corporations. Such connections can be explicit or implicit, they can be total or partial, and they form complex networks of creation, reference, adaptation, and co-adaptation. Such networks of adaptation are inherently open, meaning they are only potentially there as soon as connections are traced and agreed upon by an individual or by an "interpretive community" that then also becomes an agent in the network. This "interpretive community" accounts for both the existence of individual interpretations of a cultural product as well as for the "stability of interpretation (at least among certain groups at certain times)." Connections are thus not purely subjective but always prestructured by interpretive "strategies [that] exist prior to the act of reading and therefore determine the shape of what is read."[52] The film *No Country for Old Men*, directed by the Coen brothers, for example, makes an explicit reference to Cormac McCarthy's novel by its use of the same title and thereby connects the two media and their respective cultural discourses. Yet, not only does the film have to be highly selective in forming these connections. The film-novel connection is only one possible connection out of a dense network of inherent links to other films, genres, cultural, aesthetic, or production contexts, not to mention the extensive realm of what Genette calls "paratexts" (titles, prefaces, epigraphs etc.) and "metatexts," the discourse about the text by fans and critics that surrounds the text proper.[53] These connections form an implicit intertextual and intermedial web, yet they have the potentiality to turn into adaptations as soon as they are enacted, performed, and recognized as adaptations by a particular community.

Having established that adaptations can be regarded as networks of circulating signification, what follows from such a proposition? What is

50 Wendy Hui Kyong Chun. "Networks NOW: Belated Too Early." In *Network Theory and American Studies*, special issue of *Amerikastudien/American Studies*, ed. by Ulfried Reichardt, Heike Schäfer, and Regina Schober, 60.1 (2015), 37.

51 Alexander Galloway, "Networks." In *Critical Terms for Media Studies*, ed. by W.J.T. Mitchell and Mark B.N. Hansen (*The Univ. of Chicago Press,* 2010), 281.

52 Stanley Fish, "Interpreting the 'Variorium'," *Critical Inquiry* 2.3 (Spring 1976), 483.

53 Gerard Genette, *Palimpsests: Literature in the Second Degree* [1982], transl. by Channa Newman and Claude Doubinsky (Lincoln: University of Nebraska Press, 1997), 3; 8.

the heuristic function of applying the network metaphor to the study of convergence culture? Of the various implications the network perspective may have, I would argue that three are particularly relevant. Firstly, convergence culture "as network" focuses more on the process rather than on the result or "art work." Secondly, the decentralized quality of adaptation and convergence urges us to rethink agency and control. Thirdly, adaptation processes display emergent properties that result from complex reciprocal interaction. Taken together, these three principles shift the focus from "fidelity" and "origin" to "function" and enable a scalable, thus multidimensional, approach to the study of adaptation as a shifting configuration of ideas, media, and human actors.

While the processual nature of adaptations as evolving and circular practices of approximating the "truth" have been discussed in relation to the Pragmatist "adaptation" of Darwinian evolution, the problem of agency becomes even more pressing in relation to network theory. If adaptation takes place within interlocking semiotic, cultural, and social systems, agency has to be reconceptualized as distributed within these networks. Debates in the context of a new materialism and particularly within Actor-Network Theory prove helpful for reconsidering adaptation and convergence. Bruno Latour suggests that the social is to be understood as "a type of momentary association which is characterized by the way it gathers together into new shapes."[54] Latour claims that these agents are not necessarily human agents, but that "*any thing* that does modify a state of affairs by making a difference is an actor," including non-humans.[55] Accordingly, media can just as well be considered agents in a complex network of production and signification, as are writers, producers, recipients, or cultural institutions. Media, in fact, are perhaps closest to what Latour calls "mediators," which, due to their complexity, "transform, translate, distort, and modify the meaning or the elements they are supposed to carry," as opposed to "intermediaries" which simply carry meaning without transforming it.[56] Media therefore have two functions within the assemblage of the social, being at once conveyers of social "meaning" as well as actors generating and reflecting this meaning. If we consider media and other objects to be agents in processes of adaptation and convergence, we need to rethink the concept of creativity as a faculty reserved to the human mind. Whether we embrace such a distributed process of cultural production or whether we remain skeptical with regard to the loss

54 Latour, *Reassembling the Social*, 64–65.

55 Ibid., 71.

56 Ibid., 39.

of human power and control, such shifts in perspective put into question well-established categories such as authorship and copyright, and thus touch on one of the most vulnerable domains of culture, its value system.

Perhaps the most fundamental effect of distributed agency in complex systems is that outcomes of media production become less predictable. Through co-evolving processes that are entangled with each other, and which interact in recursive, non-linear feedback loops, new things originate which cannot be explained by an analysis of the single parts of which they consist. This is what complexity theory calls "emergence." It does not mean that innovation is purely a matter of chance (or chaos) nor that causal explanations for innovation do not exist. Instead, as Taylor has it, "its occurrence cannot be accurately predicted" because too many factors are entangled in too many interactions.[57] Emergence helps to explain phenomena based on collective behavior, for example in information technology or biology. For example, the complex architecture of an anthill cannot be explained by looking at the thousands of ants that have built it individually, but only by taking into account their interaction and thus the self-organizational tendencies of the ant colony. In the context of convergence culture, emergent patterns account for the seemingly erratic directions media adaptations often take, not only but especially visibly in the age of Web 2.0. Jenkins opens his book *Convergence Culture* with an example of emergent media behavior. In the global circulation and re-appropriation of Dino Ignacio's digital collage of *Sesame Street*'s Bert and Osama Bin Laden, which was printed off the internet, used by anti-American protesters, and eventually made its way back to the US on CNN news, the interaction of different agencies (including the images themselves) leads to multiple levels of signification in different contexts with often surprising effects. Viral videos, memes, fan culture, and crowdsourcing are other notions that display and rely on emergent properties, since they reveal and bring forth patterns of self-organization in largely decentralized media environments.

Process-orientation, distributed agency, and emergence are properties of complex systems that radically challenge the notion of "fidelity" while emphasizing the concept of "function." If adaptation is seen not as an exception but as a rule to cultural production and reception, the focus on process and development weakens the status of both "origin" and "author," thus de-temporalizing cultural consumption. Despite a paradoxical (or, one could argue, compensatory) fetish for "the original" as well as a necessarily

57 Taylor, *The Moment of Complexity*, 137.

diachronic perspective on culture from a critical point of view, the presence of the cultural product in a synchronous relationship with other media, recipients, institutions etc. has increasingly become the focus both in cultural production and in criticism. A network perspective suggests that, entangled in a dense web of influences, allusions, and socio-cultural affects, an artwork cannot be reduced to just one reference medium but, depending on the perspective taken, it exposes a myriad of connections to a whole system of adaptations. The same applies to its functions. An adaptation functions not only *as adaptation*. Depending on its context, it can be regarded as an independent work and as a potential seed for future adaptations. In alluding to the shortcomings of teleological or etiological theories of (biological) function based on cause and effect ascriptions, Bence Nanay argues that a theory of "function" (whether in the sense of biological function or in relation to artifacts) must take into account three premises, namely

1. That "a trait can have two (or more) functions at a time,"
2. That "function attributions can depend on the explanatory project at hand," and
3. That "a trait can have a function but fail to perform this function."[58]

These preconditions demand that function needs to be theorized either in relational terms, according to which the function of a trait token is associated "with the property (or properties) that the trait is being selected *for* in that regime"[59] or from within the individual adaptation itself, independent from all other "texts." Nanay argues that such a view that focuses only on the trait itself (or the adaptation, for the purpose of this argument), seems to contradict the concept of "malfunctioning" since, if there is no other trait/text this particular object can be compared to, it cannot lack any feature/function. Malfunctioning thus becomes a matter of "would."[60] If, for example, the BBC film adaptation of Jane Austen's novel *Pride and Prejudice* was to be considered primarily for what it signifies as a text in its own right (and not as an adaptation), it would have various specific functions independent from the "original" (e.g. to tell the story of Jane Bennett and her sisters in an audiovisual medium or to partake

58 Bence Nanay, "A Modal Theory of Function," *The Journal of Philosophy* 107.8 (August 2010), 412–414.

59 D.M. Walsh, "Fitness and Function," *The British Journal for the Philosophy of Science*. 47.4 (December 1996), 565.

60 Nanay, "A Modal Theory of Function," 420–421.

in a nostalgic revival of period drama in British television). The question whether this adaptation is "successful" or indeed "malfunctioning" becomes obsolete since this is what Nanay calls a "modal" question, a question that is purely hypothetical since the adaptation, from its pure existence alone, inevitably has functions bound to its own intra- and extratextual relations. Not even the frequently mentioned aspect of "aesthetic quality" (whatever this may be) is a valid criterion for judging the overall function of the adaptation, since "quality" and "function" are not necessarily the same thing. "Aesthetic quality" is itself a highly subjective and context-dependent category, thus representing one possible function for making value judgments but not the only one. Thus, aesthetic quality does not equal function, but is only an attribute ascribed to a particular adaptation based on systems of cultural distinction (which can itself be a function of the adaptation).

Both theories of "function" are effective in adaptations. The function of an adaptation depends just as much on its relation to other texts or media as on its own properties and its status as medium in its own right. The network perspective reconciles these two notions of function, since networks are defined by what Castells calls their "scalability," namely that "they can expand or shrink in size with little disruption."[61] Networks potentially encompass a multitude of perspectives; they allow us to "think *simultaneously* the singular and the multiple, the common and the unique."[62] Depending on the scale chosen, we can zoom into the level of the individual or zoom out and look at interrelations or the network as a totalizing structure, "a meshwork of overlapping cultural formations, of hybrid reinventions, cross-pollinations, and singular variations."[63] The function of adaptations as constituting a network of different agents therefore oscillates between Walsh's "relational" and Nanay's "modal" function, between the question which traces and associations the adaptation bears to past and future texts and the question how it is unique in its functions, irrespective of other media. The scalability of networks as map-like structures makes them a heuristic tool for switching between different layers of signification and between shifting cultural functions. However, networks are always abstractions, suggesting coherence and a horizontal ontology where there might be fragmentation and hierarchies.

61 Castells, "Informationalism, Networks, and the Network Society," 6.

62 Tiziana Terranova, *Network Culture: Politics for the Information Age* (London, New York: Pluto Press, 2004), 1.

63 Terranova, *Network Culture*, 2.

Regaining critical agency through adaptation

An awareness of intermedial complexity can be made productive for rethinking intermedial relations in terms of constant, reciprocal processes of interaction by human or non-human agents with emergent properties. As metaphors, both evolution and the network shift our attention towards such features of complex systems as reciprocity, self-organization, and co-adaptation as well as their interaction. Eventually, we as scholars have to note that we are also actors in the network of adaptations, since, as Humberto Maturana proclaimed, "everything said is said by an observer."[64] If we regard adaptations as a set of connections, the first connection that has to be made or, to use the terminology of neuroscience, that is *activated*, is made by the observer. Hutcheon remarks that adaptations can potentially be treated as original texts in their own right and *as adaptations*. In considering what she calls an "adaptation's double-nature" she argues that to label something as "adaptation" is already an interpretative choice made by the observer.[65] To call something an "adaptation" thus establishes a contingent connection, one that is not necessarily, or essentially, given, and could be imagined otherwise. This system-theoretical insight that our observations are bound to our own perceptual system seems to be particularly valid for adaptation studies, since the research focus of case studies is always necessarily a reduction of potential cross-links and effects. At the same time, a network approach also puts emphasis on the negotiating processes within an interpretive community. While the individual observer may be bound to an isolated perspective, adaptations function largely within more or less heterogeneous social communities. The functions of adaptations therefore have to be regarded in the context of cultural negotiation processes with competing viewpoints and functional ascriptions, a view that further complicates the contingent cultural status of adaptations (if, for example, fan communities pertain to the fidelity values much more persistently than adaptation scholars).

A perspective that takes seriously the relational and complex dynamics of adaptations foregrounds the functions of adaptations, thus undermining attempts to hierarchize, and make value judgments based on misleading notions of "origin," "fidelity," and "purpose." Instead, such an approach emphasizes the value of process, diversity, and creativity of adaptations as

64 Humberto Maturana and Francisco Valera, *Autopoesis and Cognition. The Realization of Living* (Dordrecht, Boston: D. Reidel, 1980), 8.

65 Linda Hutcheon, *A Theory of Adaptation* (New York: Routledge, 2006), 6.

necessary elements of cultural evolution. It gives weight to cultural functions, contexts, and contingency, thus taking agency away from individual authors and instead empowering other human and non-human actors in the complex web of retellings and remediations. One may even claim that networks of adaptations are self-organizing, that they function without central authority or control. However, that does not mean that networks are inherently democratic structures. Although agency is distributed in networks, it is not necessarily distributed equally. Networks show specific power laws and despite their connectivity, they are not totally inclusive. In containing an ambivalent tension between connection and disconnection, between net and the "in-between, [...] the not-net,"[66] and fundamentally operating on the "binary logic" of "inclusion/exclusion,"[67] networks can suggest highly conflicting notions of both belonging and separation, of unity and fragmentation, of anxiety and fascination.

Similarly, the question of how power is distributed in convergence culture cannot easily be answered. Both evolution and the network are models that are often associated with "organic" structures and processes. In many respects, it makes sense to regard literature and culture as equally vibrant systems that evolve in a creative and often unexpected way. However, we need to be careful not to naturalize adaptation processes. Both production and reception processes rely largely on the centralized efforts of human subjectivity as well as on intersubjective modes of social, cultural, and communal recognition. Stories only tell themselves to a certain extent. Storytelling itself is intricately connected with the human need to understand and structure the world. As long as humans ascribe meaning to stories, all narrative processes will be directed, organized, and evaluated by human beings. What is more, power resides not only in the collective intelligence of a bottom up participatory culture, but also or even largely in the hands of corporations involved in the production and dissemination of culture. The United States, in particular, displays a paradox between a culture often associated with a proclivity to decentralized structures, participation, and what I would consider a Pragmatist notion of instrumental adaptation, while at the same time depending largely on the power of media corporations. In my argument I have not focused on the politics of adaptations that are, of course, more complex than the label "participatory" suggests. At this point, let me only briefly mention some of the problematic aspects of the decentralized logic of Web 2.0 participation without going into the nuances

66 Böhme, "Einführung: Netzwerke," 21, my translation.

67 Castells, "Informationalism, Networks, and the Network Society," 4.

of the debate around amateur and professional reading and production: Tiziana Terranova addresses the capitalist exploitation of "free labour" in the New Economy, alluding to a wide range of functions that adaptations have in a global market with distributed modes of production, reception, and dissemination.[68] Evgeny Morozov dismantles the rhetoric of "participative liberation" even further by pointing to the fallacies of what he calls new media's "solutionism". Not only does this view tend to "prize participation in culture much more than culture itself," but also a delegation of cultural critique to the crowds' rating or ranking neglects complex functions of professional criticism that go beyond personal taste and appreciation.[69] While Morozov's concepts of "professional" versus "crowd" reception of culture may simplify the wide range of possible functions both on a professional and an amateur level (not to mention the contingencies of these ascriptions in general), his critique productively informs a view on adaptation beyond an ahistorical idealization of a new media culture that neither accounts for the existence of convergence phenomena before digital media nor critically reflects on the political implications of such a culture.

It is not my attempt to argue for technological determinism or for the "rule of the system" but rather the opposite: by developing an understanding of the complexities and contingencies of adaptations, audiences can become empowered to enjoy the creativity involved in decentralized systems while at the same time being able to value individual ideas and origins. The different functions of adaptations – whether aesthetic, social, economic, or political – may account for the inherent "adaptability" of adaptations. At the same time, they explain why popular and academic discourses on adaptations have always been and perhaps will always be charged with irreconcilable tensions, conflicting value ascriptions, and territorial struggles. As Fredric Jameson reminds us, adaptations display the poststructuralist notion of "Difference" on two levels: while representing the original's "other," "[d]ifference is also opposition, antagonism, struggle, and it seems possible that the differences between novel and film versions also harbor some more-active tensions between word and image, if not literature and film itself."[70] To theorize adaptation from a perspective that emphasizes process, complexity, and function means to take a fresh view on literature and culture

68 Terranova, *Network Culture*, 73.

69 Evgeny Morozov, *To Save Everything Click Here: Technology, Solutionism, and the Urge to Fix Problems That Don't Exist* (London: Penguin, 2013), 178–179.

70 Fredric Jameson, "Afterword: Adaptation as a Philosophical Problem." In *True to the Spirit: Film Adaptation and the Question of Fidelity*, ed. by Colin MacCabe, Rick Warner, and Kathleen Murray (Oxford University Press, 2011), 230.

itself, and to reflect on the ambiguities and ideologies hidden within the shifting systems of signification, knowledge production, and interaction involved in making sense of our world.

Works Cited

Albrecht-Crane, Christa, and Dennis Cutchins, eds. *Adaptation Studies: New Approaches*. Madison, NJ: Fairleigh Dickinson, 2010.

Bacon, Michael. *Pragmatism: An Introduction.* Cambridge: Polity, 2012.

Bakhtin, Mikhail M. *The Dialogic Imagination: Four Essays*, edited by Michael Holquist. Austin: University of Texas Press, 1981.

Böhme, Hartmut. "Einführung: Netzwerke. Zur Theorie und Geschichte einer Konstruktion." In *Netzwerke: Eine Kulturtechnik der Moderne*, edited by Jürgen Barkhoff, Hartmut Böhme, and Jeanne Riou, 17–36. Köln: Böhlau, 2004.

Bortolotti, Gary R., and Linda Hutcheon. "On the Origin of Adaptations: Rethinking Fidelity Discourse and "Success" – Biologically." *New Literary History* 38.3 (Summer 2007): 443–458.

Bruhn, Jørgen, Anne Gjelsvik, and Eirik Frisvold Hanssen, eds. *Adaptation Studies: New Challenges, New Directions*. London, New York: Bloomsbury, 2013.

Castells, Manuel. "Informationalism, Networks, and the Network Society. A Theoretical Blueprint." In *The Network Society. A Cross-Cultural Perspective*, edited by Manuel Castells, 3–45. Cheltenham: Edward Elgar, 2004.

—. 1996. *The Rise of the Network Society*. 2nd ed. Vol. 1. Chichester: Wiley-Blackwell, 2010.

Chun, Wendy Hui Kyong. "Networks NOW: Belated Too Early." *Network Theory and American Studies*. Special Issue, edited by Ulfried Reichardt, Heike Schäfer, and Regina Schober. *Amerikastudien/American Studies* 60.1 (2015): 37–58.

Darwin, Charles. *The Origin of Species*. 1859. London: J.M. Dent & Co, 1971.

Deleuze, Gilles, and Félix Guattari. 1980. *A Thousand Plateaus. Capitalism and Schizophrenia*. Transl. Brian Massumi. London, New York: Continuum, 2010.

Dewey, John. *Art as Experience*. 1934. New York: Penguin, 2005.

Eckstein, Lars, and Christoph Reinfandt. "On Dancing about Architecture: Words and Music between Cultural Practice and Transcendence." *Zeitschrift für Anglistik und Amerikanistik* 54.1 (2006): 1–8.

Elliott, Kamilla. *Rethinking the Novel/Film Debate*. Cambridge: Cambridge University Press, 2003.

___. "Theorizing Adaptation/Adapting Theories." In *Adaptation Studies: New Challenges, New Directions*, edited by Jørgen Bruhn, Anne Gjelsvik, and Eirik Firsvold Hannssen, 19–45. London et al.: Bloomsbury, 2013.

Fish, Stanley. "Interpreting the 'Variorium'." *Critical Inquiry* 2.3 (Spring 1976): 465–485.

Fluck, Winfried. *Das kulturelle Imaginäre. Eine Funktionsgeschichte des amerikanischen Romans 1790–1900.* Frankfurt am Main: Suhrkamp, 1997.

Galloway, Alexander R. "Networks." In *Critical Terms for Media Studies*, edited by W.J.T. Mitchell and Mark B.N. Hansen, 280–296. Chicago: The University of Chicago Press, 2010.

Gauntlett, David. *Making is Connecting: The Social Meaning of Creativity from DIY and Knitting to YouTube and Web 2.0.* Cambridge: Polity Press, 2011.

Genette, Gerard. *Palimpsests: Literature in the Second Degree.* [1982] Transl. Channa Newman and Claude Doubinsky. Lincoln: University of Nebraska Press, 1997.

Greenblatt, Stephen. "The Circulation of Social Energy." 1988. In *Modern Criticism and Theory: A Reader*, edited by David Lodge and Nigel Wood, 495–511. 2nd ed. Harlow: Longman, 2000.

Hutcheon, Linda. *A Theory of Adaptation.* New York: Routledge, 2006.

James, William. "Pragmatism's Conception of Truth." 1907. In *The Pragmatism Reader: From Peirce through the Present*, edited by Robert B. Talisse and Scott F. Aikin, 79–91. Princeton: Princeton University Press, 2011.

—. "Does 'Consciousness' Exist?" *The Journal of Philosophy, Psychology and Scientific Methods* 1.18 (1904): 477–491.

—. "Philosophical Conceptions and Practical Results." 1898. In *The Pragmatism Reader: From Peirce through the Present*, edited by Robert B. Talisse and Scott F. Aikin, 66–78. Princeton: Princeton University Press, 2011.

—. "What Pragmatism Means." In *Pragmatism: A New Name for Some Old Ways of Thinking*, 26–41. Rockville, MD: Arc Manor, 2008.

Jameson, Fredric. "Afterword: Adaptation as a Philosophical Problem." In *True to the Spirit: Film Adaptation and the Question of Fidelity*, edited by Colin MacCabe, Rick Warner, and Kathleen Murray, 215–233. Oxford: Oxford University Press, 2011.

—. *Postmodernism or, The Cultural Logic of Late Capitalism.* Durham: Duke University Press, 1991.

Jenkins, Henry. *Convergence Culture: Where Old and New Media Collide.* New York: New York University Press, 2008.

Lagerroth, Ulla Britta. "Reading Musicalized Texts as Self-Reflexive Texts." In *Word and Music Studies: Defining the Field*, edited by Walter Bernhart, Steven Paul Scher, and Werner Wolf, 205–220. Amsterdam and Atlanta: Rodopi, 1999.

Latour, Bruno. *Reassembling the Social: An Introduction to Actor-Network-Theory.* Oxford: Oxford University Press, 2007.

Leitch, Thomas. "Review Article. Adaptation Studies at a Crossroads." *Adaptation* 1.1 (2008): 63–77.

—. *Film Adaptation and Its Discontents: From Gone with the Wind to The Passion of Christ*. Baltimore: The Johns Hopkins University Press, 2007.

MacCabe, Colin, Rick Warner, and Kathleen Murray, eds. *True to the Spirit: Film Adaptation and the Question of Fidelity*. Oxford: Oxford University Press, 2011.

Maturana, Humberto R., and Francisco J. Valera. *Autopoesis and Cognition. The Realization of Living*. Dordrecht, Boston: D. Reidel, 1980.

Morozov, Evgeny. *To Save Everything Click Here: Technology, Solutionism, and the Urge to Fix Problems That Don't Exist*. London: Penguin, 2013.

Murray, Simone. *The Adaptation Industry: The Cultural Economy of Contemporary Literary Adaptation*. New York: Routledge, 2011.

Nanay, Bence. "A Modal Theory of Function." *The Journal of Philosophy* 107.8 (August 2010): 412–431.

O'Connor, Flannery. "Some Aspects of the Grotesque in Southern Fiction." In *Collected Works*, edited by Sally Fitzgerald, 813–821. New York: Library of America, 1988.

Reichardt, Ulfried. "The Network as a Category in Cultural Studies and as a Model for Conceptualizing America." *Network Theory and American Studies*. Special Issue, edited by Ulfried Reichardt, Heike Schäfer, and Regina Schober. *Amerikastudien/American Studies* 60.1 (2015): 17–35.

Sanders, Julie. *Adaptation and Appropriation*. London: Routledge, 2006.

Schober, Regina. "Adaptation as Connection: Transmediality Reconsidered." In *Adaptation Studies: New Challenges, New Directions*, edited by Bruhn, Jørgen, Anne Gjelsvik, and Eirik Frisvold Hanssen, 89–112. London and New York: Bloomsbury, 2013.

—. "'Partial Members of a Vast Natural Network': Notions of Interconnectedness in American Transcendentalism and Pragmatism." *Network Theory and American Studies*. Special Issue, edited by Ulfried Reichardt, Heike Schäfer, and Regina Schober. *Amerikastudien/American Studies* 60.1 (2015): 97–119.

Stam, Robert. "Beyond Fidelity: The Dialogics of Adaptation." In *Film Adaptation*, edited by James Naremore, 54–76. New Brunswick, NJ: Rutgers University Press, 2000.

—. "Introduction: The Theory and Practice of Adaptation." In *Literature and Film: A Guide to the Theory and Practice of Film Adaptation*, edited by Robert Stam and Alessandra Raengo, 1–52. Oxford: Blackwell, 2004.

—. *Literature through Film: Realism, Magic, and the Art of Adaptation*. Malden, MA: Blackwell, 2005.

Taylor, Mark C. *The Moment of Complexity. Emerging Network Culture*. Chicago: University of Chicago Press, 2001.

Terranova, Tiziana. *Network Culture: Politics for the Information Age*. London, New York: Pluto Press, 2004.

Walsh, D.M. "Fitness and Function." *The British Journal for the Philosophy of Science.* 47.4 (December 1996): 553–574.

Watts, Duncan J. *Six Degrees: The Science of a Connected Age.* New York: Norton, 2003.

Wolf, Werner. "Towards a Functional Analysis of Intermediality: The Case of Twentieth-Century Musicalized Fiction." In *Cultural Functions of Intermedial Exploration*, edited by Erik Hedling and Ulla Britta Lagerroth, 15–34. Amsterdam: Rodopi, 2002.

Zapf, Hubert. *Kurze Geschichte der anglo-amerikanischen Literaturtheorie.* 2nd ed. München: Fink, 1996.

About the author

Regina Schober is Associate Professor of American Studies at the University of Mannheim. She recently completed a book manuscript on the history of the network in US American literature. She is the author of *Unexpected Chords: Musicopoetic Intermediality in Amy Lowell's Poetry and Poetics* (Winter, 2011) and co-editor of *The Failed Individual: Amid Exclusion, Resistance, and the Pleasure of Non-Conformity* (Campus, 2017), and special issues of *Amerikastudien/American Studies* and *Studies in American Naturalism.*

3. Filing off the Serial Numbers: Fanfiction and its Adaptation to the Book Market

Bettina Soller

Abstract
The novel series *Fifty Shades of Grey* and *The Mortal Instruments* originated as fanfiction adaptations of the *Twilight* and *Harry Potter* series. E.L. James and Cassandra Clare published in fanfiction archives first, before they deleted their online writing, edited and rewrote their work, and removed traces of fandom so that the narratives could be adapted to the print market. This process is called "filing off the serial numbers" or "pulled to publish" by fans. Beyond the adapted texts, and writing strategies that transitioned from the fan community to the commercial book market, established practices of fan authorship have been adapted as well. The article investigates these consecutive and simultaneous processes of transposition and appropriation as "layered forms of adaptation."

Key words: Fanfiction; Harry Potter; Twilight; pulled to publish; adaptation

Introduction

After the *Fifty Shades of Grey* book series had sold more than 125 million copies worldwide, fans eagerly awaited the release of the movie adaptation in February of 2015. Building on the books' success, the opening weekend of the movie alone grossed $248 million.[1] The production and pre-production of the film was accompanied by media reports and PR announcements of the ways

1 See Ben Child, "Fifty Shades of Grey Beats Avatar with $248m Opening Weekend Box Office," *Guardian*, Feb. 16, 2015.

Fehrle, J. and W. Schäfke, *Adaptation in the Age of Media Convergence*,
Taylor & Francis Group, 2019
DOI 10.5117/9789462983663_CH03

the narrative and specifically the BDSM scenes in the book were adapted to the screen, as well as which actors were cast as the central characters Christian and Ana. Throughout this renewed interest in *Fifty Shades of Grey*, the history of layered adaptation that the text had transitioned through before it was turned into a movie receded into the background.

An earlier version of *Fifty Shades of Grey*, the *Twilight* fanfiction *Master of the Universe*, had been widely read by fans online before the text was stripped of its direct references to *Twilight* and became a commercial success in its own right. *Master of the Universe* is not the only prominent text that evolved from the realms of fanfiction writing; with Sylvain Reynard's *Gabriel's Inferno* and the writing duo Christina Lauren's *Beautiful Bastard* at least three other authors of erotic *Twilight* fanfiction made the *New York Times* bestseller list.[2] Beyond easily adaptable "all human" fanfiction from the *Twilight* fandom, fanfictions from other fandoms, including texts that revel in fantastic supernatural worlds, have successfully transitioned from the communal online and free writing context to the book market.[3] The *Harry Potter* fanfiction *The Draco Trilogy* became the hotbed for *The Mortal Instruments* series and the ensuing *Shadowhunter* franchise that includes multiple series set in its imaginary world. Several installments of these series have made it to the *New York Times* bestseller list for young adult and children's literature as well.

Fan authors, who engage with media texts, write and publish digital fanfiction and delete their online material once they are on the way to becoming professional writers, have probably increased in numbers since James' public success. Aja Romano even argues that, "many authors have been coming to the *Twilight* fandom specifically to launch their careers by 'workshopping' their writing within the *Twilight* fandom."[4] The fan community itself calls the process "pulled to publish" or, perhaps including a reference to the obfuscation of the serial nature of the texts that results

2 Actually, E.L. James followed Reynard in the process of "filing off the serial numbers," and thanked him in an early edition of *Fifty Shades of Grey* for taking the route to republishing fanfiction first. See Anne Jamison, *Fic: Why Fanfiction Is Taking over the World* (Dallas: Smart Pop, 2013), 224.

3 See Jamison, *Fic: Why Fanfiction Is Taking over the World*, 224. And Joseph Brennan and David Large, "'Let's Get a Bit of Context': Fifty Shades and the Phenomenon of 'Pulling to Publish' in Twilight Fan Fiction," *Media International Australia Incorporating Culture and Policy: Quarterly Journal of Media Research and Resources* 152 (2014): 32.
"All human" or AH is a genre designation that signals to the reader that the characters exist in the specific fanfiction without their supernatural features.

4 Aja Romano, "Fifty Shades of Grey and the Twilight Pro-fic Phenomenon," *The Mary Sue* (blog), March 23, 2012.

from the republication of fanfiction, "filing off the serial numbers." The site *twifanfictionrecs.com* provides a list of hundreds of books that are adapted *Twilight* fanfictions. While some writers try their luck with self-publishing, often via Amazon, the Australian publishing house The Writer's Coffee Shop (TWCS) and the US-based Omnific are publishers who specialize in the adaptation of fanfiction for commercial purposes and are responsible for a majority of the titles on these lists, many of which appear as e-books only. Works that have been successful in fan communities and are as issued by these smaller publishers have been purchased and then republished with little risk by larger players like Vintage.

Both Erika Leonard and Judith Rumelt and their respective fanfiction adaptations of popular series were famous in the *Twilight* and *Harry Potter* fandoms respectively before the material, or parts of it, were transposed to the book market. Like them, many fan authors start publishing their fanfictions on *Fanfiction.net*, one of the largest and oldest online fanfiction archives. The site holds fanfictions from many fandoms, among them about 773,000 *Harry Potter* and 219,000 *Twilight* fanfictions, making them two of the most proliferating fandoms on the site for years.[5] Erika Leonard began to publish the *Twilight* fanfictions *Master of the Universe I* and *II* under the pseudonym Snowqueens Icedragon, which appeared in serialized form in over 110 chapters between 2009 and 2010 until it was deleted from the archive because of its explicit content. Leonard moved the text to her webpage *50shades.com* where she continued writing. After scoring a publishing deal with TWCS, she removed all free online content. In May 2011, TWCS published an e-book version and a print-on-demand paperback book based on the fanfiction with the title *Fifty Shades of Grey* under the pen name E.L. James. The sequels *Darker* and *Freed* were published in September 2011 and January 2012 respectively. The e-book was reissued in print after Vintage Books had auctioned the rights for

5 Both franchises began as narratives that developed across multiple novels and have spurred serializations and medial appearances as adaptations into films, graphic novels and games as well as merchandise. That both of these texts have garnered such a huge amount of fan productivity, part of which is fanfiction, is no coincidence, as audience's desire for communal and productive engagement with popular serialized texts is a prevalent practice since at least the turn of the last century, specifically for science fiction and fantasy series. See Jennifer Hayward, *Consuming Pleasures. Active Audiences and Serial Fictions from Dickens to Soap Opera*, (Lexington: UP of Kentucky, 2009); Nancy Baym, *Tune in, Log on: Soaps, Fandom, and Online Community*, (Thousand Oaks, London and New Delhi: Sage Publications, 2000) and Michael Saler, *As If. Modern Enchantment and the Literary Prehistory of Virtual Reality*. (New York: Oxford University Press, 2012).

the series.[6] By now, the first book of the series alone has sold more than 65 million copies worldwide, and the success of the franchise is ongoing. In February 2015 the film version of *Fifty Shades of Grey* was released, followed by the latest book sequel *Grey* in June of the same year. The second movie, *Fifty Shades Darker*, was released in 2017 and the third one in 2018.

Like Leonard, Judith Rumelt initially published the fanfiction series *The Draco Trilogy* (*Draco Dormiens*, *Draco Sinister*, and *Draco Veritas*) on *Fanfiction.net*, beginning in 2000. In March of 2007, now writing as Cassandra Clare, she published the first book of the *Mortal Instrument* series with Simon & Schuster, set in its own imaginary world. Unlike *Fifty Shades of Grey*, *The Mortal Instruments* is not an edited version of Rumelt's fanfiction, but includes passages that are recognizably similar to *The Draco Trilogy*. As Cassandra Claire, she had garnered a substantial following on *Fanfiction.net*, and as in Leonard's case, her account was deleted, this time in 2001. The removal of her account was triggered by accusations of plagiarism, which caused a rift between different groups of fans and administrators on the site. Rumelt moved *The Draco Trilogy* to the developing *Harry Potter* related site *FictionAlley.com*, where her texts remained available until August 2006. Shortly after she concluded the series, Claire informed her readers that her fanfiction would soon no longer be available on fan sites, which allowed fans to finish reading the fanfiction and to secure copies (pdf versions of the fanfiction can easily be found online), before she deleted all of her online material.[7] Since then, Clare, increasingly in collaboration with other authors, has written sequels, prequels and a spin-off series for *The Mortal Instruments* that appeared in print and as e-books. By now, the franchise comprises 21 books, with more in production. The narrative has been adapted into a movie, graphic novels, a TV show, and a game. Online, the media change of the narrative and its characters has gone full circle, as *The Mortal Instruments*' fanfiction is currently among the top ten fandoms in the category "books" on *Fanfiction.net*.

Taken as select examples of a larger phenomenon, the genesis of *The Mortal Instruments* and *Fifty Shades of Grey* each foreground different

6 See Bethan Jones, "Fifty Shades of Exploitation: Fan Labor and Fifty Shades of Grey," *Transformative Works and Cultures* 15 (2014) and Bertrand, Natasha, "'Fifty Shades of Grey' Started Out as 'Twilight' Fan Fiction before Becoming an International Phenomenon," *Business Insider UK*, Feb. 17, 2015.

7 See "The Draco Trilogy." *Harry Potter Wiki*. Accessed Jan. 3, 2017.

aspects of what I call "layered adaptation," a term that refers to consecutive adaptations (novel series that are adapted into fanfiction, which is then transposed to the book market) and adaptations on different levels (stories and texts as well as writing practices and the performance of authorship). "Adaptation" as a concept and the perspective of adaptation studies can be made useful, first, to explain how fanfiction can be understood as a form of adaptation and to point at the differences between the adaptation and appropriation of a series of media texts into fanfiction by fan authors and the transposition of these texts to the book market. Employed to refer to the evolutionary processes of adapting practices to different writing and publishing habitats, "adaptation" also helps to illuminate the processes of adapting practices of communication and authorship performances by Leonard and Rumelt in their transition from the realm of fanfiction writing to the realm of professional authorship. "Layered adaptation" is therefore not only a linear process, but refers to the chronological activities as well as to processes of adaptations taking place simultaneously on different levels. The investigation thus includes the level of textuality on which the adaptation of (multiple) pre-texts and genre conventions takes place as well as the level of practices on which writing, reception, and authorship performances are adapted.[8]

Fanfiction and adaptation theory

In her seminal work *A Theory of Adaptation*, Linda Hutcheon struggles to include fanfiction as a form of adaptation. In the main part of the book, she argues that all fanfictions, like prequels and sequels, are mere expansions of the existing narratives, which fans write because they do not "want [...] a story to end."[9] In contrast to her treatment of fanfiction, Hutcheon includes computer or video games that engage with imaginary worlds[10] of existing media texts, its characters, events and settings, without necessarily repeating the story of the pre-text, which she argues is central for

8 I want to follow Birgit Spengler in her use of terminology using "pre-text" instead of "source" etc. to describe a "text that precedes another text temporally, but [...] can also be read in the sense of "pretext" or excuse. [...] Thus, the term raises but ultimately rejects the idea of subsidiariness," see Birgit Spengler, *Literary Spinoffs: Rewriting the Classics – Re-Imagining the Community* (Frankfurt am Main: Campus, 2015), 13 (note).

9 Linda Hutcheon and Siobhan O'Flynn, *A Theory of Adaptation*, 2nd ed. (New York: Routledge, 2013), 9.

10 Ibid., 14.

most theories of adaptation.[11] Investigating the criteria and practices that comprise her definition of adaptation, the exclusion of fanfiction seems almost arbitrary. While Hutcheon herself does not qualify her assessment in the revised version of her study, the second edition is followed by an epilogue by Siobhan O'Flynn that considers adaptation in a digital context and touches upon fan productivity, including fanfiction. This expression of unease to include fanfiction in this broad group of texts, and its appearance in the epilogue of the book, mirrors the reluctance of established literary studies to include fanfiction in its corpus. This reluctance is astonishing considering the amount of fanfiction available online, which probably outnumbers any other form of digital fiction writing, and its huge number of authors and readers, and, as the case studies at hand show, the impact of fanfiction on the contemporary literary landscape in general.

One reason for the exclusion of fanfiction is its derivative nature and its specific aesthetics, which often lead scholars and literary critics to have an overly simplified notion of fanfiction, which is opposed to the differentiated concept of the genre by its connoisseurs. The (aca-)fan-driven site *Fanlore* provides a minimal definition of fanfiction as "written by fans for other fans [...]."[12] While there are fans writing just for themselves, fanfiction "is most commonly produced within the context of a fannish community and can be shared online such as in archives or in print such as in zines" and takes "a source text or a famous person as a point of departure."[13] The open and communal nature of fanfiction, which allows for good and bad writing, has generally preserved its free availability in web archives such as *Fanfiction.net* or *Wattpad*, on personal blogs, *Tumblr,* or other sites that fans use to publish, despite the nascent presence of fanfiction in commercial spaces like Amazon's Kindle Worlds.[14] In the context of fanfiction, users can engage as readers and writers or offer to proofread and support authors as so-called "beta-readers." "Lurkers" can read fanfiction and observe the fan community online without leaving visible traces. At least potentially, readers can become authors themselves and partake in communication

11 Ibid., 10.

12 Henry Jenkins has popularized the term "aca-fan," which has since been employed by many scholars to describe their own context investigating fandom and media texts both from a critical perspective as academics and as fans and consumers of these texts, see Henry Jenkins, *Fans, Bloggers, and Gamers: Exploring Participatory Culture*, (New York: New York UP, 2006), 4.

13 "Fanfiction," *Fanlore*, accessed Jan. 3, 2017.

14 Kindle Worlds is a platform opened by Amazon in 2013. Here fans can publish and sell fanfiction for specific franchise, which are owned by Amazon, as for example *Gossip Girl* and *The Vampire Diaries*.

about the work in progress through the comment and review sections most sides provide, which fosters communication specifically in between the publications of individual chapters of a fanfiction. Fan authors often encourage collaborative engagement by asking for advice or input, but eventually remain in control of their fanfictions. Because of the importance of the comment and review practices and its interlinkage with fanfictions, Hellekson and Busse have introduced the useful term "fantext" which refers to the network of fanfictions written in a fandom and the accompanying forms of written communication, which in its entirety results from a collective effort.[15]

In this network of texts and inside the fan community, fanfiction readers approach texts with extensively different genre expectations concerning the plot and the structure of narratives than recipients of transmedial storytelling or commercial serializations. Authors and producers of prequels and sequels in existing media narratives, who often also identify as fans, must nevertheless adhere to the canon, the rules, and laws of the franchise.[16] Authors of fanfiction are not restricted in the same sense because they do not need to write fanfiction that is coherent with existing installments, as fanfictions do not necessarily work as extensions. Following a commercial impetus, while being connected to the canon, most installments of franchises can stand and be sold individually. Because digital fanfiction is embedded in a fantext, it is read as one text of several or many. Many fanfictions explore the imaginary worlds of pre-texts while others focus on romantic relationships or play with changes and appropriations to settings and characters established in the media narratives. This means that fanfictions in a fandom do not necessarily exist in the same imaginary world as the pre-text or each other, but rather, due to the innumerable changes fan authors can think of, in parallel universes which fans call AU (alternate universe). Because of fans' interest in the investigation and further creation or appropriation of fantastic worlds, fantasy and science fiction series, like *Twilight* and

15 Karen Hellekson and Kristina Busse, eds., *Fan Fiction and Fan Communities in the Age of the Internet*, (Jefferson: McFarland, 2006), 7.

16 It has been argued that works by professional authors who are fans should be included in definitions of fanfiction, e.g. Sheenagh Pugh, *The Democratic Genre: Fan Fiction in a Literary Context* (Bridgend: Seren, 2005), 25. However, considering fanfiction as a genre of writing points to the differences between professional serializations and amateur fanfiction writing, which becomes visible specifically when authors transition between realms. There are means for authors writing for an established franchise to alter the established canon, e.g. through retroactive continuity in comics. But the necessity for coherence still differs from the freedom fanfiction authors have.

Harry Potter, spur the largest amount of fanfiction that appears online. Smaller fandoms cover everything from prominent popular culture to such literary classics as the Jane Austen novels and even wrestling personas or so-called "Real Person Fiction" about politicians or boy bands. Often, through gaps and elisions in the text, fanfiction points beyond itself and cannot be understood completely without in-depth knowledge of the pre-text or fanfiction conventions. It evades closure through the possibility of ever more fans becoming writers, who can continuously add more fanfiction, more commentary, and reviews to the narrative and the fantext without being organized by an authority like the original author or copyright holders, the canon, or an official timeline. Abigail de Kosnik has discussed at length the importance of digital rogue archives for fan communities. The current state of fan fiction and its involved practices are tied to the affordances of the internet. Online archives, run often by volunteers, allow free access and downloads of texts. Here, fans can evade copyright restrictions; works are preserved and made visible as a part of popular culture (de Kosnik 77).

The uncontrollable sprawling amounts of texts, which leave much creative freedom to their authors, are at the same time structured by conventionalized practices and subgenre distinctions. The texts remain distinctively related to their pre-texts and an understanding of these texts as adaptations helps to understand their meaning and the involved practices. In her book, Linda Hutcheon explains that adaptation must be understood in a threefold manner. First, "as a *formal entity or product,* an adaptation is an announced and extensive transposition of a particular work or works," which can materialize in the same medium as the pre-text or involve a reincarnation in another medium, genre, and context.[17] Like *Master of the Universe* and *The Draco Trilogy*, all fanfictions announce themselves as adaptations implicitly through the identification *as* fanfiction, often quite obviously by being published in a fan archive, or linked to tags that allow readers to find these texts as derivative fictions of existing media narratives. They can be short (drabbles, for example, are pieces of exactly 100 words), but there are hundreds of fanfictions in the *Harry Potter* fandom alone that extend the length of the already extensive pre-text. Individual fanfictions, but even more so the total fantext in a fandom, remain extensively engaged with the pre-text, using the means of the genre.

Fanfictions' engagement with pre-texts is substantially different from a mere quote, reference, or allusion that can be felt as an intertextual influence.

17 Hutcheon and O'Flynn, 7–8.

This process can be further illuminated with Hutcheon's second criterion that defines adaptation as a "*process of creation*" consisting both of "(re) interpretation and then (re)creation."[18] For fanfiction, the relationship or connection to the pre-text is not necessarily one of prolonging, as Hutcheon assumes. Instead, fanfiction writing is the result of a process that necessarily includes the (re)reading of a pre-text and the transformation of the text or its recreation into fanfiction. The two cases at hand show that this process is also part of a reinterpretation. *Master of the Universe* eliminates all supernatural elements from its *Twilight* pre-text. The unequal and abusive dynamics between the vampire Edward and the human Bella[19] are foregrounded and challenged in the fanfiction by translating their liaison into a consensual BDSM relationship. *The Draco Trilogy,* also an AU (alternate universe) text that remains in the world of *Harry Potter* changes the events of the pre-text and features a slash (homoerotic) subtext diverging from established canon.[20] The fanfiction points at the exclusive display of heterosexual relationships in the series, yet remains faithful to most of the parameters of the established imaginary world. Events or plotlines of the canon are re-imagined, when Draco and Harry are transformed into each other after using polyjuice, a potion that allows Harry and Ron to morph into Draco's friends in the canon of *The Chamber of Secrets*. *The Draco Trilogy* has itself been an intertextual influence on other fan adaptations, as the reinterpretation of Draco as a character has been seminally influential in the fandom.

Often fanfictions are not only in dialogue with one pre-text, but create pastiches of several texts, e.g. the novel and film versions of a particular story and other fanfictions, and are additionally created to cater to the expectations of the genre.[21] In her reflection, Julie Sanders explains that beyond the adapted text, other adaptations and appropriations serve as intertexts. Therefore, it might be more fitting in relation to adaptations, especially in the context of fanfiction writing, "to think in terms of complex processes

18 Ibid., 8.

19 See Melissa Miller, "Maybe Edward Is the Most Dangerous Thing out There. The Role of Patriarchy," *Theorizing Twilight. Critical Essays on What's at Stake in a Post-Vampire World*, edited by Maggie Parke and Natalie Wilson, (Jefferson: McFarland, 2011), 165–177 and Wind Goodfriend, "Relationship Violence in 'Twilight': How 'Twilight' Teaches Teens to Love Abusive Relationships," *Psychology Today,* Nov. 9, 2011.

20 Fans consider all information, everything that is "true" and can be known by all audience members about a narrative as "canon."

21 See Louisa Stein and Kristina Busse, "Limit Play: Fan Authorship between Source Text, Intertext, and Context," *Popular Communication* 7 (2009): 192–207.

of filtration, and in terms of intertextual webs or signifying fields, rather than simplistic one-way lines of influence from source to adaptation."[22] The connections between fanfictions and the pre-texts, Sanders' intertextual webs, are actualized in the reception process. Hutcheon refers to the mode of reading in her definition of the third criterion of adaptations. As a "*process of reception*," she explains, "we experience adaptations (as adaptations) as palimpsests through our memory of other works that resonate through repetition with variation."[23] Understanding fanfiction and the involved processes of meaning making is often necessarily based on a reception practice that sees them exactly in this manner. For fanfictions there is an "interrelation between texts which is fundamental to their existence and which at times seems to get to the heart of the literary, and especially the reading, experience" that Sanders deems central.[24] The expectation of authors that their readers will read their texts as fanfiction and therefore as a specific form of adaptation is constitutive even in the structure of many texts, and certainly in the content of the comments and reviews that are part of the fantext of any given fandom.[25] Of course, not all fanfictions are written in the same fashion. Fanfictions can be written as distinct works, as for example many "all human" fanfictions, in which the knowledge of the pre-texts adds another dimension to the reception process but is not fundamental. Fanfictions can further explore motivations of canonical characters, and develop them in ways that provide continuity with the pre-text, bestowing these characters with more emotional and psychological depth. These texts then are a "means of prolonging the pleasure of the original presentation, and repeating the production of a memory" as John Ellis argues for transpositions of narratives into other media.[26] Fanfictions, written as extensions in this sense, are linked to their pre-texts in similar ways as prequels and sequels of franchises.

Yet, at its inception fanfiction is often not intended to stand by itself, even if fans turn to the texts to enjoy the same pleasures repeatedly. The authors of fanfiction can assume that their readers are familiar with the canon. This knowledge is then, as in the reception of other adaptations as well, drawn on and juxtaposed with in the reading process. Not only are the

22 Julie Sanders, *Adaptation and Appropriation* (New York: Routledge, 2006), 24.

23 Hutcheon and O'Flynn, 8.

24 Sanders, 8.

25 Judith Fathalla's *Fanfiction and the Author* provides an extensive investigation of comments and feedbacks in several fandoms. Fathallah's research highlights the cultural work inside fan communities and the complex practices of negotiation.

26 John Ellis, "The Literary Adaptation: An Introduction," *Screen* 23, no. 1 (1982): 4–5.

differences between the texts foregrounded in the juxtaposition, but the depiction of characters, events or settings allows for gaps and often remains flat or even fragmented, because fans can infer their knowledge from the pre-text. *Fanlore* implicitly points to these textual features of fanfiction in its entry "Filing off the Serial Numbers." Counting the fragmentation of depictions as being among the key difficulties when appropriating these texts for a non-fan audience, *Fanlore* explains: "[F]an fiction often depends a lot on the audience's shared knowledge of canon and thus elides a lot of information integral to plot and characterization."[27] In reviews, readers frequently comment on backstories and features or character traits that these characters possess, which are not introduced (again) in each fanfiction. Often, fan readers envision possible continuations based on their understanding of the fanfiction and its conventions by referring to the pre-text. As the adaptation of the pre-texts transitions the narratives to a space with specifically different production and reception practices, the rewritings of fan authors, and the comments and input of other fans accompanying it, highlight the practices of reading and writing itself. Because fans as readers and authors discuss the construction of the text and the act of recreation and appropriation involved in it, fanfictions are explicitly read as adaptations. The act of reading a text "*as an adaptation*," as Hutcheon explains, lets the "adapted text [...] oscillate in our memories with what we are experiencing. In the process, we inevitably fill in any gaps in the adaptation with information from the adapted text."[28] This oscillation in the reading process between fanfiction and pre-text, the filling of the gaps and recognition of the difference between the texts, is an essential part of the pleasure of fanfiction reception. The fragmentation of the fanfictions these processes allow for is probably also the reason many cursory readers and critics discard fanfiction as bad writing, without understanding its specific practices of writing and reception and the pleasures that authors and readers can experience in the process.

Scandalous adaptation and commercial success

With the deletion of her online fanfiction texts and the creation of her pen name E.L. James, Leonard distanced her professional writing identity from her former appearance as Snowqueens Icedragon and obscured the

27 "Filing off the Serial Numbers," *Fanlore*, accessed Jan. 3, 2017.
28 Hutcheon and O'Flynn, 120.

narrative's history as fanfiction adaptation. Screenshots circulate online of Leonard's webpage *50shades.com* that show how she thanked other fans for their contribution to the text, a practice that is common on fanfiction writing sites, which acknowledges the communal nature of fanfiction.[29] However, "such statements of acknowledgement were absent in both the TWCS and Vintage editions of *Fifty Shades*."[30] Leonard has come a long way from her writing in the communal and cost-free context of fan communities. Today, E.L. James is not only selling her fiction, but has been unusually active in capitalizing on the success of her books in the context of the commercial market, e.g. through the creation of a strong authorship identity that extends its power beyond her texts to authorize the film version of her book as well as merchandise that is at times related to the series rather ephemerally. On E.L. James' webpage, users can find links to branded wine, as well as information on where in the books these wines make an appearance. *Fifty Shades of Grey* has further spawned a soundtrack as well as a series of branded sex toys that are marketed with her name as "approved by E.L. James."[31]

Besides the enthusiasm of many of her readers, members of the fan community and critics have critically observed James' transition and her commercial success. In 2015, *The Washington Post* reported on the discourse with the headline: "The most scandalous part of 'Fifty Shades of Grey' isn't the sex and bondage," referring to (inaccurate) claims that the former fanfiction is an infringement of Stephenie Meyer's copyright of *Twilight*.[32] That James has been criticized because of her history as a fanfiction writer and been accused of plagiarizing *Twilight* shows that the success of an author of a derivative work, whose writing profoundly challenges ideas of high cultural notions of "originality" and the "solitary author," does not sit well with many. It probably does not help that *Fifty Shades of Grey* is written by a woman for women, openly addresses female sexual desire and leans towards pornographic descriptions, which additionally lowers the cultural status of the book. Yet, already the question of whether *Fifty Shades of Grey*

29 Jason Boog, "The Lost History of Fifty Shades of Grey," *GalleyCat*, Nov. 21, 2012.

30 See Brennan and Large, 32; also Jones.

31 The sex toys can even be bought as packages with the book. Sites like www.playpassions.com/brands/fifty-shades-of-grey-official-sex-toys also feature the trailer to the movie, accessed February 15, 2019. Therefore, these items always point beyond themselves and invite users/readers to engage further with the franchise.

32 See Christina Mulligan, "The Most Scandalous Part of 'Fifty Shades of Grey' Isn't the Sex and Bondage," *Washington Post*, Feb. 11, 2015. Mulligan, an assistant professor of law, argues that *Fifty Shades of Grey* might infringe on copyright law, but should not. Yet, her article lacks a deep understanding of fanfiction and chimes in with a larger discourse.

is plagiarism is based on a simplified notion of fanfiction, which assumes that these texts are predominantly interested in replications of a preexisting narrative.[33] Brennan and Large rightly observe that because of the fanfiction genre AU/AH (alternate universe and all human), it is obvious that *Master of the Universe* would not resemble *Twilight*. Once the explicit announcement of a connection to a pre-text is taken away, most readers lack the background knowledge to read the text as an adaptation. The commonalities between the texts, once any supernatural elements were stripped off, and the setting had been changed, were the names of the protagonists, and the inference of the features of the characters from the pre-text by its readers. In the new context, in the version of the fanfiction as reincarnated in *Fifty Shades of Grey*, the similarities between the characters Christian and Edward as well as Ana and Bella might as well be explained through the genre of the texts: if at all, they appear to be romance characters of the same type.[34] Nevertheless, the public discussion about the genesis of the text led Vintage publishing to explain that *Master of the Universe* had been edited and rewritten to an extent that resulted in the production of an "entirely original work,"[35] thereby restoring James' status as a traditional author.

Unlike the feuilleton, fanfiction readers accept and value derivative writing and collaboration as the fundament of fan authorship of texts that often center on female desire and are mostly written and read by women. For fans, a comparison between *Master of the Universe*, which was created in the communal context of fandom, and *Fifty Shades of Grey*, which was published as a book by E.L. James, is therefore paramount to a comparison of *Master of the Universe* and *Twilight*. Fans deemed it scandalous that James should claim singular authorship for a text that was created in the fan community, and sell it on the book market. On the blog *Dear Author*, Jane Little compared the texts with the help of three similarity software programs and found 89% similarity between them. Comparisons of text passages on the blog show the extensive editing, the correction of orthographic mistakes

33 On the NPR blog *On the Media*, Rebecca Tushnet, head of the legal board of The Organization of Transformative Works, explains that *Fifty Shades of Grey* is not infringing any copyrights, because it "does not actually copy any of the expression" of *Twilight*; see Rebecca Tushnet, "Fan Fiction and the Law," *On the Media*, March 8, 2013.

34 Katherine Morrissey has investigated the similarities between these texts more thoroughly. See Katherine Morrissey, "Fifty Shades of Remix: The Intersectional Pleasures of Commercial and Fan Romances," *Journal of Popular Romance Studies* 4, no. 1 (2014). Eva Illouz describes the cultural work of *Fifty Shades of Grey* and the reasons why the specific negotiation of sexuality and romance and the related gender ideology is the basis for the huge impact of the book.

35 Brennan and Large, 29.

and the changing of names. Yet, screenshots also show that most of the text remained the same and that the changes did not affect the content or plot. James' first novel transposes most of the written material in the same shape to the new context. Brennan and Large argue that James therefore profited from "a work with derivative origins" and that "the production of this work was collaboratively fostered."[36] They stress that publishing houses like TWCS or Omnific, and implicitly Leonard "exploit the free editing and beta-reading labour offered by the fan community."[37]

Like E.L. James, Judith Rumelt has turned from a popular author publishing her fanfiction for free, into an author who has become a multi-millionaire from the revenues of her franchise. In contrast to Leonard, Rumelt sustained a visible connection to her former writing identity by only dropping the "i" from her fanfiction pen name and publishing as Cassandra Clare with Simon & Schuster. Maybe because she is marketing her professional writing as Young Adult literature, Clare has seemingly come under less scrutiny than James as an author of adult fiction. Probably, there is also less interest in what Clare calls her "juvenilia," because of the extensive difference in the corpus of *The Draco Trilogy* and *The Mortal Instruments*. Yet, Claire has also been at the center of a scandal among fans that erupted as part of negotiations of plagiarism, adaptation, and originality. In her case, the discourse focused on the lack of explicitness of her intertextual references and unannounced instances of adaptation. The debate about appropriate practices of writing implicitly questions what constitutes legitimate practices of (fan) authorship and adaptation.

Accounts of Claire's plagiarism affair usually refer to an online source, a blog by a fan called Avocado (that is now only available via the Wayback Machine). On the blog, which equals about 100 print pages, Avocado retraces the connections between *The Draco Trilogy* and several pre-texts as well as reproducing email exchanges between different members of the community, including Claire, and their stance on her writing practice. According to the site, the conflict began when Avocado identified large portions of Claire's fanfiction as unmarked quotes and reproduced passages from Pamela Dean's *The Hidden Land* as well as dialogue excerpts from other books and TV shows such as *Buffy the Vampire Slayer*. In the quoted emails and comments by Claire, she explains that the hidden references and citations were part of a game between her and her readers who enjoyed tracing these passages back to their pre-text, and were therefore a legitimate form of fanfiction

36 Ibid., 27.
37 Ibid., 32.

appropriation. Beyond the established forms of adaptation and marked or at least traceable quotes that would reverberate in the cultural memory of the contemporary readers of her fiction, Claire's unmarked use of extensive phrases and even scenes from Dean's book, which was out of print at the time, did not play according to the rules of the community, and *Fanfiction.net*. In June 2001, Claire's account was deleted from the site.[38] Not all fans agreed with this penalization of Claire, and she remained a Big Name Fan for the time she continued to publish her fanfiction on the *FictionAlley.com* web page. The explicit and acknowledged reference to pre-texts is therefore central to legitimate forms of writing, at least for those fans who were invested enough to partake in this debate. Claire's ongoing success as a fanfiction writer and her successful transition to the book market also show that there is no coherent fan community that could come to a unitary understanding or evaluation of these concepts. In a similar manner, James has been successful despite all accusations directed at her work. The fan community as well as critics and literary scholars are negotiating, consciously or not, concepts of literary authorship, originality, adaptation, intertextuality, and plagiarism.

In contrast to the transition of *Master of the Universe*, the fantastic elements of the Potterverse that are part of *The Draco Trilogy* needed to be adjusted to avoid infringement on the copyright of the *Harry Potter* franchise, when Clare started to publish her work as novels. The knowledgeable reader will nevertheless see the origins of the text shine through when humans outside of the fantastic world are called "mundanes,"[39] which is reverberant of the "muggles" in the *Harry Potter* series, and the master villain, Voldemort in Rowling's series, is transformed into "Valentine." Readers and fans of Cassandra Clare have pointed out the similarities between scenes and dialogue that are part of her fanfiction and *The Mortal Instruments*.[40] The intertextual references to *The Draco Trilogy* in the book can be read as a nod to the readers who are familiar with the former fanfiction. It can also be read as an indication of the attempts of the author and publishers to create an original author performance for Rumelt or Clare, while at the same time transposing the fanfiction readership to the book market with her, which is underscored by the continuity in her pen name. Rumelt used a strategy

38 See "*The Draco Trilogy*" and Avocado, "The Cassandra Claire Plagiarism Debacle – Part XII," *Journalfen* (blog), Aug. 6, 2006.

39 The term "mundane" is also at times used in fandoms to describe non-fans.

40 See "049. Why I Have a Problem with Cassandra Clare & Why You Should Too." *Life & Whathaveyou* (blog). March 14, 2012.

quite different from Leonard's in her transition by actively sustaining her relationship to her fans, for example by giving them the chance to download her fanfiction before she deleted it. Sustaining her relationship to the readers of her fanfiction is probably one of the pillars of her success.

Sophie Einwächter argues in her doctoral thesis, which investigates fans as entrepreneurs, that the fan who has fans is a specific digital phenomenon because only in the digital sphere is the work of fans visible to a mass audience. Einwächter convincingly argues that fans are not necessarily in opposition to the media texts they transform, and that the social media and fan sites they employ for the distribution of their work already comply to the rules of markets. Additionally, the dynamics of these sites and the skills fans learn through their productions are helping those fans that transition to the commercial market. Einwächter argues that, as in the case of Rumelt and Leonard, fans can develop their own style and transcend derivative writing and emancipate themselves from the pre-texts as I have described above and therefore escape the claims of copyright holders. Einwächter further notices the importance of the established network and community, which helps authors who started out as fanfiction authors to distribute their works.[41] In the magazine *Vanity Fair*, representatives of the publishing industry are quite candid about the process of author transition and the possible profit for both authors and publishers. Journalist Shana Ting Lipton has approached the phenomenon of fanfiction authors' "filing off the serial numbers" as an opportunity for those that already work in the publishing industry and are interested in finding and marketing new authors. Literary agent Lorella Belli explains in Ting Lipton's article that one of the advantages of supporting talents out of this context is that fan authors, like Claire and Snowqueens Icedragon, already have a huge following without any extra kind of promotion. "We're seeing lots of agents, lots of publishers join Wattpad," another growing site that is used by fanfiction authors to publish their texts online, explains head of content Ashley Gardner. Authors are also using the statistics they generate through their fanfiction writing on online sites when they meet with agents. With the traffic they produce, argues Gardner, "this kind of data, along with geographical breakdowns of readership, makes fanfic appealing to both publishers and studios as it comes complete with a built-in audience."[42] Belli also indicates that these texts work on the market because they are adaptations of fanfiction, and

41 Einwächter, 107.

42 Shana Ting Lipton, "How Fifty Shades Is Dominating the Literary Scene," *Vanity Fair*, Feb. 13, 2015.

because they are based on the work of other fans as well: "Most of the original fans are actually very happy for the author because it's almost like they've helped [them] achieve financial success and are also curious to see how the book is going to be different from the original fanfiction."[43] The process of comparing the pre-text to the adaptation in the reading process is therefore not necessarily erased in the relation between fanfictions and their novel adaptations, even though many readers of these books are initially not aware of their fanfiction past. On social media sites like *Goodreads*, where users catalogue their reading, criticize, and discuss books with others, readers who encountered the narrative first as a novel then search for pdf files of the preceding fanfiction to compare *Fifty Shades of Grey* with *Master of the Universe* and *The Mortal Instruments* with *The Draco Trilogy*. Obviously, though, there remains a huge section of the audience that does not read these novels as adaptations at all.

Beyond the question of whether it is ethically questionable to transpose fanfiction to the book market, it is interesting to consider how the meaning of fanfiction changes when it is stripped of its context. Abigail de Kosnik has argued that the media change of narratives affects the meaning of fanfiction focusing on the representation of gender, sexuality, and relationships. De Kosnik explains that active fandoms create a collection of texts that "rework a common set of elements again and again, through multiple stories."[44] Like romances, while often being derided as banal and derivative exactly for their repetitiveness, fanfiction actually presents a complex process of production and reception in which this corpus offers a diversity of relationship models, gender identities, and sexuality. De Kosnik explains that this archive of texts allows "readers to make selections from numerous scenarios and versions of romance, sexuality, connection, binding, yearning, denial, rejection, and release" and offers readers, mostly women, different choices at different times. These texts then open up a diverse multitude of narratives and identity options for specific characters and thereby the chance to "explore manifold trajectories for womanhood and for personhood."[45] Outside of the fanfiction context, and no longer read as one of many adaptations that play with familiar figures, events and worlds, de Kosnik explains that the

43 Ting Lipton.

44 Abigail de Kosnik, "Fifty Shades and the Archive of Women's Culture," *Cinema Journal* 54, no. 3 (2015): 117.

45 De Kosnik, 122. I have made a similar argument in the exploration of identity options in vast narratives with a large cast of characters such as fanfiction and soap operas; see Bettina Soller, "Fan Fiction and Soap Operas: On the Seriality of Vast Narratives," *Serial Narratives. Special Issue of Literatur in Wissenschaft und Unterricht 47, no. 1–2, edited by* Kathleen Loock, (2014)*:* 191–205.

text is "denuded of all markers of its membership in an archive of explicitly intertextual stories" and "loses many, or most, of the potential meanings it can have for female readers."[46] While being popular and financially successful, many of the novels that resulted from the transition of fanfiction have been criticized for their flatness by literary critics. De Kosnik likewise argues that *The Mortal Instruments*, presented as an original work, has lost "its narrative force. Rather than being an interesting play on a set of core story elements and familiar characters, the fantext becomes meaningless, a set of seemingly empty signifiers."[47] I would not necessarily agree with de Kosnik on this point, because also as "mere" genre literature, *The Mortal Instruments* offers interesting challenges to the romance genre, for example through the introduction of homosexual attraction between some of the main characters. These changes or variations can be read in comparison to other entries in the archive of young adult fantasy fiction in a similar way as a fanfiction would be read in reference to the pre-text and other entries in the fanfiction archive. This comparative reading demands a reader experienced in the conventions of the fantasy or romance genre, one who proactively reads and compares works alongside each other. While such a comparative process is inherent in the reception and production of fanfiction, it cannot be assumed to the same extent in the reception of independently published novels. Additionally, as mentioned before, a substantial number of readers are well aware of the novels' genesis as fanfiction. Therefore, the novels remain in a liminal position. They can be read as adaptations, as fanfiction as well as distinct novels.

The performance of authorship and the adaptation of fanfiction practices

Some of the unease fanfiction provokes in its public perception lies in the challenge to established ideas of "work" and "authorship" that are triggered by the visibly divergent practices of writing and performances of authorial identities on these online sites. On profiles and personal blogs, fans usually define themselves through their affinity to specific media texts, as authors of derivative works, and thereby indicate part of the intertext in which their fanfiction is created. The writing functions for comments on fan sites foreground multiple authorship, and the collaborative nature of the genre

46 De Kosnik, 122.

47 Ibid., 123.

has in the print market and in traditional literary studies generally been credited with a lower cultural status than that of solitary authorship. The cliché of the fan as a fanatic who is too emotionally attached and in the worst case even unable to distinguish between reality and fiction adds another layer to the low status of fanfiction writing. On fan sites, many authors use pseudonyms or pen names and make little reference to their lives outside of fandom. The anonymity renders fan sites a safe space, where women can write freely about sexually explicit topics and do not have to fear the ridicule often directed at emotionally attached female fans. At the same time, fandom is a space for "insiders" where fans share knowledge about, and appreciation or love for, media texts and the practices of fanfiction writing, and friendships are fostered in private messages.

By moving outside of fanfiction writing and into the public sphere of the market, Clare and James have not simply come to inhabit their "real" author identities as names became attached to physical bodies. Rather, and this is stressed by their usage of a new set of pen names, they have created another authorship performance. "E.L. James" and "Cassandra Clare" neither continue their fan authorship nor break completely with former practices. While both authors marginalize their history as fan authors, they both adapt practices of the fan context. As argued before, the adaptation of these practices are here considered as part of *layered adaptations* that include authorship performance as well as the interaction with fans and readers but also the practices of writing and serialization that are common in fan communities.

James and Clare have created online outlets that provide a space for the staging of their authorship identities, and they have also repeatedly appeared in TV and print interviews and at public events during which specific narratives about themselves as authors are circulated. Both have short versions of an author narrative or "bio(graphy)" on their websites built on select personal information that then tend to be repeated in different contexts, often with small anecdotes or details as embellishments. James stresses on her homepage that she lives in London as a mother and wife. She states that she used to work in TV and always wanted to be a writer.[48] In the FAQ list on the site, James explains that, before it was picked up by Vintage, "[a]n earlier version of this story began as Twilight fanfiction which was posted on the internet."[49] In an ABC interview from 2012, which is exemplary for her performance, she recounts her own pleasures in the reception of the *Twilight* series ("I just sat on my sofa and

48 See James, E.L. "About Me." *E.L. James*. Accessed Sept. 15, 2015.

49 E.L. James, "Frequently Asked Questions." *E.L. James*. Accessed Sept. 15, 2015.

read them, and read them, and read them") and how she then wrote her own "novel," evading the labeling of her early writing as fanfiction and omitting this crucial step in her evolution as a writer, even though most of her work was previously published in this context. When the interviewer asked her where the idea for her novel came from, James explained: "I was inspired by Stephenie Meyer. She just flipped this switch."[50] James problematically omits the fact that the format of writing she employed (AU/AH fanfiction) existed prior to her contribution in online archives with an established tradition. Instead, she repeatedly refers to personal inspirations, for example, when she recounts in many interviews that writing has helped her through her midlife crisis.[51] In the interview with ABC, she explains that her research in BDSM practices was at least partially undertaken in her own bedroom. When talking about the details of her writing process, she mentions that much of it was done on her way to work on her Blackberry and then transferred to her Mac, providing very specific details while omitting any of the practices of publication and communication of the fan community, and the engagement between authors and readers on these sites. Even when James talks about her relationship to *Twilight*, as in the interview for ABC, she generally weaves in and privileges her past as a professional writer, a TV executive "who worked at the BBC in London."[52]

Cassandra Clare likewise provides an author's biography on her website. She explains that she traveled the world with her family, which is often referred to as the beginning of her desire to create new worlds, and that she started to write as a high school student. Clare also stresses that she began to write professionally, in her case for magazines and tabloids, after college and then immediately skips to her work "on her YA novel, City of Bones, in 2004, inspired by the urban landscape of Manhattan," and the beginning of her career as a professional fantasy writer in 2006.[53] In the FAQ section on her site, Clare never mentions fanfiction and the pre-text of her writing even while answering explicit questions concerning the inspirations for her characters and if her protagonists Clary, Jace, and Simon are based on people she knows. For fan readers Clary does not coincidentally rhyme with Harry, and Jace's physical analogies to the fandom version of Draco

50 Shana Druckerman and Sean Dooley, "Fifty Shades of Grey: Author Speaks," *ABC News*, April 20, 2012.

51 See "EL James Used Life Experience for 'Fifty Shades'," *TODAY*, NBC, Feb. 5, 2015.

52 Druckerman and Dooley, "Fifty Shades of Grey: Author Speaks."

53 Clare, Cassandra. "My Bio." *Cassandra Clare. The New York Times Bestseller Author of the Mortal Instruments*. Sept. 15, 2015.

Malfoy are obvious.[54] Like James, Clare completely omits the years she spent writing in the fan community in her author narrative and instead ties her work to her personal and professional life. In her public appearances and in communication with her readers, she narrates anecdotes about friends who were models for characters and dialogue she overheard which she than weaves into narratives. In her appearance at the National Book Festival in 2011, she identifies her work as extensively intertextual, and shows that the practices of pastiche, appropriation, and transformation that she was hailed for (as well as accused of plagiarism) in the context of fanfiction writing are still part of her writing procedure:

> [U]sually characters are a composite of people I know, [...] pure imagination, people I've read about, [...] characters I've loved and books and movies and television and historical figures, usually all so mashed up that by the time that the character hits the page, even the person it was originally based on, doesn't recognize themselves anymore.[55]

When an audience member explicitly asks her about her history as a fanfiction writer, and the merits she gained from the practice, Clare diverts from the subject, and points to her professional career as a writer again: "I think if you write fanfiction, if you write nonfiction, if you write technical writing, if you did what I did and write journalism for six or seven years, it's all helpful." Asked for her inspiration for *The Mortal Instruments* in a TV feature, Clare also refers to autobiographical anecdotes as a form of pre-text. She explains that she was interested in writing a fantasy novel set in New York when she moved there, and was inspired by tattoos based on runes, which were originally applied to warriors as symbols of protection, at a friend's tattoo parlor: "And so I thought, what about a series about a [...] group of modern day demon hunters, and they use these tattoos and they really work and so that was [...] the spark idea and I went home and started trying to develop the magic system."[56] Again, Clare provides a lot of detail and personal anecdotes to account for her writing while omitting another dimension of her circumstance like the fact that the magical tools such as wands and potions that are part of the so-called Potterverse needed to be

54 On the FAQ site, Clare explains that the characters are invented for the story and sometimes inspired by people she knows. The answer very cleverly evades any illusion to Draco by stating, "Jace, alas, is definitely not based on anyone real."

55 Cassandra Clare, *Cassandra Clare: 2011 National Book Festival. The Library of Congress*. 2011.

56 Ibid.

transformed in her own series to prevent any form of copyright infringement and to create her own brand. While both James and Clare indicate the personal inspiration for their novels, Clare specifically points at the work and artisanship that is involved in the writing process and talks a lot about the writing group that she works with, which also makes repeated appearances in TV features about her. Despite the attempts at distancing herself from all things fanfiction, the foregrounding of artisanship, the way she weaves intertextual references into the text and the communal practice of writing with her writing group, all provide similarities to her history as a fan author.

Despite their prominence as fanfiction authors, and their interest in keeping their fan readers as a readership for their professional writing, James and Clare provide an "official" performance of authorship that does not quite deny their previous writing but, to say the least, lessens its importance and impact on their succeeding texts and success. Yet, beyond the layer of adaptation identified here that accounts for the material that transitioned from one habitat to the other, which also affects reception practices that understand these texts as adaptations, on another layer, both James and Clare adapted practices of communication and writing from fanfiction processes. Clare, in particular, extensively employs social media channels to engage with her fans in feedback loops that resemble the conversations between authors and readers in the fan community and the communication among fans about the text at the center of a fandom. She extensively reposts and answers her fans' questions about the universe and specific characters in a back and forth conversation with her audience. Her posts include content, like pictures of her with the actors of the TV adaptation of *The Mortal Instruments*, that function both as part of her authorship performance and as a fan practice. Like fans, she discusses her emotional connection to the characters and provides information that dives deeper into the constituency of the imaginary world the narrative is set in, and answers questions that are left open by the text, e.g. speculations about what happens to the characters after the end of specific series, specifically on her Tumblr blog *The World of the Shadowhunters*. She posts fan art, or art inspired by the franchise and clips and photos related to it. Her Twitter and Tumblr feeds are embedded on the official website for the series, advertising a reception practice that includes the ongoing communication with and interpretation by the author. Unlike on fanfiction sites, the exchanges between her and her readers and fans are not part of a fantext but are selected so that Clare remains in control of what appears on her blog. However, because she uses hashtags and retweets posts by other Twitter users, she also points at the larger network of agents that post *The Mortal Instruments*-related content. Therefore, the exchanges between Clare and her readers function in some sense in a similar manner to those that are posted by fans in reaction to fanfiction in public spaces online. Michael Saler has observed of these public spaces where imaginary worlds are discussed that they allow audiences to engage with the texts with a "double-minded consciousness," immersing themselves in the imaginary world, yet also critically reflecting upon its creation, laws, and logic.[57] The detailed discussion with the author about the construction of the text and possible continuations of it that are so specific to the digital context of fandom are partially replicated here and integrated with the commercial drive of the series.

The usefulness of social media for the commercial success and endurance of serial fiction has been discovered by copyright holders, publishing houses, and film production companies. The communication between authors and readers is probably one of the reasons why fanfiction authors, who have practiced similar exchanges with their audiences in the context of fanfiction writing, have become so attractive for publishers. Other authors, without a history in fanfiction, of course also employ social media. After Stephenie Meyer, who has a long history of engaging with fans online, had repeatedly explained that she did not want to return to the *Twilight* universe,[58] she did get involved in a project that supported female filmmakers by providing them with the means to produce short spin-off films of the *Twilight* movies that have exclusively been shown on Facebook. The Lionsgate vice chairperson Michael Burns is quoted in a *New York Times* article, expressing the commercial impetus of the project: "We think Facebook is a great way for us to introduce the world of 'Twilight' to a whole new audience while re-energizing existing fans."[59] Brooks Barnes explains that interaction with the audience is part of keeping the value of series at a high level in between prequels and sequels, instead of "forcing marketing teams to constantly reactivate cold fan bases. Now the savviest studio marketers are using *Facebook, Tumblr, YouTube,* and other online platforms to keep fans on a constant low boil."[60] Authors and producers of series are therefore developing strategies to make use of the social networks that fan authors have been familiar with for a long time. More than that, former fan authors

57 Saler, 30.

58 Dave McNary, "Q&A Stephenie Meyer: 'Twilight' Author Trades Undead for Well-Bred in 'Austenland'," *Variety*. Aug. 13, 2013.

59 Brooks Barnes, "'Twilight' to Be Revived in Short Films on Facebook," *New York Times, Sept. 30,* 2014.

60 Ibid.

already bring audiences with them to the book market that are interested in and familiar with these forms of communication and add – through their engagement – to the value of a series or text.

Beyond the feedback loop and communication between authors and audiences, Clare and James also replicate writing strategies, specific forms of serialization and adaptation that are similar to those established in the fanfiction context. Cassandra Clare stands out as an author who extensively engages with the imaginary world that she has created. Just like the sprawling amount of fanfictions that continuously explore the world of *Harry Potter*, Clare has continued to write in the *Shadowhunter* universe of *The Mortal Instruments*, adding prequels and sequels as well as zooming in on individual characters, for example in the e-novellas that focus on the character Simon. James, on the other hand, has specifically taken up a feature of fanfiction writing by retelling the story already told in *Fifty Shades of Grey* from the perspective of a different character in *Grey*. While serialization is a common feature in popular culture in general, James' latest installment in the *Fifty Shades of Grey* series that narrates parts of the series again from the perspective of Christian instead of Ana is more common in the fan realm than in other writing contexts. On her site, she published the press announcement of the book, which was released on June 18, a date which, it is argued, is significant, and "devotees may remember as Christian's birthday." Further, the release argues: "Since the publication of Fifty Shades of Grey in 2011, thousands of readers have written to James requesting Christian's POV." The detailed knowledge of readers, the requests of readers for specific content, and the development of this content is common in the communication between authors and readers in fanfiction contexts, which is also related to the sentiment of gifting these stories to fans of, for example, a specific pairing. Fanfiction related to the *Fifty Shades of Grey* trilogy was already very popular online, and had taken on the task of relating Christian Grey's perspective before James. Alexandra Alter explains that popular fanfictions, like those published on Emine Fougner's blog, garnered an enormous readership. Fougner has generated a staggering number of 14 million views on the page.[61] By now, Fougner's writing has also transitioned to the e-book market as *Echoes in Eternity – The Pella Series Novel*, an erotic novel with fantastic elements, which not coincidentally features a relationship that resembles the power dynamics of Edward and Bella or Christian and Ana.

61 Alexandra Alter, "'Fifty Shades' Fan Fiction Assumes a Life of Its Own," *New York Times*, June 19, 2015.

By now, the authors of the pre-texts for *Fifty Shades of Grey* and *The Mortal Instruments* are also extensively invested in convergence strategies that are again part of fan writing strategies and are even taking on writing practices that are specific to fanfiction conventions. J.K. Rowling (and Sony, one might add) has been invested in keeping fans constantly on the low boil, as Barnes says, with the online platform *Pottermore*. On the site, fans can engage with the universe and the stories by being sorted into one of the houses of the Hogwarts School, playing interactive games, or joining conversations on message boards. The site has also been used to promote Rowling's renewed engagement with the franchise. She wrote a play about Harry Potter's life before the first book of the series and investigates the imaginary world further through the script of the movie prequel *Fantastic Beasts and Where to Find Them* which opened in 2016, and will form part of a new trilogy. Yet Stephenie Meyer has come even closer to emulating and cashing in on fan practices by writing *Life and Death*, a novel that retells the *Twilight* events centering on a female vampire and a male love interest for the occasion of the 10th anniversary of the first book of the series. Already in 2008, Meyer, like James did with *Grey* and like many fans before them, had released a version of *Twilight* retold from the perspective of Edward instead of Bella on her webpage. Fan practices are therefore not only adapted by fan authors who transition into professional writing but they have proven to be so successful for specific fandoms that the authors of the pre-texts are adapting them as well.

Conclusion

Fifty Shades of Grey and *The Mortal Instruments* are two examples of a larger phenomenon in which authors and texts transition from the realm of fanfiction writing to the professional and commercial book market. This chapter argues that this process involves forms of "layered adaptations," adaptations and appropriations of narratives or stories as well as practices of writing, reception, communication, and authorship performance. These processes take place at times in consecutive steps, when we consider *Master of the Universe* as an adaptation of *Twilight*, which is then transposed to the book market as *Fifty Shades of Grey*, as well as simultaneously on different levels of textuality and practices in the adaptation of authorship performances and subgenres. The fanfictions *Master of the Universe* and *The Draco Trilogy* are both adaptations of pre-texts that transpose a narrative or parts of it to the context of fanfiction writing, functioning as announced adaptations (all fanfictions are understood by their readers to be a form of transformative and derivative writing) that are part of a serialization through fanfictions with their specific forms of production and reception. These texts include recreation and often reinterpretation and are read by other fans as adaptations, something which becomes most prominently visible through the comments and reviews fans write, and in which they compare and contrast the fanfiction with the pre-text and discuss information and backstory which they have inferred from their knowledge of the pre-text.

Discussions and debates among critics and fans about the legitimacy of specific practices of writing, in the case of Clare's unannounced adaptation of Pamela Dean, and claims of authorship, both discussed in reference to James by journalists that inferred she was infringing on the copyright of *Twilight* and fans that argued that she had exploited fan labor, can be read as negotiations of legitimate forms of (fan) authorship. Both authors do not represent ideal fan authors, who understand themselves as part of a community and publish their texts including references to all pre-texts, but nor do they wholly represent established forms of professional authorship based on practices of solitary writing and originality. In their own authorship performance, as professional authors, James and Clare have marginalized their history in writing fanfiction and foregrounded their experience as professional writers in other realms. Yet both, as well as increasingly other authors with no background in fanfiction writing, have adapted practices of communication in which emotional connections to a narrative are discussed, imaginary worlds are further explored and the work is critically examined, as well as utilizing writing strategies that expand the existing narrative through sprawling extensions and refocalized retellings.

Works Cited

Alter, Alexandra. "'Fifty Shades' Fan Fiction Assumes a Life of Its Own." *New York Times*, June 19, 2015. Accessed February 15, 2019, www.nytimes.com/2015/06/20/books/fifty-shades-fan-fiction-assumes-a-life-of-its-own.html.

Avocado. "The Cassandra Claire Plagiarism Debacle – Part XII." *Journalfen* (blog), Aug. 6, 2006. Accessed February 15, 2019. https://web.archive.org/web/20141015235433/http://www.journalfen.net/community/bad_penny/8985.html.

Barnes, Brooks. "'Twilight' to Be Revived in Short Films on Facebook." *New York Times*, Sept. 30, 2014. www.nytimes.com/2014/10/01/business/media/twilight-will-be-revived-via-short-films-on-facebook.html.

Baym, Nancy. *Tune in, Log on: Soaps, Fandom, and Online Community*. Thousand Oaks, London, and New Delhi: Sage Publications, 2000.

Bertrand, Natasha. "'Fifty Shades of Grey' Started Out as 'Twilight' Fan Fiction before Becoming an International Phenomenon." *Business Insider UK*. February 17, 2015. Accessed February 15, 2019. www.businessinsider.com/fifty-shades-of-grey-started-as-twilight-fan-fiction-2015-6?IR=T.

Brennan, Joseph, and David Large. "'Let's Get a Bit of Context:' Fifty Shades and the Phenomenon of 'Pulling to Publish' in Twilight Fan Fiction." *Media International Australia Incorporating Culture and Policy: Quarterly Journal of Media Research and Resources* 152 (2014): 27–39.

Boog, Jason. "The Lost History of Fifty Shades of Grey." *GalleyCat*. November 21, 2012. Accessed February 15, 2019. www.adweek.com/galleycat/fifty-shades-of-grey-wayback-machine/50128.

Child, Ben. "Fifty Shades of Grey Beats Avatar with $248m Opening Weekend Box Office." *Guardian*, February 16, 2015. Accessed February 15, 2019. www.theguardian.com/film/2015/feb/16/fifty-shades-of-grey-beats-avatar-with-248m-opening-weekend-box-office.

Clare, Cassandra. "My Bio." *Cassandra Clare. The New York Times Bestseller Author of The Mortal* Instruments. September 15, 2015. Accessed February 15, 2019. http://cassandraclare.com/about/.

—. *Cassandra Clare: 2011 National Book Festival. The Library of Congress*. 2011. Accessed February 15, 2019. www.loc.gov/today/cyberlc/feature_wdesc.php?rec=5259.

—. "cassandraclare." *Tumblr*, Jan. 1, 2017. http://cassandraclare.tumblr.com.

De Kosnik, Abigail. "Fifty Shades and the Archive of Women's Culture." *Cinema Journal* 54, no. 3 (2015): 116–125.

—. *Rogue Archives. Digital Cultural Memory and Media Fandom*. Cambridge: The MIT Press, 2016.

Druckerman, Shana, and Sean Dooley. "Fifty Shades of Grey: Author Speaks." *ABC News*, April 20, 2012. Accessed February 15, 2019. www.youtube.com/watch?v=Fpm_1iERyoU.

Einwächter, Sophie G. "Transformationen von Fankultur: Organisatorische und Ökonomische Konsequenzen Globaler Vernetzung." PhD dissertation. Johann-Wolfgang-Goethe-Universität zu Frankfurt am Main, 2014.

"EL James Used Life Experience for 'Fifty Shades'." *TODAY*, NBC. February 5, 2015. Accessed February 15, 2019. www.youtube.com/watch?v=b4SvZoSJPqE.

Ellis, John. "The Literary Adaptation: An Introduction." *Screen* 23, no. 1 (1982): 3–5.

"Fanfiction." *Fanlore*. Accessed January 3, 2017. https://fanlore.org/wiki/Fanfiction.

Fathalla, Judith May. *Fanfiction and the Author: How Fanfic Changes Popular Cultural Texts*. Amsterdam: Amsterdam University Press, 2017.

"Filing off the Serial Numbers." *Fanlore*. Accessed January 3, 2017. https://fanlore.org/wiki/ Filing_Off_The_Serial_Numbers.

Goodfriend, Wind. "Relationship Violence in 'Twilight': How 'Twilight' Teaches Teens to Love Abusive Relationships." *Psychology Today,* November 9, 2011. Accessed February 15, 2019. www.psychologytoday.com/blog/psychologist-the-movies/201111/relationship-violence-in-twilight.

Hayward, Jennifer. *Consuming Pleasures. Active Audiences and Serial Fictions from Dickens to Soap Opera*. Lexington: University Press of Kentucky, 2009.

Hellekson, Karen, and Kristina Busse, eds. *Fan Fiction and Fan Communities in the Age of the Internet*. Jefferson: McFarland, 2006.

Hutcheon, Linda, and Siobhan O'Flynn. *A Theory of Adaptation*, 2nd ed. New York: Routledge, 2013.

Illouz, Eva. *Hard-Core Romance. Fifty Shades of Grey, Best-Sellers, and Society*. UCP, 2014.

James, E.L. "About Me." *E.L. James*. Accessed September 15, 2015. www.eljamesauthor.com/about-me/.

—. "Frequently Asked Questions." *E.L. James*. Accessed September 15, 2015. www.eljamesauthor.com/?s=faq.

Jamison, Anne. *Fic: Why Fanfiction Is Taking over the World*. Dallas: Smart Pop, 2013.

Jenkins, Henry. *Fans, Bloggers, and Gamers: Exploring Participatory Culture*. New York: New York University Press, 2006.

Jones, Bethan. "Fifty Shades of Exploitation: Fan Labor and Fifty Shades of Grey." *Transformative Works and Cultures* 15 (2014). Accessed February 15, 2019. http://journal.transformativeworks.org/index.php/twc/article/view/501/422.

Lewis, Andy. "Erotic Novel 'Beautiful Bastard' Getting Movie at Constantin Film (Exclusive)." *Hollywood Reporter*. December 2, 2013. www.hollywoodreporter.com/risky-business/erotic-novel-beautiful-bastard-getting-420776.

Little, Jane. "Master of the Universe versus Fifty Shades by E.L James Comparison." *Dear Author* (blog). March 13, 2012. Accessed February 15, 2019. http://dearauthor.com/features/industry-news/master-of-the-universe-versus-fifty-shades-by-e-l-james-comparison/.

McNary, Dave. "Q&A Stephenie Meyer: 'Twilight' Author Trades Undead for Well-Bred in 'Austenland'." *Variety*. August 13, 2013.

Miller, Melissa. "Maybe Edward Is the Most Dangerous Thing out There. The Role of Patriarchy." *Theorizing Twilight. Critical Essays on What's at Stake in a Post-Vampire World*, edited by Maggie Parke and Natalie Wilson, 165–177. Jefferson: McFarland, 2011.

Mulligan, Christina. "The Most Scandalous Part of 'Fifty Shades of Grey' Isn't the Sex and Bondage." *Washington Post,* February 11, 2015. Accessed February 15, 2019. www.washingtonpost.com/posteverything/wp/2015/02/11/the-most-scandalous-part-of-fifty-shades-of-grey-isnt-the-sex-and-bondage/?utm_term=.bc114c99eaf3.

Morrissey, Katherine. "Fifty Shades of Remix: The Intersectional Pleasures of Commercial and Fan Romances." *Journal of Popular Romance Studies* 4, no. 1 (2014). Accessed February 15, 2019. http://jprstudies.org/2014/02/fifty-shades-of-remix-the-intersecting-pleasures-of-commercial-and-fan-romancesby-katherine-morrissey/.

Romano, Aja. "Fifty Shades of Grey and the Twilight Pro-fic Phenomenon." *The Mary Sue* (blog). March 23, 2012. Accessed February 15, 2019. www.themarysue.com/50-shades-of-grey-and-the-twilight-pro-fic-phenomenon/.

Pugh, Sheenagh. *The Democratic Genre: Fan Fiction in a Literary Context.* Bridgend: Seren, 2005.

Saler, Michael. *As If. Modern Enchantment and the Literary Prehistory of Virtual Reality.* New York: Oxford University Press, 2012.

Sanders, Julie. *Adaptation and Appropriation*. New York: Routledge, 2006.

Soller, Bettina. "Fan Fiction and Soap Operas: On the Seriality of Vast Narratives." *Serial Narratives. Special Issue of Literatur in Wissenschaft und Unterricht 47, no. 1–2,* edited by Kathleen Loock, (2014)*:* 191–205.

Stein, Louisa, and Kristina Busse. "Limit Play: Fan Authorship between Source Text, Intertext, and Context." *Popular Communication* 7 (2009): 192–207. www.tandfonline.com/doi/abs/10.1080/15405700903177545.

Spengler, Birgit. *Literary Spinoffs: Rewriting the Classics – Re-Imagining the Community.* Frankfurt Am Main: Campus, 2015.

"The Draco Trilogy." *Harry Potter Wiki.* Accessed January 3, 2017. http://harrypotter.wikia.com/wiki/Draco_Trilogy.

Ting Lipton, Shana. "How Fifty Shades Is Dominating the Literary Scene." *Vanity Fair.* February 13, 2015. Accessed February 15, 2019. www.vanityfair.com/culture/2015/02/fifty-shades-literary-scene.

Tushnet, Rebecca. "Fan Fiction and the Law." *On the Media.* March 8, 2013. Accessed February 15, 2019. www.wnyc.org/story/274585-fan-fiction-and-law/.

"049. Why I Have a Problem with Cassandra Clare & Why You Should Too." *Life & Whathaveyou* (blog). March 14, 2012. Accessed February 15, 2019. https://bellumina.wordpress.com/2012/03/14/049-why-i-have-a-problem-with-cassandra-clare-why-you-should-too/.

About the author

Bettina Soller is a staff member at the American Studies department of the Carl von Ossietzky University of Oldenburg. Her work looks at online writing practices, constructions, and performances of fan authorship and "the reader," the reciprocal influence of concepts of authorship and the medial environment of fan fiction online.

4. From Paratext to Polyprocess: The "Quirky" Mashup Novel

Eckart Voigts

Abstract

Applying broad notions of adaptation, this chapter seeks to bring "recombinant adaptation" – mashups and remixes on digital platforms – in dialogue with Gérard Genette's idea of the paratext as a text's "relations with the public." It takes four steps towards investigating how literary publishing houses such as Quirk Books respond to recombinant adaptation. Firstly, it delineates the paratexts of mashup novels as performative zones of transaction. Secondly, it examines the question of how paratexts regulate the quasi-religious textuality of fandom participation. Thirdly, it looks at the role of paratextual canonization within this textuality. And finally, it argues that printed products within the field attempt to perform a nostalgic authorization and re-materialization of literature, highlighting the haptic and material qualities of the book. Adapting the term "polytext," the chapter calls these multifarious paratextual transactions the "polyprocess."

Key words: Paratext; mashup novel; recombinant adaptation; fandom; polytext/polyprocess; remix

Introduction

This essay seeks to bring the field of "recombinant adaptation" – mashups and remixes on digital platforms – in dialogue with the Genettian idea of the paratext. Genette held that paratexts shape a given text's "relations with the public."[1] More recently, Jonathan Gray has applied the notion of

1 Gérard Genette, *Paratexts: Thresholds of Interpretation*, trans. Jane E. Lewin (Cambridge: Cambridge University Press, 1997), 14.

Fehrle, J. and W. Schäfke, *Adaptation in the Age of Media Convergence*,
Taylor & Francis Group, 2019
DOI 10.5117/9789462983663_CH04

paratext to media franchises, highlighting the active role of paratexts in creating and continuing franchise texts. Dorothee Birke and Birte Christ have elaborated Genette's ideas for a situation of convergence culture and transmedia storytelling, examining how paratexts fulfill interpretive, commercial, or navigational functions in determining contemporary readers' transmedia experience of narratives.[2]

This chapter takes four steps towards investigating how literary publishing houses respond to the ubiquitous remixes and mashups to be found on low-threshold digital platforms of participation. It will, first, delineate paratexts as zones of transaction, shifting research emphases from textual towards performative concerns and highlighting the way cultures negotiate textual distribution and circulation. Secondly, it will examine the question of how paratexts regulate the quasi-religious textuality of fandom participation; thirdly, the role of paratextual canonization will be a special focus within this textuality. Finally, the chapter argues that printed products within the field attempt to perform a nostalgic authorization and re-materialization of literature, highlighting the haptic and material qualities of "bookishness."

Media Protocols: Paratexts as zones of transaction

Practices of reading are subject to a number of media protocols or a media apparatus that have been identified by both materialist apparatus theories of media (Jean-Louis Baudry, Friedrich Kittler)[3] and cultural studies' media theory, with an emphasis on the social practices emerging with media technologies (Raymond Williams, Lisa Gitelman)[4]. Classic apparatus theories would, in the wake of Michel Foucault or Louis Althusser, analyze how the apparatus wields political power via a cultural and social conglomerate of practices and "interpellations." Convergence and transmedia theories, on the other hand, have more recently tried to highlight the way in which the circulation of media products has ushered in a new phase of cultural production that is less clearly determined by top-down processes and takes

2 Jonathan Gray. *Show Sold Separately* (New York: NYU Press, 2010), 10. Dorothee Birke and Birte Christ, "Paratext and Digitized Narrative: Mapping the Field," *Narrative* 21, no. 1 (2013).

3 E.g., Jean-Louis Baudry and Alan Williams, "Ideological Effects of the Basic Cinematographic Apparatus" *Film Quarterly* 28, no. 2, (1974–1975); Friedrich Kittler, *Grammophon, Film, Typewriter* (Berlin: Brinkmann & Bose 1986).

4 Raymond Williams, *Television. Technology and Cultural Form*, 2nd ed. (London: Routledge, 1990); Lisa Gitelman *Always Already New. Media, History, and the Data of Culture* (Cambridge: MIT Press, 2006).

more notice of the more sovereign and empowered "produser" in a shared cultural space. What we can, indeed, observe is the need for publishing houses to share or, at least, to be seen as sharing with their readers. The publishing house Quirk Books and its "mashup novels" are a key example of how traditional purveyors of texts seek to participate in contemporary remix culture, using paratextual strategies to redistribute already freely circulating mashups.

In the narrow sense, research into digital textuality could investigate how one kind of text – for instance, Shakespeare's Elizabethan play *Hamlet*; more than 400 years old and obviously shaped by the textualities emerging around Elizabethan theater ("good" and "bad" quartos etc.), which can be observed in the textual discussions of various Arden editions – is molded and forced into observing the media protocol of, for instance, Facebook. This, in fact, is exactly what author and journalist Sarah Schmelling did in 2008. She published her "Facebook Hamlet" first on the blog McSweeney's Internet Tendency, and subsequently in her book of similar adaptations, *Ophelia Joined the Group Maidens Who Don't Float.*[5] In an email, Schmelling pointed out that she was in no way involved in the subsequent design adaptation of her text prepared by Angela Liao, whom she did not know and whose Photoshopping she did not authorize. The result of Schmelling's textual adaptation and Angela Liao's unauthorized adaptation to the design of Facebook can still be found on the Web[6], although Ms. Schmelling advised against republishing for possible copyright infringement of Facebook's designs. The Facebook social media apparatus positions a "distracted" viewer scrolling down her latest feed on her mobile device and clearly not prepared for a night out at the Royal Shakespeare Company. In this case, the result is an amusing parody effect: "The king poked the queen. The queen poked the king back. Hamlet and the queen are no longer friends and Marcellus is pretty sure something's rotten around here. Updated two hours ago. Comment."[7] Schmelling uses Facebook tools such as status updates, poking, commenting, posting events, going offline (i.e. dying), and joining the athletics group "Daggers."

The parody also includes further Shakespearian in-jokes such as the suggested Facebook friend William Davenant, and invokes other products

5 Sarah Schmelling. *Ophelia Joined the Group Maidens Who Don't Float: Classic Lit Signs on to Facebook* (New York: Plume, 2009).

6 Angela Liao, "Facebook Hamlet." 2008. Accessed January 6, 2017 www.angelfire.com/art2/antwerplettuce/hamlet.html

7 Ibid.

of contemporary popular culture: "Hamlet's father is now a zombie."[8] The text emerges at the cost of textual nuance and intensity of engagement, but gains in ironic intertextual and intermedial resonances, for instance when Ophelia joins the group "Maidens Who Don't Float." In fact, the limitations of Facebook are willfully invoked in a parody targeting both the play and the fairly unsubtle choices for communication in some social media environments. Either one regards this "reception in the mode of distraction" as a further nail in the coffin of art's aura or as a clever indictment of the limitations of the Facebook media protocol. It is only in Liao's reproduction, which includes the iconic Facebook design, that the adaptation develops its full and immediate parodic potential, and clearly, the case shows how authorship is diluted in the circulation of internet memes.

This emerging *Hamlet* textuality not only reformats and remixes, but in so doing at the same time diminishes and expands Shakespeare's *Hamlet*: it performs the play according to the media protocol of Facebook. We can, however, also notice a reverse tendency: contemporary mashup novels tend to invoke "old" media protocols in a particular pastiche that reiterates popular franchises such as *Star Wars* or cult movies such as *The Big Lebowski* according to the protocols of Shakespearean play texts. What is interesting is that all of these reformattings, remixes, and mashups seem to take the texts for granted and do not even attempt an interpretative engagement with the text. The desire is liturgical: the mashup novel seeks to re-perform, not to engage hermeneutically, with Shakespeare, *Star Wars,* or *The Big Lebowski*. This re-performance takes place within both the books' texts and their paratexts, which reinforce a discussion of authorization, ownership, and the writing process that supersedes any discussion of interpretative engagement.

To sum up recent approaches to paratexts in the hybridity of transmedia participation: we have to consider paratexts as a study of the pragmatics and performativity of literature, establishing "a zone not only of transition but also of *transaction*."[9] To put it quite bluntly: paratexts are done, rather than written. The key problem of the term "paratext" in this "distributed" or "circulating" textuality is the status of the literary text. It is no longer the textual center from which the "para"-textuality emerges.[10] Unlike Genette has it, paratexts do much more than primarily reinforce "the author's

8 Ibid.

9 Genette, *Paratexts*, 407.

10 Ellen McCracken, "Expanding Genette's Epitext/Peritext Model for Transitional Electronic Literature: Centrifugal and Centripetal Vectors on Kindles and iPads," *Narrative* 21, no. 1 (2013): 106.

purpose."[11] Rather than drawing readers outside or inside of texts, the literary text has become merely one element in a fluid "polytexual" or even "polyprocessual" cultural situation. The term "polytext" is taken from revisionist textual scholars Jerome McGann and Joseph Grigely who have argued since the 1980s that any text is merely apparent in a variety of manifestations (what Grigely coins "textualterity") or textual events.[12] In view of the fact, however, that both terms, polytext and paratext, actually refer to praxis, to "doing" texts, my term "polyprocess" (i.e., the potentially endless operations on textual variation) seems to be more appropriate.[13] To some extent, then, the arcane Genettian terminology of text, paratext, context, epitext, peritext, and allograph, suggesting clear-cut boundaries between textual practices, is compromised. It is probably best to use the term "paratext" with reference to transmedia phenomena to mark the threshold between a "textual core"[14] or "anchor-text"[15] from other kinds of textual engagements. It follows that dynamic concepts, such as Ellen McCracken's distinction between centrifugal and centripetal movement – which stands in for Genette's structuralist typological distinctions – work much better under the conditions of an intertwined "connectivity between markets and media practices,"[16] or "spreadable media."[17] The concepts of "canon" and "universe" suggest that, in spite of the lost Gutenbergian cultural primacy of the book, a textual center is still a major cause of disagreement and therefore remains a key factor in the field of cultural production. With McCracken, the current paratextual concern should therefore be the question of whether the connected paratexts induce centripetal and centrifugal movement with reference to one or more textual cores or anchor-texts that could be an Austen novel, a Shakespeare play, or a Disney franchise.

11 Genette, *Paratexts*, 2 (emphasis in original).

12 Joseph Grigely, "The Textual Event." In *Devils and Angels: Textual Editing and Literary Theory*, ed. Philip Cohen (Charlottesville: University of Virginia Press, 1991), 176–177; Jerome McGann, *A Critique of Modern Textual Criticism* (Chicago: University of Chicago Press, 1983), 52.

13 Cf. Eckart Voigts-Virchow, "Anti-Essentialist Versions of Aggregate Alice: A Grin without a Cat." In *Translation and Adaptation in Theatre and Film*, ed. Katja Krebs (New York: Routledge, 2013), 71.

14 Birke and Christ, "Paratext and Digitized Narrative," 80.

15 Amy Nottingham-Martin, "Thresholds of Transmedia Storytelling: Applying Gérard Genette's Paratextual Theory to *The 39 Clues* Series for Young Readers." In *Examining Paratextual Theory and its Applications in Digital Culture*, ed. Nadine Desrochers and Daniel Apollon (Hershey, PA: IGI Global, 2014), 290.

16 Mirko Tobias Schäfer, *Bastard Culture! How User Participation Transforms Cultural Production* (Amsterdam: Amsterdam University Press, 2011), 11.

17 Henry Jenkins, Sam Ford, and Joshua Green, *Spreadable Media: Creating Value and Meaning in a Networked Culture* (New York: New York University Press, 2013).

The religious textuality of fandom participation

Even the loose vectors of "centripetal" movement towards or "centrifugal" movement away from a core text seem untenable under the conditions of transmedia storytelling. The simple linear model of a triad between media producers who create media texts and media publishers who distribute them for the consumption of media users (communicator, message, and receiver) has long since been replaced by circular models in which values and meanings are shaped by producers and audiences alike.[18] After Lawrence Lessig, we know that the Read/Only (RO) culture of old media has been replaced by the Read/Write (RW) culture of new media.[19] After Henry Jenkins, we know that participation and collective intelligence are highly prized in the field of cultural production, but that the relationship between consumers and producers is often fraught.[20]

A classic field analysis à la Bourdieu might argue that high-art authors write for colleagues and critics while popular authors for the media and the general public.[21] Hence, a differentiated field analysis would be able to analyze how franchises produce texts in close negotiation with their fan communities – supposedly without any media industry interference that results from the foundational power imbalance between producers and consumers. As Bourdieu makes clear, cultural capital (which may result from authorial aloofness) is distinct from economic capital. Indeed, the less economic profit there is to be gained from cultural production, the more imperative the engagement between those who offer and those who still buy becomes. If any textual center still exists, it emerges in the centrality accorded by interpretative communities through their purses (economic capital) or their admiration (cultural capital). It is here that the, admittedly precarious and contested, religious textuality of participatory culture emerges. Religious textuality clearly implies a centripetal move towards the canonical core. I take this cue from Benjamin Poore, who recently pinpointed the friction between convergence and fandom, arguing about *Sherlock Holmes* fandom:

18 Cf. Eckart Voigts-Virchow, *Introduction to Media Studies* (Stuttgart: Klett, 2005), 31, 44.

19 Lawrence Lessig, *Remix: Making Art and Commerce Thrive in the Hybrid Economy* (London: Bloomsbury Academic, 2008).

20 Cf. Jenkins, Ford, and Green, where Jenkins updates points made at the time of the millennium and collected in his *Convergence Culture: Where Old and New Media Collide* (New York: New York UP, 2006).

21 Cf. Tilman Höss, "Kapital, Feld, Habitus und sozialer Raum: Pierre Bourdieu für Anglisten," *Zeitschrift für Anglistik und Amerikanistik* 55, no. 2 (2007): 187.

> If fandom is about preserving what is felt to be pure, true and distinctive about a given mythology or "universe," then convergence is about developing new markets, media platforms, and types of interactivity. Thus, as the case of Holmes and Watson demonstrates, given enough time, the "universes" of fan fiction – as if responding to laws of motion or evolution – will expand into new areas of the imaginary until even the original stories are dwarfed by the industrial-paced productivity of their derivatives.[22]

Poore's argument is not new: in 1994, before the advent of convergence culture and low-threshold participation on digital platforms, Michael Jindra argued that *Star Trek* fandom is a religious phenomenon in a nonconventional location, involving practices such as canon building and hierarchization. Jindra contended that by participating in *Star Trek* fandom one is set apart from the "mass" of society and becomes part of "symbolic communities [that] resist the secularization and rationalization of modern life."[23] Similarly, and without any hint of irony, the first Lucasfilm/*Star Wars* magazine referred to Lucas' authorized publications as "Gospel." The "Canon" is, variously, the seven films, Lucas Licensing, or what has been termed EU (Expanded Universe). Since the Walt Disney Company took over control of *Star Wars* in 2012, it has taken measures to control, redefine, and delimit the GWL or "George Walton Lucas" canon. These typical issues over legitimacy and continuity have a clear economic dimension, but are in line with Eugene Ulrich's religious definition of canon from the Greek "κανών," meaning "rule," as "the definitive list of inspired, authoritative books which constitute the recognized and accepted body of sacred scripture of a major religious group, that definitive list being the result of inclusive and exclusive decisions after serious deliberation."[24]

The "fandom = religion" equation has also generated its critics, however. Matt Hills, for instance, rejects this wholesale application:

> If transgressive fanfic challenging canon is often the order of the day among media fandoms, such transgression is hardly common

22 Benjamin Poore, "Sherlock Holmes and the Leap of Faith: The Forces of Fandom and Convergence in Adaptations of the Holmes and Watson Stories," *Adaptation* 6, no. 2 (2013): 159.

23 Michael Jindra, "*Star Trek* Fandom as a Religious Phenomenon," *Sociology of Religion* 55, no. 1 (1994): 38.

24 Eugene Ulrich, "The Notion and Definition of Canon." In *The Canon Debate*, ed. Lee M. McDonald and James A. Sanders (Peabody, MA: Hendrickson, 2002), 28, 34.

> within religion. [...], the "fandom = religion" discourse all too often creates a master narrative of (atomized and secularised) society along with (compensatory and functionalist) fandom marked by the "loss hypothesis."[25]

We could argue that transmedia storytelling is used primarily to "fill out" and "expand" a fictional universe, so that it becomes tangible, complete, worldly. Fans who become immersed in texts as part of a ritual (e.g. cosplay pilgrimages) also reenact a quasi-religious ceremony: "ST [*Star Trek*] is a body of knowledge that is continually being added to and revised."[26]

Neither transmedia producers nor transmedia fans are intentionally displacing the core with adapted, appropriated, and, in this sense, changed texts, but rather trying to add to it, building up the universe from that core. To the extent, however, that the added texts and paratexts begin to transgress their anchor-texts (not just in terms of textual "faith," but also in terms of the legal and textual "situation"), this kind of adaptation, appropriation, and paratextual diversity seems to be an inevitable result of their activities. In other words, Matt Hills' intervention reminds us that paratexts can add both centripetal (religious) and centrifugal (transgressive) dimensions to a given text.

It is no surprise that the two examples used in the following, the mashup novels *William Shakespeare's Star Wars* and *Two Gentlemen of Lebowski,*[27] testify to this cultish dimension of popular textual universes: one the global franchise that most fully elaborates a myth pastiche – *Star Wars* – and the other one the Coen brothers' *The Big Lebowski* (1998), "the most significant cult film of the last thirty years"[28] and a movie that has kept a faithful group of devotees which has recently become the object of academic fandom studies.[29]

Both core texts invite centripetal paratexts because they fulfill most of the existing definition of a "cult film" to a tee, as a summary of the "cult cinema" definition derived from the book series homepage *Cultographies* suggests:

25 Matt Hills, "Sacralising Fandom? From the 'Loss Hypothesis' to Fans' Media Rituals," *Kinephanos* 4, no. 1 (2013), accessed February 15, 2019,www.kinephanos.ca/2013/sacralising-fandom/.

26 Jindra, "*Star Trek* Fandom as a Religious Phenomenon," 46.

27 Ian Doescher, *William Shakespeare's Star Wars: Verily, A New Hope* (Philadelphia, PA: Quirk Books, 2013). Adam Bertocci, *Two Gentlemen of Lebowski: A Most Excellent Comedie and Tragical Romance* (New York: Simon and Schuster, 2010).

28 Zachary Ingle, Introduction to *Fan Phenomena: "The Big Lebowski,"* ed. Zachary Ingle (London: Intellect, 2014), 5.

29 Zachary Ingle, ed., *Fan Phenomena: "The Big Lebowski"* (London: Intellect, 2014).

- "[A]ctive and lively communal following."
- "Highly committed and rebellious in their appreciation, cult audiences are frequently at odds with cultural conventions [...]."
- "Cult films transgress common notions of good and bad taste, and they challenge genre conventions and coherent storytelling."
- "Among the techniques cult films use are intertextual references, gore, loose ends in storylines, or the creation of a sense of nostalgia. [...] In spite of often-limited accessibility, they have a continuous market value and a long-lasting public presence."
- Ritual consumption: Like a religion, the cult film "relies on continuous, intense participation and persistence, on the commitment of an active audience that celebrates films they see as the opposite of 'normal and dull' cinema. [...] *Active Celebration* is essential. [...] As with most rituals in society, aspects of purity, initiation, and infection play a crucial role in this celebration."[30]

It follows that, in terms of textuality, cult films invite the desire for authorization, canonization, and traditionalism – albeit the resulting canons, traditions, and authorization are frequently "anti-official," "amateurish," and "para-cinematic." Books such as the mashup novel *William Shakespeare's Star Wars* and *Two Gentlemen of Lebowski* (or similar texts such as *Bard Fiction*, a Shakespearean stage play and wikispace by Ben Tallen, Aaron Greer, and Brian Watson-Jones) are cult pastiche literature devoted to nostalgically recreating lost norms. In a variation on the famous analysis of Fredric Jameson, they mash up the imitation of two styles, wearing two stylistic masks, speaking in two dead languages. Jameson argues that pastiche is

> the imitation of a peculiar or unique style, the wearing of a stylistic mask, speech in a dead language: but it is a neutral practice of such mimicry, without parody's ulterior motive, without the satirical impulse, without laughter, without that still latent feeling that there exists something normal compared to which what is being imitated is rather comic. Pastiche is blank parody, parody that has lost its sense of humor.[31]

30 "Cultographies" Definition of Cult Cinema," *Cultographies*, accessed November 22, 2016, www.cultographies.com/definition.shtml (emphasis in original).

31 Fredric Jameson, *Postmodernism, or, the Cultural Logic of Late Capitalism* (Durham, NC: Duke University Press, 1991), 17.

The blank parody of pastiche according to Jameson is religious intertextuality, recreating the presence of its fetish or God, whereas parody is satirical, critical, so that parody obviously is undesirable in religious contexts. It is this religious dimension of fandom that helps explain how the mashup novel intervenes in all of the three areas singled out by Birke and Christ in their overview of paratexts in digital culture: materialization, boundaries, and authorization.[32]

Boundaries: Paratext and canon

According to Birke and Christ, textual boundaries have become increasingly blurred and fluid, suggesting the centrifugal textuality discussed by McCracken and others. As intertexts, both *William Shakespeare's Star Wars* and *Two Gentlemen of Lebowski* send you out to websites, blogs, Facebook pages and the paratextual as well as intertextual mayhem unleashed there in an example of transmedia storytelling. The very titles are paratexts that crucially contribute to this centrifugal gesture. Consider the confrontational genres in the parataxis of Grahame-Smith's *Pride and Prejudice and Zombies*, Doescher's clumsy and blatantly misattributive *William Shakespeare's Star Wars,* or the tacit suggestion of the Shakespearean comedy of mistaken identities, the relaxed Dude, and the wealthy Big Lebowski, in Bertocci's *Two Gentlemen of Lebowski.* In the latter case, the titular reference is clearly facetious, as it remains the only allusion to *Two Gentlemen of Verona* – a rather marginal entry in the Shakespeare canon. Textual knowledge is essential to the enjoyment of adaptations, but to be familiar with *Two Gentlemen of Verona* is no essential prerequisite to either writing or reading *Two Gentlemen of Lebowski.*

What often goes unnoticed is the strict re-demarcation that is part of fandom – in fact, control over boundaries and command of texts are two of the most contested areas in fandom textuality. This might be described as centripetal motion as all the textuality emerging around *Star Wars* and *The Big Lebowski* send you back to the canonical texts, reinforcing the authorized power of the filmmakers, the Coens and George Lucas – or, to be more precise, the companies controlling the textual universes – by reinforcing a residual notion of singular authorship, which makes the *Star Wars* Lucasfilm/Disney franchise a different case than the less controlled cult film *The Big Lebowski.* In the influential web-based peritexts of *Star*

32 Birke and Christ, "Paratext and Digitized Narrative," 68.

Wars – such as Wookieepedia – Doescher's book is marked as non-canon, that is, apocryphal (literally: hidden), excluded from the Lucasfilm canon.[33]

Similarly, Bertocci never fails to put a disclaimer in his paratexts, for instance the copyright page of his front matter:

> *Two Gentlemen of Lebowski* is not endorsed by or associated with the Coen Brothers, the writers and directors of the film *The Big Lebowski*, or Working Title or Universal Pictures, the producer and distributor of the film *The Big Lebowski*. Any and all adaptation rights in and to *The Big Lebowski* are reserved to the Coen Brothers and to Universal Pictures.[34]

Thus, we can argue that mashup novels tend to be affirmative and non-confrontational rather than transgressive or confrontational, actively seeking the cooperation and endorsement of copyright owners. The political remit of these texts of "literary popular culture" is close to zero. Refresh and reinvigorate old franchises they may well do, but they hardly signal "a mode of empowerment." Neither do they fulfill Eli Horwatt's ideal of an "appropriation art" from below."[35] This kind of mashup novel therefore is vulnerable to attacks along the lines of Jameson's argument (quoted above) that postmodernist texts are merely nostalgic pastiches.

Nostalgic re-materialization

Mashup novels re-materialize nostalgically from digital culture into print. Witness the elaborate book designs in all of the cases discussed here, in both the front and back covers, front and back matter, spine, dust jacket, and so forth. Doescher's *Star Wars*/Shakespeare pastiche comes as a dust-covered hardback with *faux*-nineteenth-century designs by Doogie Horner. The *Star Wars* cover displays the full splendors of mock-heraldic achievement in the title pages, a cartouche as shield in marble, complete with supporters, crest, columns, emblems, feathers, and draperies – the title becoming a sort of

33 "*William Shakespeare's Star Wars*," *Wookieepedia: The "Star Wars" Wiki*, last modified October 7, 2016, accessed February 15, 2019, http://starwars.wikia.com/wiki/William_Shakespeare%27s_Star_Wars.

34 Bertocci, *Two Gentlemen of Lebowski*, copyright page.

35 Eli Horwatt, "A Taxonomy of Digital Video Remixing: Contemporary Found Footage Practice on the Internet Cultural Borrowings." In *Cultural Borrowings: Appropriation, Reworking, Transformation*, edited by Iain Robert Smith. Special issue of *Scope: An Online Journal of Film and Television Studies* 15 (2009), 97. Web. 20 June 2013.

motto. The endpapers feature elaborate decorative floral patterns. Taking the slipcover off, which has a grainy mock-parchment or mock-vellum structure, the reader can touch a brownish morocco leathery vintage used-look cover style. Add to this mock-nineteenth-century bookbinding travesty the *Star Wars* logo with a visible "registered trademark" sign. As proudly announced on Amazon and the Quirk Books website blurb, all of the three *Star Wars* trilogy rewritings in Shakespearean style are now available in a "bibliophilic" boxed set, which comes in a slipcase and includes "an 8-by-34-inch full-color poster illustrating the complete cast and company of this glorious production."[36] The Bertocci paperback, though less elaborate and clearly less invested in gesturing towards the book binding process of bygone bibliophilic heydays, also has the signature iconography of Hamlet transformed into the vestiges of the Dude (clad into bowling outfit and sunglasses; cartwheel scruff, doublet and hose intact) and likewise offers some heraldic scrollwork: the media protocol here signals antiquity, respectability, importance, etc.

The Deluxe Heirloom Edition of *Pride and Prejudice and Zombies* flaunts elaborate typography, red headbands, decoratively printed, mock-antique endpapers, gilded letterings, a ribbon page marker, and a relief structure. It also features the inevitable – in this case zombified – James Andrews portrait of Austen in an oval frame, suggesting a Georgian miniature (Figure 4.1). Just as the grumpy look of the pencil and watercolor portrait by Jane Austen's sister Cassandra – the only "authenticated" portrait – was prettified by Andrews, the zombified Austen (or, implicitly, Elizabeth Bennet) portrait exposes the bloodshot eyes, neck bones, jawbones, and drops of blood on the empire dress, but gets rid of the frilly cap and exhibits traces of thinner contemporary Lizzie and Austen impersonators such as Anne Hathaway, Jennifer Ehle, or Keira Knightley.

The edition also includes an afterword by Allen Grove, Professor of English at Alfred University, New York. Grove "justifies" the mashup in a feeble argument that links Seth Grahame-Smith's remix with the Gothic horror parodies and pastiches of Austen's romantic contemporaries.[37] We can conclude that mashers, though firmly embedded in popular culture, revel in pastiche bibliophilia. They either parody literary culture and/or suggest a half-hidden desire to be taken seriously by book lovers, literati, and even

36 "*William Shakespeare's Star Wars* Trilogy: The Royal Imperial Boxed Set," product page on QuirkBooks.com, accessed November 22, 2016, www.quirkbooks.com/book/william-shakespeares-star-wars-trilogy.

37 Allen Grove, afterword to *Pride and Prejudice and Zombies: The Deluxe Heirloom Edition*, by Jane Austen and Seth Grahame-Smith (Philadelphia, PA: Quirk Books, 2009).

literary academics. Indeed, Shakespeare mashups have been assessed by scholars such as Peter Holland (who discusses the texts as narcissistic fan replay with Shakespearean knowledge as key criterion) and Paul Rogalus (who insists both Shakespeare and *The Big Lebowski* testify to a (very dubious) timeless literary universality).[38]

Figure 4.1: The "zombified" James Andrews portrait on the Deluxe Heirloom Edition of *Pride and Prejudice and Zombies*:[39] Mashing up Georgian miniatures.[40]

Through paratextual situatedness, both the print hardback and the e-book offer unique pleasures in the true spirit of transmedia storytelling à la Jenkins:

38 Cf. Michael Rogalus, "The Bard, the Knave and Sir Walter: Adapting a Modern Cult classic into a Neo-Shakespearean Stage Play." In *Fan Phenomena: "The Big Lebowski,"* edited by Zachary Ingle, 5–7. London: Intellect, 2014; Peter Holland, "Spinach and Tobacco: Making Shakespeare Unoriginals." *Shakespeare Survey* no. 68 (2015), 83–196.

39 Seth Grahame Smith and Jane Austen, *Pride and Prejudice and Zombies* (Philadelphia: Quirk Books, 2009).

40 Source: www.quirkbooks.com/sites/default/files/book_covers/PPZDeluxe_Cover_72dpi%20 copy.jpg. Accessed February 15, 2019.

> A process where integral elements of a fiction get dispersed systematically across multiple delivery channels for the purpose of creating a unified and coordinated entertainment experience. Ideally, each medium makes its own unique contribution to the unfolding of the story [...] Transmedia storytelling is the ideal aesthetic form for an era of collective intelligence.[41]

Each medium makes a unique contribution: while the print version seeks to make the most of pastiche print materiality, the e-book app of *Pride and Prejudice and Zombies* promises a different kind of reading experience, a kind of content-added, multi-sensory *Gesamtkunstwerk*:

> This interactive ebook features hundreds of illustrations, an original musical score, buckets of gory animation, and a pair of literary masterpieces: Hold your device right-side-up to enjoy *Pride and Prejudice and Zombies*. Turn it upside-down to read Jane Austen's original *Pride and Prejudice*. Turn the device 90 degrees to read both novels, side-by-side.
> Featuring:
> - Enhanced book/app version of the bestselling novel
> - Hundreds of pages of illustrated, interactive zombie mayhem
> - Complete text of Pride and Prejudice and Zombies AND Jane Austen's beloved Pride and Prejudice
> - Original musical score and sound effects
>
> This revolutionary vision of what an eBook reading should be creates the definitive user-driven experience through text, animation, music, sound, gameplay-like elements, and touchscreen technology.[42]

Ultimately, both kinds of paratextual formatting invoke a fake authenticity and traditionalism ("masterpiece," "original") to perform mashups as literary pastiche. In so doing they evince signs of Jamesonian nostalgia, even within the celebration of transmedia "enhancement." Quirk Books and other mashup novels re-perform texts as liturgy, seeking to publicly establish renewed community with canon texts.

41 Henry Jenkins, "Transmedia Storytelling 101," *Confessions of an Aca-Fan: The Official Weblog of Henry Jenkins*, last modified March 22, 2007. Accessed February 15, 2019, www.henryjenkins.org/2007/03/transmedia_storytelling_101.html.

42 "*Pride and Prejudice and Zombies*: The Interactive eBook App," product page on QuirkBooks.com, accessed November 22, 2016, www.quirkbooks.com/app/ppzapp.

Authorization

The etiology of Seth Grahame-Smith's *Pride and Prejudice and Zombies* or Ian Doescher's *William Shakespeare's Star Wars* series indicates interesting variants of authorization. Doescher's text was announced as "an officially licensed retelling of George Lucas's epic *Star Wars*" and, not coincidentally, Quirk Books is owned by Random House – just like the Del Rey publishing house that publishes *Star Wars* novelizations. Ultimately then, the "oh so quirky" Quirk Books pastiche falls well within the *Star Wars* textuality offered by Random House, as one part of the larger transmedia presence of the *Star Wars* franchise, which provides "the most voluminous entourage in entertainment history."[43] Quirk Books, thus, looks more conventional, standardized, and orthodox than the non-conformism of both the name of the publishing house and the promotional paratexts of the "wacky," "outré," or "unorthodox" mashup would have it. Whereas mashup novels emerge from paying attention to supposedly transgressive amateurs and grassroots fandom, they are, however, primarily a clever idea in literary distribution, flogging enhanced out-of-copyright texts or re-invigorating the commercially exhausted textual anchors of transmedia franchises.

Second, one may argue that Seth Grahame-Smith's mashup novel is (co) authored by Jason Rekulak, because the Quirk editor had the first idea and it is Quirk Books who supply the formula of the mashup novel. Another paratext, in this case an interview with "masher" Seth Grahame-Smith for *Pride and Prejudice and Zombies*, suggests Rekulak as the real author of the book:

> Actually the credit for this belongs to my editor, Jason Rekulak. He had had this sort of long-gestating idea of *doing some kind of mashup*, he called it. He didn't know what it was, he just knew there was something to it. He had these lists, and *on one side* he had a column of *War and Peace* and *Crime and Punishment* and *Wuthering Heights* and whatever *public domain classic literature* you can think of. And *on the other side* he would have these phenomena like werewolves and pirates and zombies and vampires. He called me one day, out of the blue, very excitedly, and he said, all I have is this title, and I can't stop thinking about this title. And he said: Pride and Prejudice and Zombies. For whatever reason, it just struck me as the most brilliant thing I'd ever heard.[44]

43 Gray, *Shows Sold Separately*, 177.

44 Lev Grossman, "*Pride and Prejudice*, now with Zombies!" *Time*, April 2, 2009, accessed February 15, 2019, http://content.time.com/time/arts/article/0,8599,1889075,00.html (emphasis added).

It is equally illuminating to assess the relationship between George Lucas and Ian Doescher, or the Coen brothers and Adam Bertocci as they are projected by the paratexts. Grahame-Smith, Doescher, and Bertocci – our second-degree mashup authors – are at the same time described as viewers, audiences, and readers. Bertocci's book apparently started when he took a book-signing photograph with Anne Hathaway after a performance of *Twelfth Night*. The mashup novels are, in fact, good examples of the polyprocess, of how the modes of literary consumption have changed in participatory culture and distributed media. A mere paratext that is structurally suggestive of doubling – the title *Two Gentlemen of Verona* – links Shakespeare's comedy to the stylistic pastiche of Bertocci's *Two Gentlemen of Lebowski*. Ian Doescher explains the genesis of his mashup novel:

> It was the morning after watching *The Very Merry Wives of Windsor, Iowa*, while we were still at the Shakespeare Festival, that I had the idea for *William Shakespeare's Star Wars®*.[45]

> [My publisher] started getting the wheels in motion with Lucasfilm to get it licensed. So I recognize how extraordinarily lucky I am to have this all happening so easily, and so quickly. I mean, the book will ultimately be published just under a year from when I first had the idea, which is kind of crazy.[46]

Under these conditions of speed publishing (Doescher wrote the text in three months), velocity is indeed a key criterion. The texts are quickly produced and rapidly forgotten. As many reviews of mashup novels point out, longevity is not their strong suit. Macy Halford's scathing critique of *Pride and Prejudice and Zombies* as an "intelligent fart joke"[47] is echoed by a reviewer of *Two Gentlemen of Lebowski*'s stage version: "Bertocci's script

45 Ian Doescher, "A Conversation with Ian Doescher, Author of *William Shakespeare's Star Wars®*," by Blair Thornburgh, *Our Blog*, QuirkBooks.com, last modified June 17, 2013, accessed February 15, 2019, www.quirkbooks.com/post/conversation-ian-doescher-author-william-shakespeare%E2%80%99s-star-wars%C2%AE.

46 Ian Doescher, "Q&A with Ian Doescher about Shakespeare on *Star Wars*," by Alisha Gorder, *Portland Monthly, June 27, 2013*, www.pdxmonthly.com/articles/2013/6/27/q-and-a-with-ian-doescher-june-2013.

47 Macy Halford, "Jane Austen Does the Monster Mash," review of *Pride and Prejudice and Zombies*, by Jane Austen and Seth Grahame-Smith, Page-Turner, *New Yorker*, April 4, 2009, accessed February 15, 2019, www.newyorker.com/books/page-turner/jane-austen-does-the-monster-mash.

is a long one-note joke whose potency has a remarkably short shelf life."[48] Doescher himself stylizes the idea to mimic the Shakespearean metrum of iambic pentameter as primarily a high school prank resulting from a creative writing task:

> We had just finished a unit on *Hamlet* and were discussing John Dryden's poem Mack Flecknoe, which is a satire against another poet, Thomas Shadwell. We were supposed to write our own version of Mack Flecknoe, writing against something we didn't like.[49]

Doescher also peddles the cliché of the innocent natural, the *poète manqué*, when he confides that he "never really studied Shakespeare, which probably helped me to continue to love it [sic, presumably Shakespeare] more."[50] Indeed, "humblebragging" and the projection of a non-literary, fannish, and non-professional identity are the key elements in the paratextual parading of mashup novelists. Adam Bertocci, when asked about the origin of *Two Gentlemen of Lebowski*, cites boredom and narcissism as the key impetus to his writing, significantly launched first via a Facebook message and cobbled together in a mere three weeks for the stage:

> In November of 2009 I posted a silly little message on Facebook where, as a joke, I "translated" a couple of famous lines from *The Big Lebowski* to amuse people. They amused pretty much only me. Undeterred, a month or so later I got bored and started typing.[51]

Bertocci's gesture is clearly meant as anti-authoritative. An English minor, he professes to know little about Shakespeare, to reject the trappings of authorship and, like other literary mashers, adopts the attitude of a humble fan vis-à-vis the towering literary author or powerful franchise – clearly in part to suggest a readerly companionship to the targeted audience:

48 Simon Abrams, "*The Two Gentlemen of Lebowski* at the Kraine Theatre," review of *Two Gentlemen of Lebowski*, by Adam Bertocci, directed by Frank Cwiklik, Kraine Theatre, New York, *The House Next Door (blog)*, *Slant Magazine*, *March* 22, 2010, accessed February 15, 2019, www.slantmagazine.com/house/article/the-two-gentlemen-of-lebowski-at-the-kraine-theatre.

49 Doescher, "A Conversation with Ian Doescher, Author of *William Shakespeare's Star Wars®*."

50 Doescher, "Q&A with Ian Doescher about Shakespeare on *Star Wars*."

51 "Frequently Asked Questions: Which, Sadly, No One Reads," official website of Adam Bertocci's *Two Gentleman of Lebowski*, accessed November 22, 2016, www.runleiarun.com/lebowski/faq.shtml.

> I mean I wrote it, I dig seeing my name on the cover. But I just don't think it is that simple. Call me a receptacle, a steward, an avatar. Call me the conduit of an important idea. [...] [M]y college reunion's coming up, and I needed something to show for the last five years.[52]

The reality is a quasi-religious, non-transgressive re-authorization. In fact, it is recognition by the "stars" involved in *The Big Lebowski* as well as the Folger Library as representatives of Shakespearean tradition that confers the breakthrough accolade on Bertocci's play, as this timeline on the promotional webpage suggests:[53]

> Thursday, January 7
> - Jeff Bridges is sent the link, reportedly reacts with amusement.
> - Tweeted by the Folger Library, Michael McKean, Harry Knowles.
>
> [...]
> - Sunday, January 24
> - Report arrives that John Goodman has been given the text and "laughed his ass off."
>
> [...]
> - Friday, March 12
> - Julianne Moore made aware of the piece and the upcoming production. Laughs at the title.

The Folger Library (Shakespeare) and the actors Jeff Bridges, John Goodman, and Julianne Moore are the key purveyors of a traditionalist pedigree and the necessary accolades in the context of Lebowski and Shakespeare fandom. In spite of the grassroots participatory culture "wreader" and "prosumer" ideology, therefore, all of the authors discussed here have deliberately sought the canonization of the franchise "church" and basked in the approval of entertainment companies. It is these companies who ultimately retain copyright. This can be seen in the simple fact that more than 100 requests for the performing rights to *William Shakespeare's Star Wars* had to be turned down. Because "Lucasfilm

52 Adam Bertocci, *Two Gentlemen of Lebowski: A Most Excellent Comedie and Tragical Romance* (New York: Simon and Schuster, 2010), 203. Cf. also Bertocci's self-fashioning in Zachary Ingle, 60–61.

53 "The Backstory: The Compleat History of a Viral Phenomenon (Abridged)," official website of Adam Bertocci's *Two Gentlemen of Lebowski*, accessed November 22, 2016, www.runleiarun.com/lebowski/viral.shtml.

still owns the rights to the story, only a few scenes can be performed at a time."[54]

In conclusion, my examination of the polyprocesses emerging in the textuality of mashup novels has highlighted the commercial and navigational, that is, "performative" functions of paratexts that seem to undercut and cancel out their presumed interpretive functions. The polyprocesses, that is, the paratextual transactions emerging with mashup novelizations exhibit both the centripetal and the centrifugal impetus of fan engagement. Mashers' authorial self-fashioning as humble fans signals a textual subservience towards the core of franchises or cult films. To establish the status of mashup novels as literary "jokes" it is mandatory to highlight the authorization and canonization of the texts. My findings support Jonathan Gray's claim that franchise paratexts tend to create "scripts of value": "author, aura, and artistry – all qualities often said to be lacking in the age of big-budget blockbusters and for-profit art – are hailed and awarded to texts by their paratexts."[55]

The literariness and bookishness of the projects is reinforced by the nostalgic re-materialization of print editions in the context of a travesty of book culture. The pastiche materiality validates and reaffirms the "classic" or "cult" status of the textual anchors, contributing to their fandom canonization rather than transgressing boundaries or challenging legal properties or aesthetic proprieties. A mashup novel need not be confrontational unless its reception indicates otherwise: aesthetic friction, political strife, and legal action, controversy and confrontation, indignation, and invective – these are the true indicators of transgression – and, so far, they are missing from the publication history of mashup novels. Existing mashup novels are, on the contrary, rather marked by strict adherence to intellectual property rights and integration into, or painstaking respectfulness towards, the economic incentives and quasi-religious fannish status of canonized works and transmedial franchises.

54 Martha Kang, "And Now, 'Star Wars' as Shakespeare Might Have Told It," *Quirksee*, last modified July 21, 2013, accessed February 15, 2019, www.quirksee.org/2013/07/21/and-now-star-wars-as-shakespeare-might-have-told-it/.

55 Gray, *Shows Sold Separately*, 18.

Works Cited

Abrams, Simon. "*The Two Gentlemen of Lebowski* at the Kraine Theatre." Review of *Two Gentlemen of Lebowski*, by Adam Bertocci, directed by Frank Cwiklik, Kraine Theatre, New York. *The House Next Door (blog), Slant Magazine, March 22, 2010*. Accessed February 15, 2019. www.slantmagazine.com/house/article/the-two-gentlemen-of-lebowski-at-the-kraine-theatre.

Baudry, Jean-Louis and Alan Williams. "Ideological Effects of the Basic Cinematographic Apparatus." *Film Quarterly* 28, no. 2 (1974–1975): 39-47.

Bertocci, Adam. *Two Gentlemen of Lebowski: A Most Excellent Comedie and Tragical Romance*. New York: Simon and Schuster, 2010.

Birke, Dorothee, and Birte Christ. "Paratext and Digitized Narrative: Mapping the Field." *Narrative* 21, no. 1 (2013): 65–87.

"Cultographies' Definition of Cult Cinema." *Cultographies*. Accessed November 22, 2016. www.cultographies.com/definition.shtml.

Doescher, Ian. "A Conversation with Ian Doescher, Author of *William Shakespeare's Star Wars®*." By Blair Thornburgh. *Our Blog*, QuirkBooks.com. Last modified June 17, 2013. Accessed February 15, 2019. www.quirkbooks.com/post/conversation-ian-doescher-author-william-shakespeare%E2%80%99s-star-wars%C2%AE.

—. "Q&A with Ian Doescher about Shakespeare on *Star Wars*." By Alisha Gorder. *Portland Monthly, June 27, 2013*. Accessed February 15, 2019. www.pdxmonthly.com/articles/2013/6/27/q-and-a-with-ian-doescher-june-2013.

—. *William Shakespeare's Star Wars: Verily, a New Hope*. Philadelphia, PA: Quirk Books, 2013.

"Frequently Asked Questions: Which, Sadly, No One Reads." Official website of Adam Bertocci's *Two Gentleman of Lebowski*. Accessed November 22, 2016. www.runleiarun.com/lebowski/faq.shtml.

Genette, Gérard. *Paratexts: Thresholds of Interpretation*. Translated by Jane E. Lewin. Cambridge: Cambridge University Press, 1997.

Gitelman, Lisa. Always Already New. Media, History, and the Data of Culture. Cambridge: MIT Press, 2006.

Grahame Smith, Seth and Jane Austen. *Pride and Prejudice and Zombies*. Philadelphia: Quirk Books, 2009.

Grigely, Joseph. "The Textual Event." In *Devils and Angels: Textual Editing and Literary Theory*, edited by Philip Cohen, 167–194. Charlottesville: University of Virginia Press, 1991.

Grossman, Lev. "*Pride and Prejudice*, now with Zombies!" *Time*, April 2, 2009. Accessed February 15, 2019. http://content.time.com/time/arts/article/0,8599,1889075,00.html.

Grove, Allen. Afterword to *Pride and Prejudice and Zombies: The Deluxe Heirloom Edition*, by Jane Austen and Seth Grahame-Smith, 354–357. Philadelphia, PA: Quirk Books, 2009.

Halford, Macy. "Jane Austen Does the Monster Mash." Review of *Pride and Prejudice and Zombies*, by Jane Austen and Seth Grahame-Smith. Page-Turner, *New Yorker*, April 4, 2009. Accessed February 15, 2019. www.newyorker.com/books/page-turner/jane-austen-does-the-monster-mash.

Hills, Matt. "Sacralising Fandom? From the 'Loss Hypothesis' to Fans' Media Rituals." *Kinephanos* 4, no. 1 (2013). Accessed February 15, 2019. www.kinephanos.ca/2013/sacralising-fandom/.

Höss, Tilman. "Kapital, Feld, Habitus und sozialer Raum: Pierre Bourdieu für Anglisten." *Zeitschrift für Anglistik und Amerikanistik* 55, no. 2 (2007): 173–189.

Holland, Peter. "Spinach and Tobacco: Making Shakespeare Unoriginals." *Shakespeare Survey* no. 68 (2015): 83–196.

Horwatt, Eli. "A Taxonomy of Digital Video Remixing: Contemporary Found Footage Practice on the Internet Cultural Borrowings." In *Cultural Borrowings: Appropriation, Reworking, Transformation, edited* by Iain Robert Smith. Special issue of *Scope: An Online Journal of Film and Television Studies* 15 (2009). Web. 20 June 2013.Web. 20 June 2013.

Ingle, Zachary, ed. *Fan Phenomena: "The Big Lebowski."* London: Intellect, 2014.

—. "Introduction." In *Fan Phenomena: "The Big Lebowski,"* edited by Zachary Ingle, 5–7. London: Intellect, 2014.

Jameson, Fredric. *Postmodernism, or, the Cultural Logic of Late Capitalism*. Durham, NC: Duke University Press, 1991.

Jenkins, Henry. "Transmedia Storytelling 101." *Confessions of an Aca-Fan: The Official Weblog of Henry Jenkins*. Last modified March 22, 2007. Accessed February 15, 2019. www.henryjenkins.org/2007/03/transmedia_storytelling_101.html.

Jenkins, Henry, Sam Ford, and Joshua Green. *Spreadable Media: Creating Value and Meaning in a Networked Culture*. New York: New York University Press, 2013.

Jindra, Michael. "*Star Trek* Fandom as a Religious Phenomenon." *Sociology of Religion* 55, no. 1 (1994): 27–51.

Kang, Martha. "And Now, 'Star Wars' as Shakespeare Might Have Told It." *Quirksee*. Last modified July 21, 2013. Accessed February 15, 2019. www.quirksee.org/2013/07/21/and-now-star-wars-as-shakespeare-might-have-told-it/.

Kittler, Friedrich. *Grammophon, Film, Typewriter*. Berlin: Brinkmann & Bose 1986.

Liao, Angela. "Facebook Hamlet." 2008. Accessed January 6, 2017 www.angelfire.com/art2/antwerplettuce/hamlet.html

McCracken, Ellen. "Expanding Genette's Epitext/Peritext Model for Transitional Electronic Literature: Centrifugal and Centripetal Vectors on Kindles and iPads." *Narrative* 21, no. 1 (2013): 105–124.

McGann, Jerome. *A Critique of Modern Textual Criticism*. Chicago: University of Chicago Press, 1983.

Nottingham-Martin, Amy. "Thresholds of Transmedia Storytelling: Applying Gérard Genette's Paratextual Theory to *The 39 Clues* Series for Young Readers'. In *Examining Paratextual Theory and its Applications in Digital Culture*, edited by Nadine Desrochers and Daniel Apollon, 287–312. Hershey, PA: IGI Global, 2014.

"Pride and Prejudice and Zombies: The Interactive eBook App." Product page on QuirkBooks.com. Accessed November 22, 2016. Accessed February 15, 2019. www.quirkbooks.com/app/ppzapp.

Poore, Benjamin. "Sherlock Holmes and the Leap of Faith: The Forces of Fandom and Convergence in Adaptations of the Holmes and Watson Stories." *Adaptation* 6, no. 2 (2013): 158–171.

Rogalus, Michael. "The Bard, the Knave and Sir Walter: Adapting a Modern Cult classic into a Neo-Shakespearean Stage Play." In *Fan Phenomena: "The Big Lebowski,"* edited by Zachary Ingle, 5–7. London: Intellect, 2014.

Schäfer, Mirko Tobias. *Bastard Culture! How User Participation Transforms Cultural Production*. Amsterdam: Amsterdam University Press, 2011.

Schmelling, Sarah. Ophelia Joined the Group Maidens Who Don't Float: Classic Lit Signs on to Facebook. New York: Plume, 2009.

—. Personal email communication. 22 December 2016.

"The Backstory: The Compleat History of a Viral Phenomenon (Abridged)." Official website of Adam Bertocci's *Two Gentlemen of Lebowski*. Accessed November 22, 2016. www.runleiarun.com/lebowski/viral.shtml.

Ulrich, Eugene. "The Notion and Definition of Canon." In *The Canon Debate*, edited by Lee M. McDonald and James A. Sanders, 21–35. Peabody, MA: Hendrickson, 2002.

Voigts-Virchow, Eckart. *Introduction to Media Studies*. Stuttgart: Klett, 2005.

—. "Anti-Essentialist Versions of Aggregate Alice: A Grin without a Cat." In *Translation and Adaptation in Theatre and Film*, edited by Katja Krebs, 63–77. New York: Routledge, 2013.

"*William Shakespeare's Star Wars*." *Wookieepedia: The "Star Wars" Wiki*. Last modified October 7, 2016. Accessed February 15, 2019. http://starwars.wikia.com/wiki/William_Shakespeare%27s_Star_Wars.

"*William Shakespeare's Star Wars* Trilogy: The Royal Imperial Boxed Set." Product page on QuirkBooks.com. Accessed November 22, 2016. www.quirkbooks.com/book/william-shakespeares-star-wars-trilogy.

Williams, Raymond. *Television: Technology and Cultural Form*. 2nd ed. London: Routledge, 1990.

About the author

Eckart Voigts is Professor of English Literature at TU Braunschweig, Germany. Most recently, he has co-edited (with Katja Krebs and Dennis Cutchins) the *Routledge Companion to Adaptation* (2018). He has written, edited and co-edited numerous further books and articles, such as the special issue of *Adaptation* (vol. 6.2, 2013) on transmedia storytelling, *Introduction to Media Studies* (Klett 2004), *Janespotting and Beyond: British Heritage Retrovisions since the Mid-1990s* (Narr 2005), *Adaptations – Performing Across Media and Genres* (WVT 2009) *Reflecting on Darwin* (Ashgate 2014) and *Dystopia, Science Fiction, Post-Apocalypse* (WVT 2015) and *Transforming Cities* (Winter 2018).

5. "You Just Got Covered": YouTube Cover Song Videos as Examples of Para-Adaptation

Costas Constandinides

Abstract
Cover songs are broadly viewed as adaptations within the context of relevant scholarly debates, yet little has been written about user-made YouTube cover song videos as adaptations. Scholarly work outside adaptation studies mainly describes such videos as derivative or fan-made videos. This chapter revisits the concept of *para-adaptation* as a first step in understanding how these videos form a multi-layered dialogue with other media forms developed within and around YouTube. User-made YouTube cover song videos do not visually emulate (unless the video falls under the category of parody) the official music video of the song covered, yet the visual settings may also be viewed as adaptations since they borrow familiar elements from other participatory or industry-driven practices. Para-adaptation is a more fitting term to describe such videos: no-budget user-generated content that creatively "disturbs" commercial source products, and may eventually achieve a status that surpasses the "ordinary" expectations of its creator(s). These videos, deliberately or due to a lack of media production competencies and/or space availability other than a bedroom, "fail" to establish a look closer to industry standards. Rather than subtracting from their appeal, these "failures" not only enrich the culture of "ordinary" creativity, but become a source of inspiration for re-energized forms of commercial entertainment.

Key words: Cover; YouTube; adaptation; para-adaptation

Fehrle, J. and W. Schäfke, *Adaptation in the Age of Media Convergence*,
Taylor & Francis Group, 2019
DOI 10.5117/9789462983663_CH05

Introduction

In 2012 Walk off the Earth (WOTE), a rock band based in Canada uploaded on YouTube a video of their cover of the hit single "Somebody That I Used to Know" by Gotye. The playful combination of the vocal and musical abilities of the band members and their staging in front of the camera (five musicians playing one guitar) as well as the deadpan performance of one of the members of the band (Mike Taylor, also known as the Beard Guy) made the video go viral within days. The same arrangement was later presented on *The Ellen DeGeneres Show*. However, the replication of the same arrangement in a TV studio was awkward in many ways. The transference of the WOTE arrangement from the *Between two Ferns*-like décor of their do-it-ourselves (DIO) cover to the larger stage of the TV show inevitably restricted their otherwise novel and globally celebrated YouTube video to an old school variety-like act.

WOTE's TV appearance was simply "non-televisual" when compared to the staging – fully utilizing the studio's spatial and technical possibilities – of other bands appearing on the same show such as the Thirty Seconds to Mars "Do or Die" performance or the adaptation of the official music video of Sia's "Chandelier."[1] WOTE's TV presentation of their YouTube cover remained faithful to the original staging of the musicians' bodies simply because the "five-musicians-playing-one-guitar" arrangement is the basis of the cover's success. The less "confident" TV adaptation of the same arrangement reaffirms that the deliberate use of limitations and possibilities featured in WOTE's no-budget cover video can be "better viewed on YouTube"; in other words, the key characteristics of the video are examples of how YouTube enables a type of creativity, which is not fully prescribed by gatekeepers.

The key reason I am introducing the "five-musicians-one-guitar" video is because it has become a paradigmatic case of a YouTube cover song video; a cover that according to Mosser's[2] classification of covers has become a

1 Sia talks about the specific performance in an interview she gave to *Dazed*. Sia states that her "fantasy at the beginning of this process was to marry reality television with Nordic arthouse cinema." During the performance Sia is positioned on the far back right corner of the TV set (which is a direct reference to the dilapidated apartment in the music video) and sings the song facing her back facing to the camera, while the young dancer Maddie Zeigler, as mini-Sia (wearing the characteristic blond Sia wig), recreates the music video's choreography. "Sia on taking performance art to the masses: Behind the scenes as the blonde-bobbed artist explains her visionary 'Chandelier' video and Ellen performance." *Dazed*, accessed October 1, 2015, www.dazeddigital.com/music/article/19982/1/sia-on-taking-performance-art-to-the-masses.

2 Kurt Mosser, "Cover songs": Ambiguity, Multivalence, Polysemy," *Popular Musicology Online* 2 (2008), accessed December 27, 2016, www.popular-musicology-online.com/issues/02/mosser.html.

"base" performance, primarily, because of the visual mediation of the musical performance. One of the aims of this article is to focus on the visual form and style of do-it-yourself (DIY) or DIO covers on the same social media platform to highlight certain common characteristics. The specific band also exhibits a process of "evolution" in the making of their DIO music videos uploaded to YouTube and this is something that a number of YouTube users[3] go through in order to attract a larger viewership and potentially come to enjoy the financial benefits of YouTube's Partner Program.

In addition, the comparison between WOTE's YouTube and their *Ellen DeGeneres* performance illustrates that self-made YouTube music videos featuring amateur, unknown, or aspiring recording artists performing familiar songs form a YouTube genre in its own right. Many of these videos are small-scale musical and visual productions, whose appeal depends on elements that innovatively marry limitations, inadequacies, and possibilities as illustrated by WOTE's YouTube cover. The word "genre" instead of "trend" is already being used to describe such videos.[4] In addition, the publication of guides to YouTube such as *Social Media for Musicians: YouTube*,[5] which aim to help aspiring musicians to improve the quality of their video presentations as well as build a "brand" that would possibly secure a successful monetization of their cover song videos, further illustrates the fact that such videos need to meet certain criteria. Small-scale does not of course imply an inferior form of the music video genre or of the source performance of the song being covered. Furthermore, some of these self-made videos may also be read as a form of personal expression that combines the intimacy of the home video, the confessional elements of online video diaries or video blogs (also known as vlogs),[6] and performance elements that may be closer to the process of a technical exercise or educational process,[7] rather than an attempt to get noticed by talent producers. YouTube cover song videos predominantly establish a connection with a preexisting commercial product, but at the same time follow YouTube-based communicative patterns and thus form a cultural phenomenon outside industry favored practices and

3 See also Cayari's case study about Wade Johnston, a teenage YouTube musician. Christopher Cayari, "The YouTube effect: How YouTube has provided new ways to consume, create, and share music." I*nternational Journal of Education & the Arts* 12.6 (2011): 1–30.

4 Jean Burgess, "'All your Chocolate Rain are Belong to Us?' Viral Video, YouTube and the Dynamics of Participatory Culture." In *Video Vortex Reader: Responses to YouTube*, ed. Geert Lovink and Sabine Niederer (Amsterdam: Institute of Network Cultures, 2008), 101–109.

5 Gary Hiebner, *Social Media for Musicians: YouTube* (Boston: Cengage Learning PTR, 2014).

6 See Strangelove's discussion on the confessional elements of online video diaries. Michael Strangelove, *Watching YouTube: Extraordinary Videos by Ordinary People* (Toronto: University of Toronto Press, 2010).

7 See Cayari, "The YouTube Effect."

closer to processes found in media fandoms. YouTube-based popularity may become a mainstream media reference, which may in turn expand a user's earning potential, lead to major-label record deals, or generate an invitation to audition for a hit TV talent show such as *The Voice*.

YouTube cover song videos (as discussed here) should not be confused with the aesthetics and practices specific to fannish vidding or parodies of the official music video of a commercial song. According to Francesca Coppa, "vidding is a form of grassroots filmmaking in which clips from television shows and movies are set to music. The result is called a vid or a songvid [...]. [F]annish vidders use music in order to comment on or analyze a set of preexisting visuals, to stage a reading, or occasionally to use the footage to tell new stories."[8] YouTube cover song videos by contrast are amateur, sometimes sophisticated, video productions featuring an aspiring singer/ musician, who performs a version of a preexisting song. The video is usually self-made, and such videos are predominantly shared on YouTube. Coppa argues that a vid "is a visual essay that stages an argument, and thus it is more akin to arts criticism than to traditional music video."[9] The examples discussed here are musical performances that showcase the vocal abilities and creativity of the performer(s) appearing in the video, tested against a popular commercial product. However, similar to Turk's work on vids and vidding, YouTube cover song videos also "respond to and repurpose commercial media [...] in ways that the producers and copyright holders did not intend and may not approve."[10] Furthermore, YouTube cover song videos are examined outside the context of fan studies, and are thus viewed as a DIY process that appropriates amateur or industry-made practices to visually communicate and inexpensively promote a musician.

George Plasketes[11] is one of the few scholars to have published consistently on the topic of covers. In his influential article "Re-flections on the Cover

8 Francesca Coppa, "Women, Star Trek, and the early development of fannish vidding," *Transformative Works and Cultures*, 1, (2008), accessed July 21, 2017, http://journal.transformativeworks.org/index.php/twc/article/view/44/64

9 Ibid.

10 Tisha Turk, "Transformation in a New Key: Music in Vids and Vidding," *Music, Sound, and the Moving Image* 9.2 (2015): 174.

11 George Plasketes, ed., *Play it Again: Cover Songs in Popular Music* (Surrey: Ashgate Publishing, Ltd., 2010);

George Plasketes, "Re-flections on the Cover Age: A Collage of Continuous Coverage in Popular Music," *Popular Music and Society* 28.2 (2005): 137–161; George Plasketes, "Look What They've Done to my Song: Covers and Tributes, an Annotated Discography, 1980–1995," *Popular Music & Society* 19.1 (1995): 79–106; George Plasketes, "Like a Version: Cover Songs and the Tribute Trend in Popular Music," *Studies in Popular Culture* (1992): 1–18.

Age: A Collage of Continuous Coverage in Popular Music," Plasketes notes, "by the early 1990s, cover song momentum as a musical movement was well established. Whether due to an overreaction to a fad, leftover excess from the 1980s, artistic convenience, or the industry's profit motivation, covers proliferated creatively and commercially, transcending trend status into a surging, re-sounding subgenre."[12] Plasketes interestingly connects his understanding of cover songs to processes of adaptation:

> The process of covering a song is essentially an adaptation, in which much of the value lies in the artists' interpretation. A song travels a slightly different course than a piece, which evolves from page to stage to screen, whether silver or small. With music, the song undergoes a recontextualization, remaining in the same medium, with the artists translating the material into a particular style.[13]

Plasketes' statement that the song undergoes a recontextualization within the same medium is not incorrect as a general observation, but it limits the understanding of the cover song performance to elements specific to music. Burns, Dubuc, and Lafrance's[14] basic model of analyzing covers as adaptations takes into consideration the visual elements of a cover song's (music) video. The authors acknowledge "the circulation of multiple versions and manipulations of a given popular song or video. Through the medium of the Internet, music consumers are exposed to a seemingly endless stream of song and video versions."[15] This is particularly evident on YouTube, where the image is undoubtedly an intrinsic part of covering processes by non-commercial musicians and offers an interpretative challenge that Plasketes omits from his basic comparison between covering processes and page-to-screen adaptation. YouTube-based cover videos as a form of adaptation entail a twofold process. The musical settings refer to an existing song, but the visual settings refer to or borrow from a set of practices that are a combination of YouTube and music video aesthetics. Both the musical and visual settings may consciously or otherwise refer to or mimic the arrangement of other YouTube videos (not exclusively amateur-made) covering the same song.

12 Plasketes, "Re-flections on the Cover Age" 146.

13 Ibid., 150.

14 Lori Burns, Tamar Dubuc and Marc Lafrance, "Cotextuality in Music Video: Covering and Sampling in the Cover Art Video of "Umbrella." In *Pop-Culture Pedagogy in the Music Classroom: Teaching Tools from American Idol to YouTube*, ed. Nicole Biamonte (Lanham MD: Scarecrow Press, 2010), 233–264.

15 Burns, Dubuc and Lafrance, "Cotextuality in Music Video," 233.

Mosser notes that the term cover song "is used without the recognition that there are many different kinds of 'covers'."[16] In order to avoid a narrow definition of what an original song may be, Mosser proposes the term "base song" instead, which may be read as a term that is analogous to the "source text" or "hypotext," or a term that at first glance wishes to deprioritize values associated with the use of the word "original." He explains that he uses the term "base" to refer to a song "that, due to its status, popularity, or possibly other reasons, is taken to be paradigmatic, and thus the version to which all other recordings or performances are compared."[17] The base song is to a certain extent an inclusive term, since a cover song may become itself a base song as in the paradigmatic case of WOTE's "Somebody That I Used to Know" YouTube cover song video. In other words, Mosser's working definition of the base song entails the possibility that at a certain moment in the history of a song, which holds the status of the base song, a paradigmatic cover may take the original song's position as a base song or base song performance due to its popularity or charismatic performance of the covering artist. Ingham uses the term "adaptation displacement" to describe such covers.[18]

Burns et al. introduce the category "versions by fans performing the song"[19] together with other categories that may fall under a broader understanding of cover videos, but they do not offer an elaborate understanding of what this may entail or how it may function as a form of adaptation. The key aim here is to discuss covering processes outside industry-controlled contexts of remaking music and making music videos. Terms such as adaptation displacement or base song as a case of adaptation displacement have been used by the above authors to refer to commercially successful covers, clearly positioning the phenomenon within an adaptation framework. Aligning my own work with this trend of studying covers as adaptations, I propose to revisit the term para-adaptation[20] as a first step in understanding how small-scale YouTube cover videos such as WOTE's video can also be read as adaptations and not solely as fan versions of popular songs. The success of WOTE's video has led to a new relationship between the source and the cover song that is not strictly determined by the order of release, or where and how the source song or cover song were released. Para-adaptations are therefore

16 Kurt Mosser, "Cover songs."

17 Ibid.

18 Mike Ingham, "Popular Song and Adaptation." In *The Oxford Handbook of Adaptation Studies*, ed. Thomas Leitch (New York: Oxford University Press, 2017), 324–339.

19 Burns, Dubuc and Lafrance. "Cotextuality in Music Video," 233.

20 Costas Constandinides, "Para-adaptation: Or How I Learned to Stop Worrying and Love Convergence Culture," *Adaptation* 6.2 (2013): 143–157.

user-generated creative contributions that, on the one hand, are associated with a specific industry-created product and, on the other, wish to feature creative talents or responses in a way that is not limited to paratextual or fan video functions. Such user-generated content may eventually achieve the status of "base" content within and around its *ordinary* context of production.

Stylistic features of YouTube cover songs

Self-made cover song videos on YouTube share key aspects of musical and visual elements. Many performances are acoustic renditions of popular songs or are emulations of a defining cover version of a base song by a popular artist. However, the visual aspects of a cover song video do not usually incorporate elements of the official music video of a base song. The visual elements of such videos mainly follow "norms" that reflect the attractive aspects of YouTube, which according to Michael Strangelove are "dialogue, access to opinions and people, and the sense that we are seeing things that cannot be seen within the regular fare of commercial media."[21] Self-made YouTube cover song videos may also establish a visual connection to types of industry-driven online music videos such as the video recordings of live radio performances by popular artists covering other artists or singing an acoustic version of one of their own songs (e.g. BBC Radio 1's *Live Lounge* segment). These complementary visual offerings of radio performances have been described by Berry as examples of "radio visualization," which is itself a process developed to meet the challenges of transmedia engagement.[22]

The video recording of live radio performances as a form of music video is not an elaborate or costly audiovisual production, and it is not a new visual experience as official music videos that use a recording studio as their décor existed pre-2000s (The official music video of "We are the World" [1985] is a classic example). The location is the studio of the radio station where the live performance takes place and the video is usually published online after the completion of the radio segment. Bits from the radio interview with the artist and the artist's preparation moments before the performance may be included in these video segments, but the focus of the video is the live performance. These video segments also form another popular YouTube genre, which may be described as a non-visually elaborate

21 Strangelove, *Watching YouTube*, 48.

22 Richard Berry, "Radio with Pictures: Radio Visualization in BBC National Radio," *Radio Journal: International Studies in Broadcast & Audio Media* 11.2 (2013): 169–184.

music video featuring a commercially successful artist and forming part of radio stations' transmedia storytelling strategies. Interestingly, the visual elements of visualized radio covers are closer to self-made YouTube covers as their medial characteristics adhere to the possibilities and limitations of YouTube and online videos in general. Even though self-made cover videos published on YouTube are not always recorded as live performances, the small-scale production of visualized radio covers and the singing-head shot are the two main characteristics that these music video subgenres share. The small scale and what appears to be a less controlled arrangement (of an artist's performance) of visualized radio covers invites a viewing of these performances that equally suggests access to an event that, as Strangelove notes,[23] cannot be seen within the context of large-scale productions or traditional media presentations. Even though the performer is a popular recording artist, the visual informality of the video recording, the acoustic nature of the cover and the usually comfy clothing selection offer a homier atmosphere.

Covering is a process that is closely related to industry practices, but can now originate from outside the industry as a form of "everyday creativity"[24] at the level of video production, and as a kind of demo at the level of musical talent display. It may be argued, then, that the practice of self-made YouTube cover videos is an evolution of the demo tape. Unedited and non-pre-recorded YouTube cover videos may refer back to the sometimes poor quality of the demo tape or in certain cases the DIO image-making of aspiring artists and bands, but the publication of contemporary demo material by young musicians goes beyond the limited circulation of the demo tape. Unlike music track sharing websites (e.g. SoundCloud and Bandcamp), YouTube covers are multi-media examples, but they may also engage in a kind of transmedia relationship with the aforementioned music track sharing sites. For example, YouTube user Mia Wray, whose music video cover is discussed in the final part of this article, also has a SoundCloud account, where she publishes her covers and original music. Wray lip-syncs to her pre-recorded cover of "No Diggity vs. Thrift Shop," which she also shares on her SoundCloud account as a music track. Wray covers the base-status acoustic mashup by Ed Sheeran and Passenger, which was performed live by the two artists during a radio show, titled *Fifi and Jules*. Its visualized version was shared on YouTube by a number of users.

23 Strangelove, *Watching YouTube*.

24 Jean Burgess and Joshua Green, YouTube: Online Video and Participatory Culture (Cambridge: Polity Press, 2009).

The intention of this study is not to evaluate online videos of song covers in terms of success or failure, departure from or fidelity to an original song, but to take into account the visual aspects of the phenomenon of YouTube cover song videos made by non-professional videographers/non-commercially successful musicians, and to illustrate that the visual elements of these videos also establish a dialogue with existing industry-related and other user-generated practices such as radio visualizations, home videos, and vlogging. This phenomenon could be read as a form of para-adaptation because a great number of these videos are no-budget productions, which surround, or become a defining adaptation of, a commercial source product, and deliberately or due to a lack of media production competencies "fail" to meet the aesthetics or quality of industry standards. Rather than subtracting from their appeal, these "failures" in essence underpin the success of these videos. Therefore, the visual relationship of these cover song videos with the entertainment industry is to a certain extent one of aesthetic difference, which is in no small part the result of recognizable technical and technological limitations nonetheless deemed acceptable by the YouTube community. This difference is sometimes adopted by "lo-fi" commercial entertainment, and YouTube-inspired shows or show segments often become a space where celebrities can themselves perform everyday "fails" or display a different set of talents such as lip-syncing mastery (e.g. *Lip Sync Battle*).[25]

The covering process by amateur musicians can be described as "parasitic" since YouTube performers feed off the popularity of commercial music videos or performances also hosted on YouTube. Existing research indicates that authorized "music videos are among the most popular content shared on YouTube."[26] According to a 2012 Nielsen report the teen's dominant choice for discovering music in the US is YouTube.[27] Liikkanen and Salovaara also note that YouTube is "the most recognized digital music brand."[28] The same authors write that derivative videos (covers being a subcategory of this broader category proposed by the authors) are "the most heterogeneous of all the primary music video types. These videos were inspired by the

25 See also Edmond's discussion of the music video of the song "Here We Go Again" (2006) by the group OK Go. Maura Edmond, "Here We Go Again Music Videos after YouTube," *Television & New Media* 15.4 (2014): 305–320.

26 Christopher J. Schneider, "Music Videos on YouTube: Exploring Participatory Culture on Social Media." *Symbolic Interactionist Takes on Music* 47 (2016): 98.

27 www.nielsen.com/us/en/press-room/2012/music-discovery-still-dominated-by-radio--says-nielsen-music-360.html. Accessed February 15, 2019.

28 Lassi A. Liikkanen and Antti Salovaara, "Music on YouTube: User Engagement with Traditional, User-appropriated and Derivative Videos," *Computers in Human Behavior* 50 (2015): 108.

Classic music videos, but they included novel elements in their video, audio, or embedded content."[29] They conclude, "traditional videos receive more views but derivative videos invite more active viewer participation through commenting and voting."[30] However, amateur-made covering is far from being a deadly threat to the survival of the music industry. The relationship between the phenomenon of amateur YouTube covers and the industry can be more accurately described as mutually symbiotic since mainstream cultural products (e.g. talent shows) also benefit from the platform's talent discovery possibilities, not to mention YouTube's licensing deals. It could also be argued that user-generated creativity is no longer a "revolutionary" alternative to commercial channels that promote media content but an "extension of the cultural industries,"[31] which have evolved into platforms that host both amateur and professional creativity. For example, the Starmaker 3.0 App (launched in June 2014) by Starmaker Interactive (a company that has established a partnership with The Voice franchise among other similar partnerships) allows users to make a "music video selfie" and then upload their video to YouTube. The company sells this product using the slogan "Be discovered or discover the next music star." This example illustrates Schäfer's understanding of how new business models benefit from the activities of users through implicit participation, "where social interaction and user activities are channeled and controlled by design."[32] Still, a number of these videos remain explicitly peripheral and sometimes become defining cultural contributions standing in contrast to the kind of videos the Starmaker App seems geared towards – with its offer of backing tracks of mainstream songs and auto-tune possibilities to pre-record a user's vocal performance.

In order to offer an understanding of the aesthetic differences between YouTube user-generated music videos and industry-related visual forms of musical performances I will return to the comparison between WOTE's YouTube cover of "Somebody That I Used to Know" and their performance on the *Ellen* show. The key problem of WOTE's recreation on television is one of production scale. In *Unruly Media* Carol Vernallis identifies scale as one of the defining characteristics of YouTube clips.[33] One of her key

29 Liikkanen and Salovaara, "Music on YouTube," 114.

30 Ibid., 123.

31 Mirko Tobias Schäfer, Bastard Culture!: How User Participation Transforms Cultural Production (Amsterdam: Amsterdam University Press, 2011), 11.

32 Ibid., 44.

33 Carol Vernallis, *Unruly Media: YouTube, Music Video, and the New Digital Cinema* (Oxford: Oxford University Press, 2013).

observations is that post-2000s audio-visual culture is influenced by the music video; in order to make this point, she identifies the sonic and visual connections between YouTube videos, digital cinema and music videos. The large-scale audiovisual examples she uses to support her argument are the filmic works of David Fincher, Spike Jonze, and Michel Gondry, who started their filmmaking career as music video directors. Vernallis describes YouTube as the "new digital cinema's shadowy twin"[34] and lists some of the key smaller-scale values (limited length, low resolution, impromptu lighting and design, etc.) of YouTube, which along with their variations are also characteristic of cover song music videos:

> YouTube's aesthetic values include bold graphic design and well-judged scale. This may be related to the medium and its mode of delivery – a clip's limited length, its level of resolution, and the forms of attention it encourages. Poorly lit small environments shot and uploaded with low resolution may tend toward fuzziness [...] YouTube clips must often garner attention in a competitive environment; many that struggle to gain legibility, go bold.[35]

WOTE's YouTube video shares some of these small-scale characteristics; an uninterrupted still shot, dressed with non-professional lighting, indoor plants and window shutters acts as a background in order to enhance the boldness and playfulness of their attempt. This conscious, yet successful pairing of self-made elements with the band's skillful performance led to the popularity of the video, and hence the transposition of this pairing from a small-scale production to a larger-scale context, in this case the set of a mainstream television show, inevitably feels odd. Vernallis observes that "some of the most popular clips' particularity must be locked in the ways these figures reside exactly where they are within their flat, miniature cubicles."[36] Interestingly, this locking of multi-bodies in front of a still camera has become a kind of trademark arrangement in many of the band's YouTube videos. WOTE smartly established a dialogue between their YouTube performances and their more polished appearance in the official music video for their song "Red Hands," which even though it uses a dolly-out/pull-back shot and displays the energetic movement of the musicians amidst an obviously larger-scale set, also includes moments

34 Ibid., 134.
35 Ibid., 135.
36 Ibid.

where the bodies of the five members coexist in the frame in a way that refers back to their YouTube videos.

Many user-created cover song videos on YouTube share the low-res, poorly lit and under-decorated DIY characteristics described by Vernallis in *Unruly Media*.[37] At the level of visual characteristics, these videos usually do not establish a dialogue with an official music video of a base song. Instead, they establish a dialogue with a broader "movement" of online video production, which is often the result of autodidactic activities to master the process of creating videos; in this case, music videos that aim to share, express, and display a set of musical skills using familiar songs.

While many aspiring recording artists upload their performances on YouTube hoping to be noticed by talent producers of shows such as *The Voice*, the predominantly self-made video recordings of amateur-made YouTube performances are evidently contributions to what Plasketes describes as a diversified and accelerated cover age.[38] These small-scale contributions also form part of an accelerated and diversified online arena that is shaped around the core of the commercial music industry, and yet they may become popular through an adaptation process that is not tightly linked to the power structures of the music industry. Therefore, the non-involvement of industry-driven image-making processes is, to a significant extent, the reason why amateur-made YouTube cover videos are para-adaptations. These videos exist in an intermediate position. They are neither subcultural nor entirely monitored by the industry, but they "exploit" the success of base songs to generate views, as well as utilizing the tools that YouTube provides to meet the needs of its users such as the Music Insights tool. The production of these videos is usually characterized by technical and creative "inadequacies," yet the "likeable" quality of these videos is precisely the result of their inadequacies or small-scale settings. In this fashion, they echo the manner in which other cultural products (e.g. Jeffrey Sconce's understanding of paracinema[39]) that differ from mainstream forms of entertainment are celebrated for their aesthetic "lows."

Interestingly, not all YouTube cover song videos feature low-grade qualities. Many user-generated cover song videos try to create the feeling of a studio setting, or mimic the visual settings of professionally-made

37 Ibid.

38 Plasketes, "Re-flections on the Cover Age."

39 Jeffrey Sconce, "Trashing the Academy: Taste, Excess and an Emerging Politics of Cinematic Style," *Screen* 36.4 (1995): 371–393.

recordings of music videos in a manner similar to the video recordings of live radio performances or artists' acoustic covers of their own songs, or through the use of spaces such as abandoned indoor spaces, warehouses, or residential garages familiar from professional productions. Many creators of cover song videos invite comments that will help them improve their skills and videos, thus there is also an apprenticeship process, which renders the cover song, and cover song video, as non-professional but still part of a creative growth process that welcomes criticism. The basis of this criticism is often the result of a comparison to the base song. Amateur performers of cover songs also learn from other performers, who upload covers on YouTube. More experienced performers and video makers tend to upload "making of" videos to explain the process of covering or to comment on the dos and don'ts of the same process. For example, YouTube user JonDittertMusic uploaded a video in 2013 titled "How to Make Cover Songs on YouTube" in which he explained the basic process of uploading a cover video to YouTube in the form of a stand-up comedy. His humorous description of some of the steps of the process refers to key visual and sometimes confessional characteristics of amateur-made cover videos: "Step 4 is to set up your camera, anywhere is fine [...] it doesn't matter [about] the lighting," "It's time for crucial Step 5, Apologize. Hey guys I just actually started to learn this song today so forgive me if I make any mistakes" and "Step 7: Upload your video, some cameras will even let you upload straight from your camera to YouTube, which will keep you from feeling bad about skipping that tedious editing part."

YouTube viewers may follow the channel of an amateur performer, who serially covers mainstream songs, and tend to make requests; some of these followers might even request an original song by their favorite YouTube performer. These practices form a hybrid aesthetic, which combines home video and radio visualization settings; even though covering is associated (unofficially or otherwise) with a source product, the visual and the familiar musical settings usually function as ways to bring to the fore an unknown artist's personality and musical talent. The covering process in this case is not usually an homage or an attempt to establish a profound dialogic process, but a hook, that is, a way to grab someone's attention. Furthermore, the title of a popular song as part of the video's title will possibly help the discoverability of the performer on YouTube. Such forms of talent display are now well established; therefore, it is worth bearing in mind that this hybrid aesthetic may simply be a choice that results from a conscious assessment of the rewards of covering songs on YouTube. Even so, it remains part of a practice that, unlike industry paradigms, can be self-/user-managed.

YouTube cover song videos of "No Diggity" and "Titanium" as para-adaptations

For a closer examination of YouTube cover song videos as para-adaptations, I will discuss music videos created by amateur or unknown musicians covering the songs "No Diggity" by the American R&B group Blackstreet featuring Dr. Dre and Queen Pen and "Titanium" by French DJ and music producer David Guetta, featuring vocals by Australian recording artist Sia, who is also one of the writers of the song. The search "No Diggity cover" on YouTube returns about 1,920,000 results and the search "Titanium cover" returns about 3,920,000 results (29/04/2018). A capella versions of both songs were featured in the film *Pitch Perfect*,[40] and this may have contributed to the popular selection of these songs as cover material for the creation of YouTube cover videos by young musicians. In addition, most of the covers are inspired by acoustic versions or ballad versions of the songs performed by recording artists, e.g. "No Diggity" mashed up with "Thrift Shop" by Ed Sheeran and The Passenger or Chet Faker's commercially recorded cover of "No Diggity" or Sia's ballad version of "Titanium."

The key type of YouTube cover video discussed in this section is described by Burgess as the "virtuosic bedroom musical performance."[41] This mainly refers to the unedited and low image quality type of video that the user JonDittertMusic playfully comments on in his "making of cover songs" video. According to Burgess, "the everydayness of the genre is all the more evident because of its situatedness in the bedroom."[42] Burgess adds that "the bedroom music genre demonstrates how relatively simple uses of video technology (recording straight to camera and uploading without much editing) and highly constrained genres (the musical cover), while not necessarily contributing to the aesthetic advancement of the medium, can invite further participation by establishing clear rules"[43] for other YouTube users who may want to start covering or advance to the next level of making cover videos. These "rules" are formulated through what Burgess describes as operations of play and learning that also involve the showcasing of talent and in effect the "setting of standards for other players in the game to attain or beat."[44] "Making of" videos such as the one created by JonDittertMusic in the form

40 Moore, *Pitch Perfect*.

41 Burgess, "All your Chocolate Rain are Belong to Us?"

42 Ibid., 7.

43 Ibid.

44 Ibid.

of parody or J Sharnie's video tutorial titled "How to Make/Record Cover Songs for YouTube" are examples of videos that aim to communicate a set of acceptable standards in terms of video production and audio production. J Sharnie introduces three levels of YouTube cover song production: Basic, Intermediate, and Advanced. A key musical element of many bedroom music videos that somewhat establishes a closer rapport between the viewers and the performer is that the musicians sing and play an instrument live while a web camera records them (a basic form of a YouTube cover song according to J Sharnie); in this case performers do not lip-synch to their pre-recorded version of the cover or sing to a backing track (elements which are usually met by intermediate and advanced YouTube users).

Sunn St. Claire's cover video of "Titanium" (published in 2011) is an example that shares the "basic" characteristics of YouTube covers. Sunn introduces herself at the beginning of the video and informs the viewers that this is the first time she will play the guitar instead of the keyboard as in her previous videos. In the description of the video, she notes that this attempt is part of a learning experience and confesses that she sang the wrong lyrics adding a "haha" as a cute way to apologize. Her introduction and the medium-to-close-up framing reflect settings associated with vlogging, "a form whose persistent direct address to the viewer inherently invites feedback."[45] Sunn's endearing direct address also echoes the "sweetness" and intimacy which Vernallis nostalgically associates with early professional music videos of the 1980s.[46] Sunn closes her performance with what seems to be a spontaneous shy face that may suggest vulnerability, as she is not in a position to receive an immediate response from her potential online viewers, as she would be in the case of performing live for an audience.

Intimacy, vulnerability, and sweetness are key characteristics of many cover song videos uploaded on YouTube. Burgess and Green note that many user-made music videos "adopt a conversational mode, as artists preface their work with a discussion of the motivations or context of the piece they have written or will perform, respond to suggestions and feedback, often drawing the audience into the intimacy afforded by direct address."[47] Timid introductory comments prior to a performance, the silences before and after unedited performances, which include the process of pressing the record button, casual appearance, quick glances at the lyrics sheet, and the framing of homely surroundings, are all elements that do not visually

45 Burgess and Green, *YouTube*,54.
46 Vernallis, *Unruly Media*.
47 Burgess and Green, *YouTube*, 54.

emulate 1980s' music videos but are nevertheless components that meet the entry level standards of YouTube covering musicians and communicate the exploratory relationship between a musician and their video production tools as well as online audience (whose reaction might not always be friendly).

Radio visualization trends on YouTube channels operated by radio stations and their emulation by YouTube performers are an interesting development, as both recording artists and amateur musicians put their skills to the test and "battle" for online attention. The visual elements of many amateur and independently made online music videos (which are mainly composed of close-up shots of a performer wearing a headset with half of his/her face, off center, covered by the pop filter of the microphone and close-up shots framing hands playing a variety of musical instruments) are closer to the visualized covers published by radio shows such as BBC Radio 1's *Live Lounge*. The sound of radio visualization-like YouTube cover videos is usually pre-recorded, as performers tend to create a multitrack audiovisual production. In addition, artists whose music videos are self-made cannot afford/manage a two-camera shoot (which will provide them with a variety of shot sizes and angles to play with in the editing part) if they decide to video record a live performance; hence a pre-recorded sound track allows for a better visual arrangement. Mia Wray's cover of "No Diggity vs. Thrift Shop" is an example of a pre-recorded multi-tracked YouTube cover featuring vocals by herself that emphasizes the arrangement of visual elements, in turn hinting at the non-elaborate characteristics of visualized radio covers or official music videos that often use a recording studio as their visual setting. The opening shot features Wray in a medium-to-close-up shot preparing for her performance. A dominant visual element is the microphone she appears to sing into while playing the guitar. Wray attempts to establish depth of field by adding a legible and slightly out of focus line of musical instruments behind her, leading to the closed door of what seems to be a bedroom. The second shot of the video frames her hands playing the guitar and then a third shot is a side view of her lip-syncing the backing vocals of the track into the microphone. This obviously affirms that the pre-recording was edited by, for instance, adding additional vocal tracks in the mix.

YouTube performers like the examples discussed here attempt to improve their video skills or visual settings (separate from their music skills) over time, or collaborate with other creators to mediate more effectively their personality and creativity. Mia Wray's first uploads are examples of basic bedroom covers and Sunn's improvement in the making of cover videos is evident over time, possibly after her realization that her performances were attracting a good number of viewers. Sunn's "Rather Be" cover published three years after her "Titanium" video is shot outdoors, and includes titles instead of a verbal introduction. In addition, Sunn has turned her shyness (the cute bite of her tongue after the completion of her performances) into a sort of "bold" trademark or branding element that is added after the completion of the performance (a cartoonish portrait of herself biting her tongue and wearing heart-shaped sunglasses, graded with warm yellowish colors against a black background. Her face appears in a yellow circle and her name, all in capital letters, appears in red, bold, and rounded letters under her chin).

Interestingly, the artists participating in Radio 1's *Live Lounge* sessions also introduce themselves before they perform and invite viewers to subscribe to *Live Lounge*'s YouTube channel. The arrangement of these introductions sometimes leads to playful yet delicate slapstick moments since well-known artists try to accurately point to the "click here to subscribe" graphic; this is reminiscent of the "intimate" intros and the silences of YouTube performers before and after their bedroom performance. The less polished version of a popular artist's image aims to communicate that the visualized radio cover is not simply just another media appearance of the artist, but a form of presentation that is closer to the stylistic features of online content, and a request for a form of interaction that is closer to the habits and experiences of social media users. Strangelove suggests that "the act of putting content on the Internet often results in dialogue" and that "YouTube amateur videos often take the form of requests of communication."[48] Radio visualizations aim to enhance the listener's or follower's experience as they provide opportunities for social interaction through accessibility to refashioned content that users can comment on or share via social media platforms.[49] At another level, the circulation of visualized radio covers or acoustic performances by commercial artists on YouTube becomes part of a more complex, and not simply clickable, dialogic process as a number of non-commercial YouTube artists borrow from the visuals of such videos and respond through their own musical renditions or emulations of acoustic arrangements, which may become "base" arrangements within and outside the YouTube community.

Conclusion

The case studies discussed in the previous section show that YouTube cover song videos are particular cases of para-adaptation as they creatively

48 Strangelove, *Watching YouTube*, 48.
49 Berry, "Radio with Pictures."

perform popular songs and mediate these performances in ways that cannot compete with large-scale industry aesthetics. Instead, they communicate a specific set of skills using tools that adhere to the particularity of YouTube as a social media platform. These videos are democratically available to the mass audience and therefore may become as popular as commercial products, like WOTE's paradigmatic cover of "Somebody That I Used to Know." The process of adaptation in this case is twofold since the performance may be identified as a cover, but the visual settings are not adaptations of the source song's official music video. Instead, the visual settings of these videos sometimes borrow visual codes from practices specific to radio visualization or are simply variations of the bedroom musical performance, which may include vlogging elements. Therefore, these videos provide a visual experience independent from industry practices of commercial music video production, or they relate more significantly to professional material that is also made for the purposes of online viewing, such as visualized radio covers.

Unlike the classification systems proposed by Mosser[50] and Magnus et al.,[51] YouTube cover song videos are, to a certain extent, examples of adaptations that may not have a clear "departure" or "destination" and this is partly because of today's frequency and variety of *re-covering*, which is not limited to well-known artists. YouTube performers may reference the source song (wrongly or otherwise), but they don't always wish to communicate the (hi)story of this song or express a sense of devotion to the "owner" of the song, as the above examples illustrate; rather, they wish to promote their talents through a deliberate performance of the song. The above exchanges point toward useful ways of looking at the journeys of familiar content across media, especially those that are associated with how viewers view, consume, and partake in the recycling of such content. While adaptation studies scholars introduce or reintroduce models of study that highlight dialogic processes and non-hierarchical ways of looking at adaptations,[52] YouTube viewers and users tell us that this might already be the norm in some areas.

50 Mosser, "Cover songs."

51 Cristyn Magnus, P.D. Magnus, and Christy Mag Uidhir, "Judging Covers," *The Journal of Aesthetics and Art Criticism* 71.4 (2013): 361–370.

52 See Deborah Cartmell and Imelda Whelehan's influential edited volume *Adaptations: From Text to Screen and Screen to Text* (London: Routledge, 1999) and Robert Stam's essay "Beyond Fidelity," which introduces the intertextual dialogism approach within the context of adaptation studies. Robert Stam. "Beyond Fidelity: The Dialogics of Adaptation." In *Film Adaptation,* edited by James Naremore (London: The Athlone Press, 2000), 54–78.

Works Cited

Berry, Richard. "Radio with Pictures: Radio Visualization in BBC National Radio." *Radio Journal: International Studies in Broadcast & Audio Media* 11.2 (2013): 169–184.

Biamonte, Nicole, ed., *Pop-Culture Pedagogy in the Music Classroom: Teaching Tools from American Idol to YouTube*. Lanham, MD: Scarecrow Press, 2010.

Burgess, Jean. "All your Chocolate Rain are Belong to Us? Viral Video, YouTube and the Dynamics of Participatory Culture." In *Video Vortex Reader: Responses to YouTube* edited by Geert Lovink and Sabine Niederer, 101–109. Amsterdam: Institute of Network Cultures, 2008.

Burgess, Jean, and Green, Joshua. *YouTube: Online Video and Participatory Culture*. Cambridge: Polity Press, 2009.

Burns, Lori, Tamar Dubuc, and Marc Lafrance. "Cotextuality in Music Video: Covering and Sampling in the Cover Art Video of "Umbrella." In *Pop-Culture Pedagogy in the Music Classroom: Teaching Tools from American Idol to YouTube*, edited by Nicole Biamonte, 233–264. Lanham, MD: Scarecrow Press, 2010.

Cartmell, Deborah, and Imelda Whelehan, eds. *Adaptations: From Text to Screen, Screen to Text*. London: Routledge, 1999.

Cayari, Christopher. "The YouTube effect: How YouTube has provided new ways to consume, create, and share music." *International Journal of Education & the Arts* 12.6 (2011): 1–30.

Constandinides, Costas. "Para-adaptation: Or How I Learned to Stop Worrying and Love Convergence Culture." *Adaptation* 6.2 (2013): 143–157.

Coppa, Francesca. "Women, Star Trek, and the Early Development of Fannish Vidding." *Transformative Works and Cultures* 2 (2008). Accessed July 21, 2017. http://journal.transformativeworks.org/index.php/twc/article/view/44/64

Dazed. "Sia on taking performance art to the masses: Behind the scenes as the blonde-bobbed artist explains her visionary 'Chandelier' video and Ellen performance." Accessed October 1, 2015. www.dazeddigital.com/music/article/19982/1/sia-on-taking-performance-art-to-the-masses.

De Backer, Wally. "Somebody That I Used to Know" Recorded by Gotye featuring Kimbra In *Making Mirrors*. Eleven, 2011.

Edmond, Maura. "Here We Go Again Music Videos after YouTube." *Television & New Media* 15.4 (2014): 305–320.

Furler, Sia, and Jesse Shatkin (2014). "Chandelier" Recorded by Sia. Inertia, Monkey Puzzle, RCA.

Furler, Sia, David Guetta, Giorgio Tuinfort, and Nick Van De Wall (2011). "Titanium" Recorded by David Guetta featuring Sia. Virgin, EMI.

Haggerty, Ben, and Ryan Lewis (2012). "Thrift Shop" Recorded by Macklemore & Ryan Lewis featuring Wanz. Macklemore LLC.

Hiebner, Gary. *Social Media for Musicians: YouTube.* Boston: Cengage Learning PTR, 2014.

Ingham, Mike. "Popular Song and Adaptation." In *The Oxford Handbook of Adaptation Studies*, edited by Thomas Leitch, 324–339. New York: Oxford University Press, 2017.

Jackson, Michael and Lionel Richie (1985). "We Are the World" Recorded by the United Support of Artists (USA) for Africa. Columbia.

JonDittertMusic. (22/01/2013). "How to Make Cover Songs on YouTube." Accessed October 1, 2015. www.youtube.com/watch?v=i6Q_MwOk70c

Leto, Jarred (2013). "Do Or Die" Recorded by Thirty Seconds to Mars. Virgin Records.

Liikkanen, Lassi A. and Antti Salovaara. "Music on YouTube: User Engagement with Traditional, User-appropriated and Derivative Videos." *Computers in Human Behavior* 50 (2015): 108–124.

Magnus, Cristyn, P.D. Magnus, and Christy Mag Uidhir. "Judging Covers." *The Journal of Aesthetics and Art Criticism* 71.4 (2013): 361–370.

Marshall, Ryan, Gianni "Luminati" Nicassio, Sarah Blackwood, and Thomas "Tawgs" Salter (2012). "Red Hands" Recorded by Walk off the Earth. Columbia.

Moore, Jason. *Pitch Perfect.* Universal Studios Home Entertainment. 2012. DVD.

Mosser, Kurt. "'Cover songs': Ambiguity, Multivalence, Polysemy." *Popular Musicology Online* 2 (2008). Accessed December 27, 2016. www.popular-musicology-online.com/issues/02/mosser.html

Patterson, Jack, James Napier, Nicole Marshall, and Grace Chatto (2014). "Rather Be" Recorded by Clean Bandit featuring Jess Glynne. WMG and Atlantic.

Plasketes, George, ed., *Play it again: Cover Songs in Popular Music.* Surrey: Ashgate Publishing, Ltd., 2010.

—. "Like a Version: Cover Songs and the Tribute Trend in Popular Music." *Studies in Popular Culture* 15.1 (1992): 1–18.

—. "Look What They've Done to my Song: Covers and Tributes, an Annotated Discography, 1980–1995." *Popular Music & Society* 19.1 (1995): 79–106.

—. "Re-flections on the Cover Age: A Collage of Continuous Coverage in Popular Music." *Popular Music and Society* 28.2 (2005): 137–161.

Scharnweber, Joe (24/06/2015). "How to Make/Record Cover Songs for YouTube." Accessed October 1, 2015. www.youtube.com/watch?v=T91Dus-gww4

Schäfer, Mirko Tobias. *Bastard Culture!: How User Participation Transforms Cultural Production.* Amsterdam: Amsterdam University Press, 2011.

Schneider, Christopher J. "Music Videos on YouTube: Exploring Participatory Culture on Social Media." *Symbolic Interactionist Takes on Music* 47 (2016): 97–117.

Sconce, Jeffrey. "'Trashing' the Academy: Taste, Excess, and an Emerging Politics of Cinematic Style." *Screen* 36.4 (1995): 371–393.

"Season 9, Episode 84/2 *Ellen: The Ellen DeGeneres Show* (Produced by Telepictures, Distributed by Warner Bros. Television) January 23, 2012.

Sheeran, Ed & Passenger Cover No Diggity *Fifi and Jules* (Today's Hit Network, FOX FM). Uploaded March 6, 2013. Accessed January 10, 2015. www.fox.com.au/shows/fifi-and-jules/video/ed-sheeran-covers-no-diggity/#disqus_thread. *Live Lounge* (BBC Radio 1).

St. Claire, Sunn. (07/09/2014). "Rather Be Clean Bandit Cover by SUNN." Accessed October 1, 2015. www.youtube.com/watch?v=ezhJa-lhbeQ.

—. (14/09/2011). "Titanium David Guetta ft. Sia Cover singing by SUNN." Accessed October 1, 2015. www.youtube.com/watch?v=KrQb8JIDCxM.

Stam, Robert. "Beyond Fidelity: The Dialogics of Adaptation." In *Film Adaptation*, edited by James Naremore, 54–78. London: The Athlone Press, 2000.

Strangelove, Michael. *Watching YouTube: Extraordinary Videos by Ordinary People*. Toronto: University of Toronto Press, 2010.

Turk, Tisha. "Transformation in a New Key: Music in Vids and Vidding." *Music, Sound, and the Moving Image* 9.2 (2015): 163–176.

Vernallis, Carol. *Unruly Media: YouTube, Music Video, and the New Digital Cinema*. Oxford: Oxford University Press, 2013.

Walk off the Earth. (05/01/2015). "Somebody That I Used to Know – Walk off the Earth." Accessed October 1, 2015. www.youtube.com/watch?v=d9NF2edxy-M

Wray, Mia. (26/03/2013). "No Diggity vs. Thrift Shop (Ed Sheeran + Passenger) – Mia Wray." Accessed October 1, 2015. www.youtube.com/watch?v=74vyMJc8Rgo

Young, Andre et al. (1996). "No Diggity" Recorded by Blackstreet featuring Dr. Dre and Queen Pen. Interscope.

About the author

Costas Constandinides is Assistant Professor of Film and Digital Media Studies in the Department of Communications at the University of Nicosia. He is the author of *From Film Adaptation to Post-celluloid Adaptation* (2010) and co-editor of *Cypriot Cinemas: Memory, Conflict, and Identity in the Margins of Europe* (2015).

6. Masters of the Universe? Viewers, the Media, and *Sherlock's* Lead Writers

Benjamin Poore

Abstract
This chapter focuses on the representation of the tabloid press in the second and third series of *Sherlock* and, in turn, on the series' lead writers and their handling of publicity for *Sherlock*'s third series in January 2014. Expectations for the new series were high, as *Sherlock*'s popularity had grown and intensified in the two-year hiatus between series two and three. Gatiss and Moffat became increasingly visible as public figures, as interest in *Sherlock* spilled over into press and fan interest in the making of *Sherlock*. The chapter raises the question of whether *Sherlock* itself took a political stance in response to news events of the time, and whether its two lead writers acted as political agents, as well as cultural agents.

Key words: Sherlock; Mark Gatiss; Steven Moffat; showrunners; adaptation; villains

Introduction

During the publicity surrounding the screening of series three of *Sherlock*, the BBC's modernized adaptation of the Sherlock Holmes stories, in January 2014, a great deal was heard from the show's co-creators, Mark Gatiss and Steven Moffat. Moffat in particular appeared in several public fora, defending the show's new direction. Series three marked a turning point for *Sherlock* where the actors' off-screen lives suddenly became much more visible on-screen: in addition to lead writer Gatiss also playing Sherlock's brother Mycroft, Martin Freeman (John Watson)'s then-wife in real life, Amanda Abbington, joined the cast as John's wife Mary, and the real-life parents of Benedict Cumberbatch (Sherlock), Timothy Carlton and Wanda Ventham, made cameo

Fehrle, J. and W. Schäfke, *Adaptation in the Age of Media Convergence*, Taylor & Francis Group, 2019
DOI 10.5117/9789462983663_CH06

appearances as Sherlock and Mycroft's parents. In addition, this was the first series to feature a final villain who was not Jim Moriarty. Gatiss and Moffat chose a media magnate, Charles Augustus Magnussen, as their designated super-villain, a character based on a blackmailer in the Conan Doyle stories, Charles Augustus Milverton. Such a modernizing character adaptation was bound to attract interest for its topicality, especially given the recently concluded Leveson Inquiry, set up by the British government to investigate the ethics and practices of the British press. To underline this connection, Magnussen is first seen on screen giving evidence in front of some kind of official inquiry. Indeed, at the time of the show's airing, criminal trials of senior News International figures were still ongoing. Finally, discussion in Q&A sessions after the premieres of the series' three episodes often returned to the subject of *Sherlock*'s international success, the fan responses that it has inspired, and the logistics of filming. Again, Moffat and Gatiss have had sometimes surprising and controversial views on the series' fans, reflected both in post-show discussions and discernible in the program itself.

Given the increasing visibility of Gatiss and Moffat as public figures, then, as interest in *Sherlock* spilled over into press and fan interest in the making of *Sherlock*, this chapter raises the question of whether *Sherlock* itself had developed a political position, and whether its two lead writers acted as political agents, as well as cultural agents, in the positions they publicly took up at this point in the show's history. In brief, I intend to explore whether the attitude of anti-media populism in *Sherlock* series two and three is taken up in a politically cohesive way. In order to do this, I begin by defining more closely Gatiss and Moffat's status as *Sherlock* co-creators and lead writers; I will then analyze in more detail two aspects of series three, which attracted press attention for their political overtones, and will compare these with the show's use of the reporter Kitty Reilly in series two. The chapter then considers *Sherlock*'s treatment of its fans, both within the show itself and in the lead writers' comments. Drawing on these two strands – politics and the fandom – I go on to argue that what connects the lead writers' reaction on these issues is a need to control *Sherlock*'s central "story," and not to have that storytelling function challenged or contested by either fans or journalists. It is this insistence on "framing the narrative," I conclude, that ultimately most reflects the politics of the period.

Showrunners versus lead writers

To begin, it may be useful to specify the role of Gatiss and Moffat in *Sherlock*'s creative process. The two men are frequently referred to in press and online commentary as *Sherlock*'s showrunners, but I will avoid the term in this essay, since its use oversimplifies Gatiss and Moffat's relationship to their source material, and the institutional dynamics of producing a commercially successful show for an independent company that is broadcast and distributed by the BBC.

As Kate Harwood, former BBC Head of Drama for England, has expressed it, British television tends to have lead writers rather than showrunners in the American sense. The difference, for Harwood, is that American showrunners have much greater autonomy, being responsible for the hiring and firing on their shows, and leading a large team of writers whose output they oversee for consistency of tone.[1] Examples of showrunners in American television with a considerable degree of institutional power have included Matthew Weiner (*Mad Men*), David Chase (*The Sopranos*), David Simon (*The Wire*), and David Milch (*Deadwood*).[2] Although Moffat, in particular, carried a good deal of institutional power as series co-creator of *Sherlock* as well as being, at the time, executive producer and lead writer of *Doctor Who* (the BBC's two most lucrative television exports), in *Sherlock* the writing team so far has consisted only of Moffat, Gatiss, and Stephen Thompson. Moffat's account of the writing process, given in the Q&A session after the premiere of "His Last Vow," suggests that for an episode like "The Sign of Three" all three writers collaborated extensively: "we all did everything."[3] So, while the term "lead writer" may be misleading in the sense that these two writers lead a writing team consisting of only one other person (Thompson, whose role in any case appears to have diminished since the earlier series), it does at least have the virtue of identifying Gatiss and Moffat's role as writers (and adaptors of Conan Doyle) without necessarily allowing the screenwriting function to overshadow the creative contributions of others.[4] An alternative label, "auteurs," might be applied to Gatiss and Moffat, but I have opted for "lead writers" instead on the grounds that "auteur" suggests a history of film directing that is potentially misleading,[5] and which again may conflate a range of different creative contributions to the show's success (those of, say,

1 Poore, "Neverending Stories," 73.

2 See Martin, *Difficult Men*, 8–9, 72–73, 147–148, and 252.

3 Mellor, "Sherlock: His Last Vow Q&A."

4 For example, Paul McGuigan, who directed two episodes of series one and two, was responsible for key elements of *Sherlock's* visual style, including the placing of text on the screen to convey information read either on smartphones or in Sherlock's head. See Tribe, *Sherlock Chronicles*, 65–66, 102–105.

5 "The film director is king – on television, it's the writer, so you have to get your head around that," remarks Paul McGuigan. Tribe, *Sherlock Chronicles*, 96.

the designers, editors, composers, and directors) with an overall auteurist, authorial vision.[6]

Furthermore, despite their status as successful writers in their own right, and as co-creators of *Sherlock*, Moffat and Gatiss lack the autonomy of the powerful US showrunner, or of the filmic auteur. For example, as Steve Tribe explains, the series was conceived as consisting of 60-minute episodes, but a BBC staffing change resulted in a request for the unusual format of 90-minute episodes.[7] Another aspect of the writers' relative lack of power is the (un)availability of *Sherlock*'s lead actors. Moffat and Thompson have made no secret of the fact that the small number of episodes of *Sherlock* is due in large part to the busy schedules of Benedict Cumberbatch and Martin Freeman, whose Hollywood film careers have both taken off in recent years.[8] Thompson even quotes Moffat as saying, in respect of the time constraints placed on *Sherlock* by such factors, "no script is ever properly finished – it's just transmitted."[9]

Moffat, Gatiss, and the psychic concept of adaptation

On one level, then, *Sherlock*'s writers freely allude to their relative lack of creative control, and present the show's immense success as akin to a happy accident. However, there is a second discourse, which runs in contradiction to this, a discourse mostly constructed by Moffat, which strongly suggests that he and Gatiss are uniquely qualified to adapt Conan Doyle for the twenty-first century. This self-fashioning, as the chapter will go on to explore, can easily shade into a slight impatience or intolerance of anything but the lead writers' own approved storylines and interpretations.

In explaining this pattern, it is significant that *Sherlock* seemed at this point to enjoy a symbiotic relationship with *Doctor Who*, the BBC's other flagship action drama.[10] In part, this could be because the characters of

6 Stephen Crofts refers to the way that in the "auterist critical enterprise, the author is impressionistically read off from thematic and/or stylistic properties in the film(s)," emphasizing the way that, in a Foucauldian sense, the idea of a single auteur is constructed by the viewer or critic. Crofts, "Authorship and Hollywood," 313.

7 Tribe, *Sherlock Chronicles*, 61–64.

8 Mellor, "Sherlock: His Last Vow Q&A"; Tribe, *Sherlock Chronicles*, 81.

9 Quoted in Tribe, *Sherlock Chronicles*, 81.

10 There has even been persistent talk of a crossover project in which Sherlock would meet the Doctor. See Hooton, "Doctor Who Sherlock Crossover."

the Doctor and Holmes have some marked features of the "maverick" or "trickster" hero in common.[11] However, a more salient reason is that during *Doctor Who*'s period off-air between 1989 and 2005 (one is tempted to call it a Great Hiatus, in mimicry of the period from 1891 to 1894 when Conan Doyle's Sherlock Holmes was presumed dead), Gatiss wrote for Virgin Books' *New Adventures of Doctor Who* series and contributed radio dramas for Big Finish Productions, and Moffat wrote a *Doctor Who* short story for Virgin Books and a TV parody.[12] This, as Christopher Marlow points out, means that Gatiss, Moffat, and Russell T. Davies, among others, who contributed to the *Doctor Who* universe(s) during the show's "wilderness years," have in later years "achieved the very positions of institutional authority and expertise that [Henry] Jenkins supposes to be beyond the grasp of the disenfranchised fan writer."[13] Such a trajectory makes it even more galling, for some fans of *Sherlock* and *Doctor Who*, that Moffat should at times voice dismissive opinions about appreciation for the series that goes beyond the officially branded merchandise.[14] Sue Vertue, manager of Hartswood Films, which produces *Sherlock*, makes the series creators' fan status clear when she recalls that at the project's inception, "you [Moffat] and Mark knew everything about it and I knew nothing about it."[15] Moffat himself recalls, in a 2010 interview, his first reading of Sherlock Holmes as a boy and being "Utterly, utterly, utterly thrilled."[16]

This childhood enthusiasm for the Holmes and Watson stories shared by Gatiss and Moffat ("this schoolboy infatuation for Sherlock Holmes [...] It's the Sherlock Homes Club," says Thompson of his co-writers)[17] at times manifests itself as a suggestion that the two writers are uniquely placed to adapt Conan Doyle's most famous creations. Even at the moment of the show's conception, by Moffat's account, "we just thought *of course* it should

11 See Charles, "Three Characters," 83–102.

12 See Marlow, "The Folding Text," 55.

13 See Marlow, "The Folding Text," 54–55. This point warrants some qualification. Moffat and Gatiss were not writing fanfiction in the sense of producing amateur works, as their stories were commissioned work, and constituted paid labour. Nevertheless, Marlow points out, for the revived *Doctor Who* television series from 2005 on, "only those who had written *Doctor Who* material that most viewers would consider non-canonical were employed." See Marlow, "The Folding Text," 49. Thus, Moffat and Gatiss can be seen as a new wave of *Doctor Who* writers who have displaced the "old guard" of scriptwriters for the original series, which was canceled in 1989.

14 See Robinson, "Do *Sherlock* and *Doctor Who* really have a 'bad fan' problem?"

15 Mellor, "Sherlock: His Last Vow Q&A."

16 "Unlocking Sherlock."

17 Quoted in Tribe, *Sherlock Chronicles*, 72.

be modernized. And we nodded and drank our tea [...] saying someone was going to do that," and that furthermore, "we were going to be cross" because "[i]t should have been us!"[18] The account of *Sherlock*'s development given in the companion book to the series, *Sherlock Chronicles*, makes clear the competitive element: Gatiss is purported to have emailed Moffat in 2008 with the news that Guy Ritchie was to direct a "funky" modern Sherlock Holmes film, and to have urged, "Let's get the scripts in now!"[19]

Kamilla Elliott's "six concepts of adaptation," which she elucidates with reference to adaptations of *Wuthering Heights*,[20] is a useful framework through which to examine these claims by the lead writers. What Moffat is implying with his "utterly thrilled" and "It should have been us!" remarks is akin to Elliott's psychic concept of adaptation, where the assertion is made that the adapter is uniquely qualified to convey the "spirit of the text" into the new medium.[21] As Elliott goes on to point out, many critics "render the spirit of a text synonymous with authorial intent," and in Gatiss' comments about how modern the Holmes and Watson stories were at the time of their first publication, and wanting to "blow away the Victorian fog" to get back to how "Doyle thought of [the stories] himself," there is the same assertion of recapturing the spirit of Doyle's original conception.[22] Finally, as Elliott indicates, "Fidelity to the spirit of a text is almost always accompanied by an insistence on the necessity of *in*fidelity to its letter or form,"[23] and this is true of *Sherlock*'s lead writers, who argue that modernizing Sherlock Homes allows them to be more faithful, not only to Doyle's characters, but to the context in which he was writing.

There is also, in the presentation of *Sherlock* as an adaptation, an element of what Elliott calls "The Trumping Concept of Adaptation."[24] Where Elliott defines this practice as "correcting a novel's material historical inaccuracies and its ideological ones,"[25] however, I have shown how *Sherlock*'s lead writers have instead sought to trump the Guy Ritchie adaptation (which turned out not to be set in modern times after all) and older attempts at historically accurate adaptations, swathed in "Victorian fog."

18 Quoted in ibid., 13.
19 Quoted in ibid., 29.
20 Elliott, "Literary Film Adaptation," 221.
21 Ibid. 222.
22 Quoted in Tribe, *Sherlock Chronicles*, 23–24.
23 Elliott, "Literary Film Adaptation," 224.
24 Ibid. 237.
25 Ibid. 238.

The Press in *Sherlock*

The paradox of modernizing a Victorian detective series in order to stay true to its "spirit" is also reflected in the modernization of Charles Augustus Milverton (from the Conan Doyle story "The Adventure of Charles Augustus Milverton") as Charles Augustus Magnussen in *Sherlock*. Why, we may ask, in a show so obsessed with cutting-edge technology and innovation – "a new sleuth for the 21st century," as the DVD packaging for series one says – did series three select an old-fashioned press baron as 2014's most dangerous man in London? Even the expression "press baron" evokes the powerful newspaper figures of the late nineteenth and early twentieth century: Lord Rothermere, Lord Northcliffe, William Randolph Hearst, and Lord Beaverbrook. Why then, in 2014, with the print operations of so many newspapers running at a loss, and the long-term future of print newspapers in doubt, did *Sherlock* cast a newspaper magnate as a super-villain, just when the power of real-life news and media bosses like Rupert Murdoch were under powerful governmental and legal scrutiny? To consolidate the sense that this is a villain from an earlier point in history, it may be recalled that Jared Harris' Moriarty in Guy Ritchie's 2011 film *Sherlock Holmes: A Game of Shadows* has comparable international influence to Magnussen; he is an *agent provocateur* industrialist with the ear of governments, who can pull the strings to provoke a world war. Ritchie's movies are set in a fantasy alternative Victorian universe, of course, but they still play up to the idea of Moriarty as a "hidden hand" itching to start the First World War.

One answer to these questions is that the visual medium of television can only survive for so long by picturing screen shots, floating text, and data streams; it needs the materiality of old-fashioned newsprint to embody the threat of the media magnate, especially since the villainous twist to Magnussen's operation turns out to be that he has no physical files after all in his "Appledore vaults," only his own prodigious memory. Thus, the misleading shots of Magnussen wandering through his extensive filing system are another way for the narrative to pull the rug from under the viewer. We are led to believe that Magnussen is dependent on "Google Glass" spectacles (or a similar device) feeding him information, then we are shown him exploring his physical vaults, and only at the climax of "His Last Vow" do we find that Magnussen's secret weapon is neither analog nor digital but, like Sherlock, his mind itself. The modernizing adaptation sets up the expectation of a technological solution (Magnussen's knowledge comes from Google Glass), then hints that there has been no modernization at all (it comes from filing cabinets and papers), before finally settling on a humanist position (the human mind is a more devious mechanism than any technology, Victorian or modern).

Despite this piece of misdirection, Magnussen is clearly, and extensively, set up as the series' major villain. Indeed, the script for "His Last Vow" works very hard to make viewers perceive Charles Augustus Magnussen as both repulsive and a major threat. Before the opening titles, Lady Smallwood explains the problem: "There isn't a man or woman in England capable of stopping that disgusting creature" (which raises the specter of Holmes being called on to save the nation, as was the rhetoric of the wartime Holmes films).[26] We see Magnussen at a fictional version of the Leveson Inquiry, on-screen information, supposedly visible to him, listing his interlocutors' level of indebtedness, porn preferences, relationship status, and "pressure point[s]."[27] The first MP who questions him has a disabled daughter, and that becomes a pressure point, a way of gaining an advantage; Magnussen has no scruples, goes the implication. He is given slippery, sweaty hands, which he insists on placing on Lady Smallwood, explaining: "I have a condition [...] the whole world is wet to my touch."[28] He licks Lady Smallwood's face, and comments on how her perfume tastes. He is compared to a shark, floating around with a flat face and dead eyes. To further aid the preparatory framing for us, Sherlock tells John, "I've dealt with murderers, psychopaths, terrorists, serial killers; none of them could turn my stomach like Charles Augustus Magnussen."[29] Perhaps most clinchingly, Magnussen tells Sherlock and John that the English are "a nation of herbivores."[30] He also urinates in the Baker Street fireplace: an ideological and physical desecration of English (or British?) ideas of national sovereignty.

Sherlock later elaborates that he hates Magnussen because "he attacks people who are different and preys on their secrets," but this seems an inaccurate description of Magnussen's *modus operandi*.[31] Magnussen, by his own account, is not looking for conformity or to silence the "different"; he is looking for leverage, and will take whatever he can get. Sherlock's statement appears, rather, to have been placed here as a marker of Sherlock's own social liberalism and enlightenment.[32] Where the Victorian Sherlock

26 See Field, *England's Secret Weapon*, 115.

27 *Sherlock*, "His Last Vow."

28 Ibid.

29 Ibid.

30 Ibid.

31 Ibid.

32 Another interpretation of Sherlock's use of the word "different" here is that it references the homoerotic subtext in the show, which seems particularly powerful in this episode. For

Holmes may have had a bohemian streak but was essentially carrying out work which could be associated with the defense of London against foreign invaders and the subjects of Empire,[33] here Moffatt and Gatiss put down a marker to remind viewers that this Sherlock has an up-to-date ethical code. In addition, bearing in mind Sherlock's summary execution of Magnussen at the end of the episode, it implies that Sherlock loathes Magnussen for more noble reasons than simply wanting to protect his friends' secrets.

Indeed, if we think back to series two, it is clear that Moriarty could not have triggered his reputation-ruining campaign against Sherlock without a compliant, sensationalist press. In that sense, series three reveals the media magnate to be the power behind Moriarty's destructive will; where Moriarty was fired by a hot-blooded rivalry with Sherlock, the newspaper boss seems only cold-heartedly interested in power. In the transition from series two to series three, *Sherlock* moves from a personal to a structural analysis of evil.[34]

Kitty Reilly

Viewed from the perspective of the attack on media magnates in "His Last Vow," then, the final episode of series two, "The Reichenbach Fall," can also be read as an anti-newspaper story. It is through the tabloid press that Sherlock unwillingly finds fame as the "Hat Detective," photographed leaving Baker Street wearing a hat as a disguise, which is then misinterpreted by the press as a fashion choice and becomes his Sherlockian trademark. It is also through the newspapers that Moriarty, baiting Sherlock via his sequence of outrageous crimes committed to the strains of "The Thieving Magpie" at the start of the episode, seeks to ruin Sherlock. Kitty Reilly (Katherine Parkinson), the undercover reporter posing as a fan (wearing a deerstalker in apparent tribute), turns on Sherlock when he rejects her approaches, and her newspaper runs Moriarty's false allegations of Sherlock being a fantasist and a fraud.

example, the "Google Glasses" confrontation can be read as a seduction scene over a romantic dinner, with strong overtones of aggression. Such a reading also resonates with fan interest in creating slash fiction encounters between *Sherlock*'s characters.

33 Michael Allen Gillespie and John Samuel Harpham, "Sherlock Holmes, Crime, and the Anxieties of Globalization," 449–474.

34 In series four, of course, Sherlock and Mycroft's sister Eurus is revealed to be the ultimate power shaping Sherlock's adventures and adversaries, which might be read in turn as a return to the personal, or even psychoanalytical, sphere where everything is explained by childhood trauma.

Journalist Kitty Reilly is a wolf in sheep's clothing, initially asking Sherlock to sign her shirt but then, when Sherlock penetrates her disguise, shifting register into what sounds like a well-worn tabloid journalist's pitch, a smaller-scale version of Magnussen's blackmailing: "There's all sorts of gossip in the press about you. Sooner or later, you're gonna need someone on your side, someone to set the record straight."[35] When she adds, "I'm smart, and you can trust me [...] totally," we know to expect that by the end of the episode Kitty will have been revealed to be double-crossing, and to be quite gullible in siding with Moriarty, who is posing as the innocent actor Rich Brook.

This reflection on series two from the perspective of the series three finale, then, reveals that in both series newspapers were meant to be the weapon to bring about Sherlock's ruin. In both series finales, Sherlock is being pressured or blackmailed into losing life or liberty to protect his friends. The format limitations which *Sherlock* has had imposed on it from series one – only three ninety-minute episodes per series – perhaps help to explain why this formula has repeated itself across the series two and three climaxes. Especially given the necessity, in series three, of reuniting Sherlock and John, introducing Mary, having John marry her, and revealing her past, there was relatively little space to develop an overarching villain figure. Given this packed itinerary, introducing a newspaper proprietor as villain was topical, considering the correspondences with the Leveson Inquiry. As noted, the idea was also a familiar one, in that Sherlock's revulsion against the popular news media was already a well-established trope in the show. He seeks information in the public interest; they, *Sherlock*'s rhetoric implies, make up stories to sell copies. Good journalism should be detective work, but with the news media in its current sick state, the true detective is mocked like a prophet in the wilderness.

The Spoof Newspapers

Having analyzed series three's "headline" attack on the press, we might now examine a related incident, which created a minor furor in the pages of the *Daily Mail* newspaper when the episode aired. At the beginning of "The Sign of Three," the second episode of series three, we are shown a series of occasions on which Inspector Lestrade fails to apprehend a group of high-profile thieves, the Waters gang. Each time, we see the relevant newspaper front pages, which superficially catalogue the unbroken run of

35 *Sherlock*, "The Reichenbach Fall."

success of the Waters gang's robberies. If the video player is "paused," the front pages can be read in considerable detail. They contain, in smaller articles, an *ad hominem* attack on Boris Johnson, the then Mayor of London ("Thames to become watery motorway"),[36] and other material that could be read as preoccupied with social, rather than criminal, justice. As there is no masthead on these newspapers, we do not know if they are meant to be left- or right-wing publications, to belong to Magnussen's roster of titles or to be his rivals in the field.

As tabloid parodies, they are hard to decode; although the writers aim for the salient stylistic features of a tabloid report, in one sentence there is a disjointed syntax that is rare in tabloid journalism: "The hair-brained scheme involved chartering disused boats, paying for their conversion into a version of London's famous bus, the Routemaster, but this plan has already foundered after pilot schemes revealed that customers were walking straight off the bus and into the icy currents of the Thames."[37] Although the article savages Johnson's populist, upper-class buffoon persona (the Mayor was "at a self-promotion event" and "was found to be dithering, incoherent and self-interested"), it quotes him as shouting "Hussar!" (a noun denoting a light cavalryman) instead of "huzzah!" (an interjection meaning "hooray").[38]

A further article legible in these front pages is called "Potential freezing spell puts funeral directors on red alert." Like the Johnson news items, it is unclear whether the article is parodying the news with satirical intent, or pastiching it for broad comedy purposes. The quoting of a "Funeral home spokesman" called "Stephen Deadman" suggests the latter, while the later line, "A Tory spokesman responded rather tersely to the potential crisis, saying, 'This is a problem that we inherited from the last government'," implies the former.[39]

Although the right-wing UK tabloid *The Daily Mail* reported these spoof newspapers as evidence of *Sherlock*, Moffat, and the BBC's left-wing bias,[40] such an interpretation shuts down the spoof tabloids' considerable

36 Johnson was subsequently appointed Foreign Secretary in the May government in 2016.

37 *Sherlock*, "The Sign of Three." We are left to wonder whether the spelling "hair-brained" is a misprint, a misunderstanding of the meaning of the expression "hare-brained," or a weak pun on Johnson's famously unruly blond hair.

38 *Sherlock*, "The Sign of Three." A further ambiguity: this could either be a transcription error on behalf of the fictional newspaper, or else an indication that Johnson, for all his talk in the article of "our great history" and his fame as an Oxford-educated old Etonian, actually knows and cares little about British traditions, rather like Magnussen.

39 *Sherlock*, "The Sign of Three."

40 Kelly, "Sherlock's new press baron foe."

ambiguities. If these tabloids are meant to be newspapers that Magnussen owns, then his journalists are subverting the neoliberal attitudes of the owner, and his cold, controlling genius is rather comically undermined by his copy-editors' questionable competence. If they are meant to be the publications of his rivals, one almost feels a twinge of sympathy for Magnussen's papers: presumably, they will be better produced and more coherent than the patchy journalism we have been shown.

Rather than being an ideological attack on Johnson and the Conservative party, as the *Mail* reads it, I suggest that with this comic opening to the episode, writers Thompson, Gatiss, and Moffat are providing additional, knockabout material to reward attentive, engaged viewers. The priority is to entertain rather than provide cohesive arguments. Rather like a clown or a comic jig at an Elizabethan playhouse, its "meaning" is expressed in its liminal status, half in the fictional world, and half out of it (that is, occurring prior to the title sequence, in a storyline concerning peripheral character Greg Lestrade).

Courting engaged viewers through added value

This willingness to push against the show's own formal intentions (to portray Magnussen as a master manipulator) in pursuit of a joke for attentive viewers shows how important such engaged (or, to borrow Shari Laster's term, "privileged") audiences are to *Sherlock*'s lead writers.[41]

In this respect then, *Sherlock* is certainly not antithetical to or dismissive of its fans. From the beginning, it has offered the engaged viewer a transmedia viewing and reading experience. John Watson's blog, which featured in the show, was a real blog accessible online, as was Sherlock's own blog in the series, "The Science of Deduction." Both offered supplementary material to the televised cases and suggestions of Sherlock and John's broader casework, which viewers have not seen. They also, of course, provide a digital analog (as it were) for the dismissive way in which Holmes responds to Watson's recording of their cases in the Conan Doyle stories, and an insight into both characters' *Weltanschauung*. Additional contextual color to life at 221B Baker Street is also provided by the official spin-off book, *Sherlock: The Casebook*, containing notes supposedly passed between Sherlock and John.[42]

41 Laster, "The Reichenbach Feels," 226.
42 Adams, *Sherlock: The Casebook*.

Similar examples of *Sherlock*'s writers creating small rewards for the intrepid transmedia viewer include the interactive trailer for series three, released in December 2013, featuring unlockable content for those able to solve clues in the trailer. Or there was the picking out, in the end credit sequence of the US broadcast of "The Empty Hearse," of red letters, which spelled "Weng Chiang," Gatiss and Moffat's playful reference to a 1977 *Doctor Who* story ("The Talons of Weng Chiang") set in Victorian London, in which Tom Baker's Doctor wears a deerstalker and Inverness cape.[43] References like this, plus some of the case names on Sherlock and John's blogs, which (like the show's episode titles) adapt Conan Doyle's story titles with an additional modern twist,[44] reveal *Sherlock* to be a strong example of what Jason Mittell has called a "drillable text."[45] Certain television shows with complex characters or storytelling patterns, Mittell proposes, encourage a form of "forensic fandom" where engaged viewers can "drill down" into deeper layers of content, find and exchange clues with other fans, compare notes, and trade interpretations.[46] In *Sherlock*'s case, in addition to the hidden or deeper content of the series itself, there is the pleasure for viewers of comparing this Sherlock Holmes adaptation with the characters and stories in the Conan Doyle source text and its many other adaptations.

For Shari Laster, fandom uses the expression "the feels" to explore the emotional resonances of climactic dramatic situations of the sort that shows like *Sherlock* routinely construct: situations in which only the audience is aware of all the calculations, deceptions, behavioral curbs, promises, secret hopes, and so on of each of the characters involved, and possess the necessary contextual information to see the incident in the round. Using the example of the series two climax where John watches Sherlock appear to commit suicide, Laster remarks "real life is rarely this perfectly constructed, and when it is the consequences are often too horrible to iteratively contemplate."[47] Moffat and Gatiss seem particularly skilled in engineering such moments in *Sherlock* (and arguably in *Doctor Who*, too) where the more the viewer knows, the more emotionally complex and resonant a narrative moment becomes.

43 Jones, "Sherlock and the mystery of the *Doctor Who* message."

44 For example, "The Geek Interpreter" for "The Greek Interpreter," "The Speckled Blonde" for "The Speckled Band," and "The Six Thatchers" for "The Six Napoleons."

45 Jenkins, Ford, and Green, *Spreadable Media*, 135.

46 Quoted in ibid., 135–136.

47 Laster, "The Reichenbach Feels," 231.

Bad fans

Nevertheless, as far as the lead writers are concerned, this mode of informed consumption should be the pinnacle of engagement for *Sherlock*'s ideal viewer. To quote Moffat responding to the question of whether fan ideas and preferences influenced them as writers: "It's hugely important, but it's a one-way thing."[48] To take fandom any further than one-way consumption is to risk the lead writers' mockery. Within the show itself, series three's opening episode, "The Empty Hearse," features a meeting of members of Anderson's conspiracy theorist group, which gathers to discuss how Sherlock survived his fall from the hospital roof at the end of series two. Their flagging levels of engagement with Anderson's campaign, and the fact that they understand so little about Sherlock that they apparently believe he wears the hat as a fashion choice, and copy it, seems to mark them out for engaged viewers as "bad fans." Perhaps that is its deliberate pitch: even viewers who do not know much about the Sherlock fandom can recognize Anderson's group as poor, sloppy members of the fandom. They believe in the hat (one piece of tabloid misinformation) but disbelieve claims of Sherlock's fraudulence (a second piece of tabloid misinformation), when from the privileged perspective of the informed viewer – who knows Sherlock's return will be widely known any moment now – they would have been better off disbelieving both.

In the days around the initial screenings of *Sherlock* series three, *Sherlock* fanfiction writers were also mocked by Caitlin Moran's stunt (at the BFI screening of "The Empty Hearse") of asking actors Cumberbatch and Freeman to read a piece of "JohnLock" slash fiction (an event at which Gatiss was present on stage). In the BFI post-screening discussion for "His Last Vow," Moffat did suggest that the microblogging site Tumblr was full of "lunatics" who wanted to kill him, but on the whole was slightly more conciliatory towards fan writers, saying, "you see something you love, you start doing your own version of it. Then you start disagreeing with the actual version and think 'my version's better,' and then you discover you've made something entirely different and you go off and do your own thing."[49] This statement, however, seems to contradict Moffat's own experience as a *Doctor Who* fan who became a writer for the show, to which he was referring in the passage quoted. Moffat and Gatiss did not make "something entirely different"; what they achieved – and what Moffat seems to be reluctant to acknowledge – is the transition from being fans of *Doctor* Who and the Sherlock Holmes

48 Mellor, "Sherlock: His Last Vow Q&A."
49 Ibid.

stories to producing a type of adaptation that Anne Jamison calls "pro-fic": professionally produced derivative works.[50] Hence, as Judith May Fathallah notes, Moffat is "stressing his own fannishness as a credential" yet on the other hand, "dismissing fannish desire as trivial and over-invested" when it constitutes a response to his and Gatiss' own derivative works.[51] For Melissa A. Click and Nettie Brock, in behaving this way Gatiss and Moffat "serve to uphold the familiar power imbalance between industry and audience."[52]

In a sense, it is as if the lead writers regard *Sherlock* fans as a lesser breed precisely because they may favor the modern adaptation over the Conan Doyle originals, because modern fans may identify as "Sherlocked" – fans of the television series primarily – rather than "Sherlockian," fans of the Conan Doyle canon.[53] As Moffat said in an early interview, part of the show is the creators "constantly wanting to say, 'Have you any idea how good this is? How good Doyle is? How good these characters are?'"[54] It is as if the approved response to enjoying episodes of *Sherlock* is to return to Conan Doyle's stories, not to engage with any of the characters or situations in a creatively open-ended way. Moffat is again invoking the "psychic model" where only he and Gatiss, the expert interpreters, are authorized to communicate Conan Doyle's talents, achievements, and intentions by adapting them into something else. Yet at the same time, there is also an element in this statement of Moffat endorsing the fidelity imperative, where screen adaptation provides a conduit back to the (implicitly superior) original.[55]

To complicate the picture further, *Sherlock* contains elements of Elliott's "De(re)composing Concept of Adaptation [...] a (de)composite of textual and filmic signs merging in audience consciousness together with other cultural narratives."[56] We have seen one aspect of this in the way that episode titles reference Conan Doyle's story titles, but the key point here is that there is no direct adaptation of any one of the source texts. Instead, each 90-minute episode contains elements of several Canonical Sherlock Holmes adventures. For example, "His Last Vow" contains references to, and appropriations of, "His Last Bow," "The Adventure of Charles Augustus Milverton," and "The Man with the Twisted Lip," among others.

50 Jamison, *Fic*, 3.
51 Fathallah, *Fanfiction and the Author*, 51
52 Click and Brock, "Marking the Line," 125
53 See Stieva, "We solve crimes," 242.
54 "Unlocking Sherlock."
55 See Elliott, "Literary Film Adaptation," 220; Murray, *The Adaptation Industry*, 8.
56 Elliott, "Literary Film Adaptation," 233.

Finally, the "Setlock" phenomenon, where *Sherlock* fans exchange information and travel to where filming of the new series is taking place, further tests the borders of acceptable fan behavior as far as the *Sherlock* production team is concerned.[57] Jenkins, Ford, and Green end their book *Spreadable Media* on a discussion of *Twilight* fans commenting on the new film's production design while it was still being filmed, seemingly regarding this as a new frontier in the standoff between fans and producers.[58] The stakes are perhaps higher still with *Sherlock*, where there is such a small window for filming due to the constraints of the actors' availability, and where the streets of London – and particularly the Baker Street stand-in, Speedy's Café on North Gower Street – have traditionally played such a key role in the series. Mark Gatiss recently remarked that the presence of fans on filming locations would change the way the program is made. Although his remarks have a "more in sorrow than in anger" ring to them,[59] it could be argued that Gatiss and Moffat stoked expectations by killing off Sherlock in series two, and then, for the following series, filming multiple explanations – such as the "Sherlock and Moriarty kiss" that made it into one counterfactual sequence in "The Empty Hearse" – to keep the fans guessing (and the press speculating) about his "resurrection." The lead writers could be accused of toying with the fans as long as "Setlock" operates on their own terms, and then issuing warnings about its threat to future series as soon as it becomes inconvenient.

Is it the case then, as Joanna Robinson surmises, that, for Moffat in particular, "there's a certain *kind* of fan, the kind that fetishizes catchphrases and iconography like [...] the deerstalker, the scarves and bow ties, that Moffat considers a bad fan," deserving of ridicule and even destruction within the shows themselves?[60] I would suggest that the pattern is more complex than this. *Sherlock*'s relative scarcity of episodes – only thirteen in seven years – and lengthy periods off-screen, along with the pace and density of episode content, encourage a "drillable text" approach, where there is time to unpack the "many layers of meaning" in a single episode.[61] Moreover, the plentiful rewards offered by *Sherlock* for the engaged viewer represent a good example of a show encouraging "behaviours that were once

57 See Garside, "A Study in 'Setlock'."

58 Jenkins, Ford, and Green, *Spreadable Media*, 300–302.

59 Jones, "Sherlock fans."

60 Robinson, "Do *Sherlock* and *Doctor Who* really have a 'bad fan' problem?" (emphasis in original). Robinson is referring, in part, to the deaths of Osgood and Seb in the series eight finale of *Doctor Who*.

61 Jenkins, Ford, and Green, *Spreadable Media*, 137.

considered 'cult' or marginal," which are now, as Jenkins, Ford, and Green argue, "becoming how more people engage with television texts."[62] Not only this, but *Sherlock* itself is a detective series, where guessing (or deducing) the outcome is part of the viewing experience, and where the hero himself models this restless intellectual energy that the show stimulates amongst viewers. Given these conditions, it seems bizarre that the show and its lead writers, in their public appearances, should combine to criticize press and fan power. This situation can be seen as what Fathallah calls the "*legitimation paradox*", where fan activity "is legitimated and empowered – *because and so far as the author says so.*"[63] What is objected to in particular by Moffat and Gatiss is any attempt to tell other stories about the show, which from their point of view are inaccurate, unauthorized, and incorrect stories.[64]

Moffat, in particular, relishes this aspect of his job as lead writer: the ability to tell gripping, surprising stories that give privileged viewers "the feels," but also to withhold key information, to mislead, to tease and taunt. In an interview alongside Gatiss for the series three return of *Sherlock*, Moffat speaks of wanting to "pull the rug one more time" from under viewers' understanding of what happened to Sherlock and how he survived, by making the final explanation given by Sherlock to Anderson – after all the red herrings in "The Empty Hearse" – deliberately implausible in several key respects.[65] Having played with viewer expectations of an explanation for Sherlock's survival, Moffat and Gatiss initially bombard us with theories within the show, and then leave us without a single one that fits the facts. As Gatiss puts it, giving a similar account to Moffat but phrasing it in diplomatic, almost Mycroftian language, "In 'The Empty Hearse', Sherlock presents a perfectly acceptable and rational theory as to how he faked his death. Anderson, quite rightly, has some questions about the method but there's no reason why it didn't happen like that. You may believe what you want!"[66]

In the BAFTA Q&A after the screening of "His Last Vow," Moffat makes it even clearer how much he relishes this power that he and Gatiss hold

62 Ibid., 142.

63 Fathallah, *Fanfiction and the Author*, 10

64 As we have seen, this is an eccentric position to hold for a show, which is itself openly an adaptation of multiple sources. Gatiss and Moffat make no secret of having been inspired by the wartime Holmes films starring Basil Rathbone and Nigel Bruce, and also by Billy Wilder's film *The Private Life of Sherlock Homes*. See Tribe, *Sherlock Chronicles*, 20. Mark Gatiss' famous comment regarding the team's inclusive principle of adaptation, "everything is canonical," clearly applies only as far as the moment of *Sherlock*'s creation. See Mumford, "Sherlock returns to the BBC."

65 "Unlocking Sherlock."

66 "Live Q&A with Steven Moffat and Mark Gatiss."

over viewers, almost to the point of mild sadism:[67] "You don't know what's going on there [with Moriarty's apparent return]. You don't know what's going on there. *We* know what's going on there but we're not telling you... for bloody ages! [laughter]. It must be hell watching this show."[68] In the same reply, he jokes sarcastically that "I've always given this grand commitment to telling the truth," making it plain that, like Moriarty, even his supposedly straightforward answers are calculated to deceive, or else may be subject to complete revision without notice.

The political rhetoric of *Sherlock*'s lead writers

Is such behavior, on the part of the lead writers, political? Well, it certainly calls for what I will argue are political presentational techniques. British politics since Margaret Thatcher, according to several commentators, has been, in part, a story of the growing influence of the Prime Minister's Press Secretary and his various media advisers (see Jones 1999; Rawnsley 2001; Cohen 2004). This influence reached its peak in the early years of the New Labour government of 1997–2010. How might New Labour's spin be connected with *Sherlock*'s lead writers, beyond the adoption of similar rhetorical methods of impression management? I will leave aside the obvious fact that Mark Gatiss played New Labour architect Peter Mandelson in a comedy drama about the aftermath of the 2010 UK general election, *Coalition*. Instead, I suggest that it is in the repeated assertion of control of an overarching narrative against a backdrop of other, overwhelmingly powerful global forces that the significant parallel between "New Sherlock Holmes" and "New Labour" really lies.

Now, clearly, Moffat and Gatiss are far more important to *Sherlock*'s success than mere Press Secretaries or "spin doctors." Both Moffat and Gatiss are lead writers and co-creators, and one is also an actor in the show. Yet, for example, there is something of the politician's technique of foregrounding family in an attempt to communicate a certain down-to-earth honesty in Moffat's public use of his own family and friends.[69] Moffat commented directly on the casting of Cumberbatch and Freeman's family (as discussed in this chapter's introduction) at the BBC Q&A: "Why look elsewhere? The

67 As Click and Brock also note, Moffat "revels in" and "becomes giddy" at these moments of withholding key information from fans. Click and Brock, "Marking the Line," 123.

68 Mellor, "Sherlock: His Last Vow Q&A."

69 See, for example, Nick Jones on Blair's use of his family in personal publicity to communicate an impression of transparent normality and trustworthiness. Jones, *Sultans of Spin*, 22, 44,

show has always been like that – it was born, after all, out of a friendship and a marriage. Choosing to work with the people you love isn't a stupid or a sentimental decision – it's one of the smartest decisions you can make."[70]

Here, Moffat refers to his friendship with Gatiss, and his marriage to Sue Vertue, a producer and Board Director at Hartswood Films, which produces *Sherlock,* amongst many other successful television programs.[71] Certainly, it is tempting to reflect, working with these people he loves is clearly a smart decision to have made. However, the statement, on the surface seemingly so punchily emotional and direct, is open to at least two interpretations. Either it makes Moffat the neoliberal child of Thatcher, promoting family values and the entrepreneurial model of the (large) family business; or (an unlikely vision perhaps), it gives Moffat the air of a utopian socialist, promoting the family relationship as cottage industry, in preference to the alienated, capitalist labor of working for people one does not love. Or does it appear to promote the virtues of meritocracy ("smart, not sentimental"), while actually practicing a mild strain of nepotism, of the sort which enables the successful middle class to entrench their economic and cultural advantages? After all, in Marxian terms, Moffat could be said to have married into the means of production: the "smart" move of endogamy.

As well as skillfully using rhetoric to reframe *Sherlock*'s casting decisions, Moffat also displays a press officer's impatience with potentially critical reporting. At the BAFTA screening of "His Last Vow" Maggie Brown from *The Guardian* newspaper asks: "Despite the record ratings, the first episode in particular was not a universal success with critics or with some viewers who branded it rather self-indulgent and self-referential. I wonder how you would respond to that criticism?" Moffat's reply is instructive:

> Any reply I give to you would allow you to write an article in which you'd say "Steven Moffat responds to the critics" or to the critical reaction, Maggie, stop it! [laughter]. We had a brilliant response from the critics as you well know, I read the press reaction, and I read as much as I can of the other stuff. That's not true, so don't put me in the position where I'm saying "I defend…" a sensationally good record which is what it was, come on. [Big round of applause].[72]

70 In pre-publicity for *Sherlock* series four, Abbington and Freeman revealed that they had separated after 16 years together. See Foster, "Martin Freeman."

71 Alongside Moffat, Sue Vertue, and Moffat's sister-in-law Debbie Vertue are the Board Directors, and Moffat's mother-in-law Beryl Vertue is the company's Chairman.

72 Mellor, "Sherlock: His Last Vow Q&A."

Moffat responds to the question by engaging in meta-commentary, anticipating how any answer he gives will be "spun," and denying the grounds for the question in the first place. As a masterstroke, he appeals to the authority of the crowd – which he knows will be sympathetic in the context of a preview screening – to applaud the show and its success, shutting down any further questioning in this line.

The metalinguistic commentary of his reply is testament to the significance of language to both the news reporter and to the account that the lead writer gives of himself and his production. It is reminiscent of the techniques of Prime Minister Tony Blair's Director of Communications and Strategy, Alastair Campbell, in the 1990s and early 2000s. He, too, affected contempt for journalists who asked unfavorable questions, using them as a pretext to criticize in turn the news media's low standards of investigative reporting and "trivialised news agenda."[73] Therefore, it may be no coincidence that Moffat's choice for the twelfth Doctor in *Doctor Who*, announced in August 2013, was Peter Capaldi, the actor whose most recognizable television role had been as the spin doctor Malcolm Tucker in the satirical sitcom *The Thick of It* (2005–2012). Tucker, an abrasive government enforcer, is widely regarded as being based on Alastair Campbell (although Capaldi himself also credits Peter Mandelson as a model).[74]

Significantly, it was Mandelson who identified a key aspect of the New Labour spin machine. In what, for Nick Jones, is a highly revealing statement, Mandelson remarked: "I'm trying to avoid gaffes or setbacks and I'm trying to create the truth – if that's news management, I plead guilty."[75] The idea of "creating the truth" through language, however disingenuous or dissembling it may seem, connects with a point made by Norman Fairclough in his discussion of the rhetoric of New Labour: that New Labour's "Third Way" political philosophy was always in the process of being "forged" in language, and New Labour politicians were "constantly forming and formulating it."[76] For Fairclough, this sense of New Labour's malleable rhetoric is linked to the idea that "New Labour seeks to reconcile in language what cannot be reconciled in reality given their commitment to neoliberalism."[77] In other words, New Labour's "commitment to the neoliberal global economy" meant that nothing fundamental could change and the function of New Labour

73 Jones, *Sultans of Spin*, 291.

74 Dee, "Peter Capaldi: Malcolm Tucker is Alastair Campbell."

75 Jones, *Sultans of Spin*, 31.

76 Fairclough, *New Labour, New Language?*, 4.

77 Ibid., 157.

rhetoric was therefore to present a narrative of transformation to cover up this capitulation to global capital.[78]

In Rawnsley's analysis of the downfall of Peter Mandelson, he writes that "[s]o long as everyone involved subscribed to an agreed 'truth' about events – however true or not this 'truth' was – then they could spin their way to safety," and calls Campbell and Mandelson the "two great storytellers of New Labour."[79] While, again, it would be crass to draw exact parallels between Moffat's abrasive, Campbellian (or Tuckeresque) public persona and Gatiss' smoother, more Mandelsonian manner, the idea of an agreed "truth" about events in *Sherlock* – whether or not this truth turns out to be true – is a suggestive one. As Gatiss has smilingly yet tellingly remarked to a *Newsbeat* reporter, "I've become a politician [...] *Sherlock* has made me one."[80]

Conclusion

Why should the lead writers place such a strange, simultaneous emphasis on rejecting press stories and fan stories while indicating the correct "line to take"[81] about what happens in *Sherlock*? Put another way, why do they write a series in which powerful, manipulative news corporations are not to be trusted, while outside the series, grassroots activity which challenges the hegemony of Gatiss and Moffat's version of *Sherlock* is not to be tolerated?

I suggest that control of the narrative, holding the secrets of the story yet to be revealed, are all that *Sherlock*'s lead writers truly have of their own. This is why they guard it so jealously, withholding information but then telling us how we should feel about that information's absence, controlling what is and is not valid speculation (that Moriarty may be alive, yes; that Moriarty, Sherlock, and/or John are gay or bisexual, no). To borrow once again from Elliott's categories, Gatiss and Moffat can only lay claim to their own "decomposed composite" of Conan Doyle and *Sherlock*, to its unique redistribution of the elements of the source text.[82]

As we have seen, aside from story, Gatiss and Moffat have few of the conveniences and privileges of the showrunner in US television. They do not own the source material, even though the *Sherlock* branding

78 Ibid., 8.

79 Rawnsley, *Servants of the People*, 444.

80 Jamieson, "Benedict Cumberbatch's Sherlock goes back to 1895."

81 See Rawnsley, *Servants of the People*, 444.

82 Elliott, "Literary Film Adaptation," 233.

has been widely marketed and disseminated (with the BBC receiving much of the financial benefit).[83] As has also been noted, Cumberbatch and Freeman are too much in demand as film and stage actors to be able to commit to regular shooting schedules of the kind that have seen *Sherlock*'s American rival, *Elementary*, clock up well over one hundred episodes to *Sherlock*'s mere thirteen. As this chapter has further argued, *Sherlock*'s creators now feel they have to make allowances for the fans who will congregate to watch location sequences being shot, in addition to the ongoing pressures of time and money on any filming schedule. The longer it takes for new series to be filmed, too, the more likely it is that a fan writer will come up with a story that anticipates the "official" Sherlock narrative, getting there first and making a new series seem already played-out by the time it airs.

Perhaps most significantly, as *Sherlock*'s global audience grows, with most of these new viewers (in China for example) accessing the show online, Gatiss and Moffat are unable to control the way that the show is consumed and interpreted in other cultures.[84] Due to the delay in international broadcasting of series three (it was not shown on PBS in the USA, for instance, until nearly three weeks later), the initial reaction to the series came from British viewers and critics, and this essay has followed that line in highlighting some British contexts for the series' jokes about Boris Johnson and Rupert Murdoch. However, the growing international popularity of Freeman and Cumberbatch – their success in the neoliberal global market for actors – may place the determination of meaning even further out of the series' creators' grasp.

Works Cited

Adams, Guy. *Sherlock: The Casebook*. London: BBC Books, 2012.

BBC. "Commercial Activity." 2014. Accessed April 27, 2015. www.bbc.co.uk/annualreport/2014/executive/finances/commercial.html.

—. "Live Q&A with Steven Moffat and Mark Gatiss." Last modified January 12, 2014. Accessed December 27, 2014. www.bbc.co.uk/programmes/b03pzpgy/live.

83 The BBC's Annual Report for 2013/14 notes that "BBC Worldwide's best performing programme of the year was *Sherlock* Series 3," and that this contributed strongly to BBC Worldwide's headline profit of £157m, up by 1% from the previous year. See "Commercial Activity."

84 See Lori Morimoto's article on the dynamics of Benedict Cumberbatch's global fame and how it is affecting casting choices. Morimoto, "Doctor Strange in a Strange Land."

Charles, Alec. "Three characters in search of an archetype: Aspects of the trickster and the flâneur in the characterizations of Sherlock Holmes, Gregory House and Doctor Who." *Journal of Popular Television* 1 (2013): 83–102.

Click, Melissa A., and Nettie Brock. "Marking the Line Between Producers and Fans: Representations of Fannish-ness in *Doctor Who* and *Sherlock*." In *Seeing Fans: Representations of Fandom in Media and Popular Culture*, edited by Lucy Bennett and Paul Booth, 117–126. London: Bloomsbury, 2016.

Cohen, Nick. *Pretty Straight Guys*. London: Faber, 2004.

Crofts, Stephen. "Authorship and Hollywood." In *The Oxford Guide to Film Studies*, edited by John Hill and Pamela Church Gibson, 310–324. Oxford: Oxford University Press, 1998.

Dee, Johnny. "Peter Capaldi: Malcolm Tucker is Alastair Campbell. But Mandelson is in there, too." *The Guardian*, October 17, 2009. Accessed December 27, 2014. www.theguardian.com/tv-and-radio/2009/oct/17/peter-capaldi-malcolm-tucker-tv.

Elliott, Kamilla. "Literary Film Adaptation and the Form/Content Dilemma." In *Narrative Across Media: The Languages of Storytelling*, edited by Marie-Laure Ryan, 220–243. Lincoln, NE and London: University of Nebraska Press, 2004.

Fairclough, Norman. *New Labour, New Language?* Abingdon: Routledge, 2000.

Fathallah, Judith May. *Fanfiction and the Author: How Fanfic Changes Popular Cultural Texts*. Amsterdam: Amsterdam University Press, 2017.

Field, Amanda. *England's Secret Weapon: The Wartime Films of Sherlock Holmes*. London: Middlesex University Press, 2009.

Foster, Patrick. "Martin Freeman and Amanda Abbington split as she reveals 'weird' real-life coincidence behind Sherlock scenes they filmed together." *The Telegraph*, December 23, 2016. Accessed December 26, 2016. www.telegraph.co.uk/news/2016/12/22/martin-freeman-amanda-abbington-split-reveals-weird-real-life/.

Garside, Emily. "A Study in 'Setlock': Fans, filming and *Sherlock*." Paper presented at the New Directions in *Sherlock* conference, University College, London, April 11, 2014.

Gillespie, Michael Allen, and John Samuel Harpham, "Sherlock Holmes, Crime, and the Anxieties of Globalization." *Critical Review: A Journal of Politics and Society*, 23 (2011): 449–474.

Hooton, Christopher. "Doctor Who Sherlock Crossover: I would do 'Wholock' says Steven Moffat." *The Independent*, August 11, 2014. Accessed April 28, 2015. www.independent.co.uk/arts-entertainment/tv/news/doctor-who-sherlock-crossover--i-would-do-it-says-steven-moffat-9660793.html.

Jamieson, Natalie. "Benedict Cumberbatch's Sherlock goes back to 1895." *Newsbeat*, April 21, 2015. Accessed April 22, 2015. www.bbc.co.uk/newsbeat/article/32380304/benedict-cumberbatchs-sherlock-goes-back-to-1895.

Jamison, Anne. *Fic: Why Fan Fiction is Taking Over the World.* Dallas, TX: Smart Pop, 2013.

Jenkins, Henry, Sam Ford, and Joshua Green. *Spreadable Media: Creating Value and Meaning in a Networked Culture.* New York: New York University Press, 2013.

Jones, Nick. *Sultans of Spin: The Media and the New Labour Government.* London: Gollancz, 1999.

Jones, Paul. "Sherlock and the mystery of the *Doctor Who* message in the closing credits." *Radio Times*, July 9, 2014. Accessed December 27, 2014. www.radiotimes.com/news/2014-07-09/sherlock-and-the-mystery-of-the-doctor-who-message-in-the-closing-credits.

—. "Sherlock fans have changed the way we make the show says Mark Gatiss." *RadioTimes.* November 25, 2014. Accessed December 27, 2014. www.radiotimes.com/news/2014-11-25/sherlock-fans-have-changed-the-way-we-make-the-show-says-mark-gatiss.

Kelly, John. "Sherlock's new press baron foe and more evidence of Left-wing bias." *Daily Mail Online*, January 13, 2014. Accessed December 27, 2014. www.dailymail.co.uk/news/article-2538350/Sherlocks-new-press-baron-foe-evidence-Left-wing-bias.html.

Laster, Shari. "The Reichenbach Feels." In *The One Fixed Point in a Changing Age: A New Generation on Sherlock Holmes*, edited by Kristina Manente, Maria Fleischhack, Sarah Roy, and Taylor Blumenberg, 223–238. Indianapolis, IN: Gasogene, 2014.

Marlow, Christopher. "The Folding Text: *Doctor* Who, Adaptation and Fan Fiction." In *Adaptation in Contemporary Culture: Textual Infidelities*, edited by Rachael Carroll, 46–57. London: Continuum, 2009.

Martin, Brett. *Difficult Men: From The Sopranos and The Wire to Mad Men and Breaking Bad: Behind the Scenes of a Creative Revolution.* London: Faber, 2013.

Mellor, Louisa. "Sherlock: His Last Vow Q&A." Transcript of BAFTA screening event. *Den of Geek.* January 14, 2014. Accessed December 27, 2014. www.denofgeek.com/tv/sherlock/28843/sherlock-his-last-vow-qa-with-steven-moffat-amanda-abbington-lars-mikkelsen-more#ixzz3MkiUrLhu.

Morimoto, Lori. "Doctor Strange in a Strange Land, or The Transnational Logics of Blockbuster Casting." *Some of us are looking at the stars.* Blog. Posted December 10, 2014. Accessed December 16, 2014. http://lorimorimoto.wordpress.com/2014/12/10/doctor-strange-in-a-strange-land-or-the-transnational-logics-of-blockbuster-casting-part-one/.

Mumford, Gwilym. "Sherlock returns to the BBC: 'He's definitely devilish.'" *The Guardian.* December 17, 2011. Accessed April 18, 2015. www.theguardian.com/tv-and-radio/2011/dec/17/sherlock-bbc-cumberbatch-freeman-interview.

Murray, Simone. *The Adaptation Industry: The Cultural Economy of Contemporary Literary Adaptation*. Abingdon: Routledge, 2013.

Poore, Benjamin. "Neverending Stories? *The Paradise* and the Period Drama Series." In *Upstairs and Downstairs*, edited by James Leggott and Julie Taddeo, 67–79. New York: Rowman and Littlefield, 2015.

Rawnsley, Andrew. *Servants of the People: The Inside Story of New Labour*. Harmondsworth: Penguin, 2001.

Robinson, Joanna. "Do *Sherlock* and *Doctor Who* really have a 'bad fan' problem?" *VanityFair*. November 10, 2014. Accessed December 17, 2014. www.vanityfair.com/vf-hollywood/2014/11/sherlock-doctor-who-steven-moffat-hate-his-fans?mbid=social_twitter.

Sherlock. "The Reichenbach Fall." Series two, episode three. Directed by Toby Haynes. Written by Stephen Thompson. BBC, January 15, 2012.

Sherlock. "The Sign of Three." Series three, episode two. Directed by Colm McCarthy. Written by Stephen Thomspon, Steven Moffat, and Mark Gartiss. BBC, January 5, 2014.

Sherlock. "The Empty Hearse." Series three, episode one. Directed by Jeremy Lovering. Written by Mark Gatiss. BBC, January 1, 2014.

Sherlock. "His Last Vow." Series three, episode three. Directed by Nick Hurran. Written by Steven Moffat. BBC, January 12, 2014.

Stieva, Rebecca. "'We solve crimes, I blog about it, he forgets his pants': Balancing Traditional and Non-Traditional Sherlockians in a Modern World." In *The One Fixed Point in a Changing Age: A New Generation on Sherlock Holmes*, edited by Kristina Manente, Maria Fleischhack, Sarah Roy, and Taylor Blumenberg, 239–252. Indianapolis, IN: Gasogene, 2014.

Tribe, Steve. *Sherlock Chronicles*. London: BBC Books, 2014.

"Unlocking Sherlock." Directed and produced by Susannah Ward. Special feature. In *Sherlock: Complete Series Three*. Midnight Oil Productions/BBC, 2014. DVD.

About the author

Benjamin Poore is Senior Lecturer in Theatre at the Department of Theatre, Film, Television and Interactive Media, University of York, UK. His books include *Heritage, Nostalgia and Modern British Theatre: Staging the Victorians*, *Theatre & Empire*, and *Sherlock Holmes from Screen to Stage: Post-Millennial Adaptations in British Theatre*.

7. *Alien* Adapted (Again and Again): Fictional Universes between Difference and Repetition

Rüdiger Heinze

Abstract
By adding storyworld upon storyworld, franchises create fictional universes. These are contested territory in terms of their constitution and the meaningfulness and ascendancy of their various elements. The very fact that fictional universes can be contested points to their defining characteristics: they are open, dynamic, flexible, and heterogeneous. This begs the question of semantic and pragmatic control over such universes in terms of production, access, permanence, and reception. Considering that franchises usually span a host of different media, they deserve a closer look in relation to adaptation, remaking, intermediality, and transmediality. This essay uses the fictional universe of the *Alien* franchise as an example to make a fundamental argument about the dynamics of fictional universes and their storyworlds.

Key words: Fictional universes; franchises; adaptation; transmediality; remakes

Introduction

On June 1, 2012, one day after the premiere of the film *Prometheus* in London, the BBC conducted a radio interview with the film's director Ridley Scott. In the course of the interview, the radio host asked Scott whether the film, although clearly being "in the same constellation, the same galaxy," was a direct prequel to Scott's 1979 film *Alien*, to which Scott replied "absolutely

Fehrle, J. and W. Schäfke, *Adaptation in the Age of Media Convergence*,
Taylor & Francis Group, 2019
DOI 10.5117/9789462983663_CH07

not."[1] The comment prompted a lively debate in numerous fanzines, magazines, and newspapers (e.g. *The Guardian, New York Post, Scientific American,* and *Huffington Post*). Whether or not one considers *Prometheus* a prequel to *Alien* wholly depends, of course, on one's definition of "prequel." A general definition of a prequel, as a fiction chronologically situated prior to, but in the same fictional universe as, that of another (already released/published) text's storyworld would make *Prometheus* a prequel.[2] A specified definition of prequel that additionally requires fairly close temporal proximity between the two narratives, a (logical or causal) connection of their plots, and the inclusion of some key characters at an earlier age/stage (say, the young Ellen Ripley or Bishop), would make *Prometheus* indeed part of "the same constellation, the same galaxy" as *Alien*, but not a prequel.

As inconsequential as it is, this little quibble illustrates a number of interesting points, authorial intention not being chief among them. For one, by adding textual storyworld upon storyworld, franchises inevitably create fictional universes.[3] These, it appears, are contested territory in terms of their particular constitution and the meaningfulness and ascendancy of their various elements (characters/creatures, locations, storylines, events, etc.) both within and across the various storyworlds that make up a universe. Moreover, the very fact that fictional universes can reasonably be contested in the first place points to what I would argue is a defining and inevitable characteristic of fictional universes that consist of multiple texts and storyworlds: they are open, dynamic, flexible, and heterogeneous, much more so than is frequently acknowledged; only in recent years have critics begun to criticize the idea of fictional universes as more or less coherent, consistent, and homogeneous. This heterogeneity, in turn, begs the question of semantic and pragmatic control over this universe in terms of production, access, permanence, and reception. As Henry Jenkins writes early on in his book *Convergence Culture* (a caveat that is sometimes overlooked),

1 Ridley Scott, "Ridley Scott says *Prometheus* is not a prequel to *Alien*," *BBC Radio 5 Live* interview, 2:51, last modified June 1, 2012, accessed February 15, 2019, www.bbc.com/news/entertainment-arts-18298709.

2 I follow David Herman's definition of storyworlds as "mental models of who did what to and with whom, when, where, why, and in what fashion in the world to which interpreters relocate – or make a deictic shift – as they work to comprehend a narrative." David Herman, "Regrounding Narratology: The Study of Narratively Organized Systems of Thinking." In *What is Narratology? Questions and Answers regarding the Status of a Theory*, ed. Tom Kindt and Hans-Harald Müller (Berlin: de Gruyter, 2003), 306 n.10.

3 I am obviously talking about fiction franchises and not the business method of trademark licensing *per se*, although, of course, all fiction franchises entail trademark licensing (for the legally sanctioned products).

participation in the creation of cultural content is almost always unequal.[4] Lastly, considering that franchises usually span a host of different media, with different representational techniques and different cultural prestige at a given point in time, they deserve a closer look by anyone interested in adaptation, remaking, intermediality, and transmediality.

In this essay, I will use the fictional universe of the *Alien* franchise as an example to make a fundamental argument about the dynamics – i.e. constitution, extension, modification, etc. – of fictional universes and the storyworld(s) they consist of.

Expansion of fictional universes and semantic inconsistency

As is indicated in the opening paragraph, the first heuristic (but logical) distinction I make is between "fictional universe" and "storyworld" in order to account for the fact that franchises usually consist of numerous products and/or storyworlds (more on this difference below) that all make a more or less extensive deictic shift to the same fictional universe. Each *Alien* film, novel, comic, computer game, and so on constitutes one *ontologically* distinct storyworld within the universe of the *Alien* franchise, even if the particular storyworld in question is an adaptation of another one in another medium, for example the novelization of the first *Alien* film, or a direct narrative continuation, for example *Aliens* and *Alien 3*.[5] As Carlos Scolari points out, transmedia storytelling is never "just an adaptation from one media to another. The story that the comics tell is not the same as that told on television or in cinema; the different media and languages participate and contribute to the construction of the transmedia narrative world."[6]

I am following Clare Parody's definition of franchise storytelling "as the creation of narratives, characters, and settings that can be used both to generate and give identity to vast quantities of interlinked media products

4 Henry Jenkins, *Convergence Culture: Where Old and New Media Collide* (New York: New York University Press, 2006), 3. His admonition is made in the context of media convergence and participatory culture.

5 Mark Wolf distinguishes between adaptation (a story moving from one medium to another) and growth: "when another medium is used to present new canonical material of a world, expanding the world and what we know about it." Mark J.P. Wolf, *Building Imaginary Worlds: The Theory and History of Subcreation* (New York: Routledge, 2012), 245–246.

6 Carlos Alberto Scolari, "Transmedia Storytelling: Implicit Consumers, Narrative Worlds, and Branding in Contemporary Media Production." I*nternational Journal of Communication* 3 (2009): 587.

and merchandise, resulting in a prolonged, multitextual, multimedial fictional experience."[7] A franchise thus constitutes what Lisbeth Klastrup and Susana Tosca call a "transmedial world":[8]

> Transmedial worlds are abstract content systems from which a repertoire of fictional stories and characters can be actualized or derived across a variety of media forms. What characterizes a transmedial world is that audience and designers share a mental image of the "worldness" (a number of distinguishing features of its universe). The idea of a specific world's worldness mostly originates from the first version of the world presented, but can be elaborated and changed over time.[9]

Clearly, not all products of a franchise constitute elaborated storyworlds, for example artwork or illustrations. Notice that while both definitions above focus on the narrative dimension of franchises/transmedial worlds (Parody: "franchise *storytelling*," "creation of *narratives*"; Klastrup and Tosca: "fictional *stories* and characters"), they do not *per se* preclude non-narrative elements. Parody includes "settings" and "merchandise" as part of the fictional universe; Klastrup and Tosca premise their definition on an "abstract content [system]," "a mental image of the worldness." It would indeed be inconsistent to exclude artwork, designs, drawings, and other non-narrative elements from fictional universes when they can actually be – and often are – powerful constituents of these universes; after all, the single most defining elements of the *Alien* franchise are the *Alien* creature and the artwork by H.R. Giger, both of which are non-narrative.[10] In fact, some hallmark design element or other non-narrative constituent

7 Clare Parody, "Franchising/Adaptation," *Adaptation* 4, no. 2 (2011): 211.

8 Wolf provides a concise overview of existing research on transmedia worlds in *Building Imaginary Worlds* (4–14), pointing out that the circulating terms – secondary, diegetic, imaginary, etc. – each emphasize a different aspect of transmedia worlds. The term "subcreation" that he himself uses in the subtitle of his monograph is taken from J.R.R. Tolkien (6).

9 Lisbeth Klastrup and Susana Tosca, "Transmedial Worlds – Rethinking Cyberworld Design." In *International Conference on Cyberworlds 2004: Proceedings*, ed. Masayuki Nakajima, Yoshinori Hatori, and Alexei Sourin (Los Alamitos, CA: IEEE Computer Society, 2004), 409.

10 It is yet another point of debate to which degree drawings and graphic artwork can be considered to have a narrative dimension. I would cede the point that some drawings may have a narrative dimension, not only in a series, but also in themselves: it is obvious in some of Giger's drawings that something must have happened for the depicted state of affairs to be possible, for example a crash-landed spaceship. However, I would argue that the narrative dimension is not the defining characteristic of drawings and illustrations, and it is usually minimal.

significantly characterizes almost all fictional universes. As Mark Wolf points out, aesthetics, infrastructures, and logic also "must be carried over."[11] In order to avoid confusion, however, I will not call these elements "storyworlds," but "storyworld constituents."

Nonetheless, it is arguable whether some merchandise is even that. The Superman-icon on a t-shirt, the Duff beer bottle in the real world, or the PEZ dispenser with an *Alien* head definitely point to the respective fictional universe (that is their customer appeal); but their signification – i.e. function and meaning – is much more a part of the real world than of the fictional universe. For Parody, such merchandise is still part of franchise storytelling, since it is "give[n] identity" by the transmedial world (see above). However, they are at the most secondary or "weak" constituents and not of primary importance for my argument.

Parody further differentiates between two main variants of franchises: a "co-ordinated act of transmedia storytelling" that is systematic and controlled; and a "palimpsest of a storyworld and its inhabitants [that is] built-up over time."[12] The *Alien* franchise predominantly shows the characteristics of the second variant – which is unsurprising, considering when and how it started, namely as a single film long before the advent of multimedia conglomerates, computer consoles, Web 2.0, and media convergence – although it appears to have become more systematic and controlled during the past decade with increasing media convergence. It is worth noting that computer games (arcade and PC), novelizations, and comics were surprisingly quick to appear.

11 Wolf, *Building Imaginary Worlds*, 246.

12 Parody, "Franchising/Adaptation," 211. In an interesting essay on *Doctor Who*, Matt Hills points out that many fictional universes, among them prominently the *Doctor Who* franchise (which has been going on and off for more than fifty years), are actually "rickety" and survive almost by accident, in large part due to die-hard fans. Matt Hills, "Traversing the 'Whoniverse': *Doctor Who*'s Hyperdiegesis and Transmedia Discontinuity/Diachrony." In *World Building. Transmedia, Fans, Industries*, edited Marta Boni (Amsterdam: Amsterdam University Press, 2017), 343. In the introduction to the collection in which Hills' essay is found, Marta Boni, like Parody, distinguishes two basic types of transmedial universes: "first, mixing business and design stresses the predictability of a world's development; the other highlights semiotic processes that evolve for years after the apparition of a matrix text. The former is inclusive, centripetal, and marked by the need to balance unity and order, typical of storytelling, with users' accessibility. The latter is centrifugal, and open to unpredictable results that exceed and dilate the borders of a system." Marta Boni, "Introduction." In *World Building. Transmedia, Fans, Industries*, 18. In an earlier monograph on fan cultures and cult texts, Hills suggests the concept of "hyperdiegesis" for sprawling fictional universes: "a vast and detailed narrative space, only a fraction of which is ever directly seen or encountered within the text, but which nevertheless appears to operate according to principles of internal logic and extension." Matt Hills, *Fan Cultures* (London and New York: Routledge, 2002), 137.

For my latter argument, it is necessary to take a closer look at the storyworlds, products, and elements that make up the fictional universe of the *Alien* creature so far. At this point, there are:

- Six films: *Alien* (1979), *Aliens* (1986), *Alien 3* (1992), *Alien Resurrection* (1997), *Prometheus* (2012), and *Alien: Covenant* (2017);
- Novelizations of the first four films, and more than a dozen other novels situated in the same universe;
- A host of comics, some of which are adaptations of specific films, others situated in the same universe;
- Various computer games on different consoles, some adaptations of specific films (at least by title), others, again, are situated in the same universe;
- Toys, sculptures, board games, theme park rides, a PEZ dispenser (!), etc.

Many of these are non-narrative and rather transient, and so, for the most part, are not relevant storyworld constituents. However, they do testify to the pervasiveness and iconic impact of the fictional universe and its key design elements. In addition, it has to be kept in mind that Giger's artwork, which much of the fictional universe of the *Alien* draws on, precedes the first film; at this point, books of his artwork, including "making-of" books, of course also include images of the *Alien* universe, creating an interesting feedback loop.

Notably, there are two crossover films that combine the *Alien* and *Predator* franchises[13] in one storyworld and, by implication, in one joint fictional universe: *Alien vs. Predator* (*AvP*; 2004) and *Alien vs. Predator: Requiem* (*AvP 2*; 2007). These films, as well as the earlier video games, pit the two "creatures" against each other (and of course against humanity) and in turn have their "own" comic and computer game re-adaptations, as well as various other merchandise.

Predictably, the legally sanctioned universe of the franchise is expanded, modified, and appropriated (more or less transiently, and with more or less feedback to the "official" universe) by various fanfictions and other

13 *Predator* is a 1987 Arnold Schwarzenegger film that itself has spawned two sequels, the last one as recent as 2010, with the attending fictional universe and an entire franchise (comics, computer games, etc.). A little detail for the connoisseurs: *Predator 2* (1990) already makes a subtle reference to the *Alien* universe by displaying an Alien skull as a trophy of the predators at the end of the film, thus predating the actual film *AvP*. Comics and computer games based on the same premise were already extant and quite popular in the early 1990s. Since Twentieth Century Fox owned the rights both to the *Alien* and the *Predator* films, copyright was not an issue. In the medium of comics, crossovers have thrived in particular. Here, the aliens and the predators meet the Terminator, Superman, Batman, and so on.

interventions (avpuniverse.com), with attending acrimonious debates over creative ownership, originality, authenticity, and storyworld logic. One reason I have limited my discussion to the official franchise is the sheer mass of non-sanctioned contributions: there are dozens of fanfiction sites with hundreds of stories about the *Alien* universe alone, and much more if we include the *Predator* universe, the AvP crossover, and the various non-sanctioned crossovers that fans have generated, not to mention graphic artwork and other media.

An abridged and a-chronic graphic approximation of this fictional universe might look as follows:

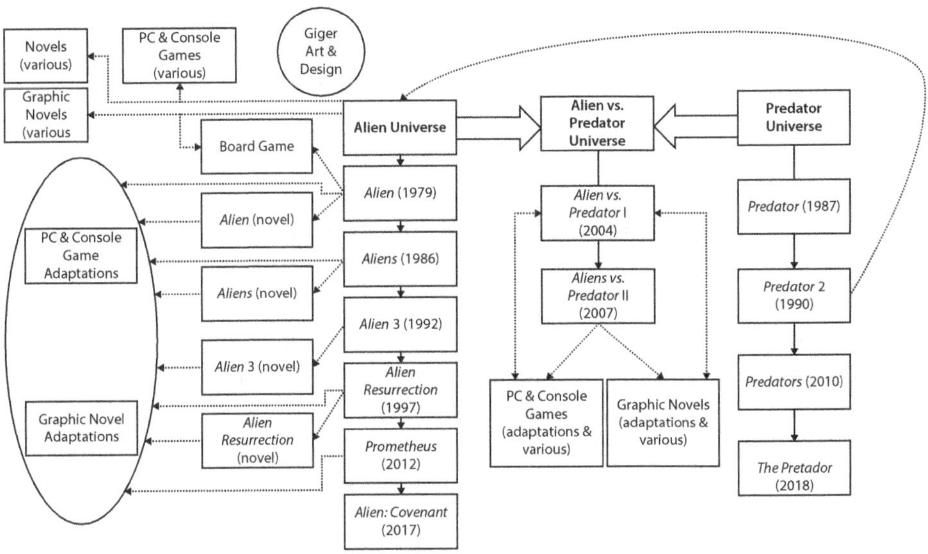

Figure 9.1: Approximation of the *Alien* Universe.

In other words – and I think the point is clear by now – the fictional universe of the alien creature and its various biological permutations (face hugger, chestburster, queen, predalien, deacon, etc.) span a host of different narrative and non-narrative manifestations and media (what Jenkins calls "corporate convergence" wherever it is legally sanctioned) in a constant – formal, medial, content-related, contextual – tension of difference and repetition, of feedback and recursion, and of seeking to maintain at least some semblance of logic and coherence. Considering the numerous storyworlds that make up this fictional universe, this is clearly not easy: the intradiegetic timeline alone covers several centuries, not to mention places, characters, creatures, and dozens of non-actualized backstories/disnarrations (e.g. of the various cybernetic organisms, the Weyland company, Ripley's family, the space jockey species), "re-versioned" or "de-narrated" stories (aspects, events, or stories that are first presented as given and then denied or modified, most significantly Ripley's "ultimate" death in *Alien 3*), as well as many smaller divergences, incongruities, gaps, and indeterminacies that do not "make sense," so to speak.[14] As Colin Harvey points out, "transmedia articulations are allowed to remember, misremember, forget and even non-remember diegetic elements from elsewhere in a specific transmedia network."[15]

Examples of these narrative gaps, incongruities, and indeterminacies abound. An example of a significant gap would be the question of how the Weyland Company that sends the unknowing crew of the Nostromo to its lethal fate knows about the alien eggs in the first place (*Alien*). This is only explained in the recent film *Prometheus*. An apparent incongruity would be the fact that the company is more interested in the creature than in the clearly advanced technology of the space ship in which the eggs are planted; and why does the company install costly terraforming devices on the planet instead of simply starting another attempt at collecting the eggs (*Aliens*)? It remains indeterminate why the *Alien* queen would lay an egg in Ripley's head, and how this is consistent with everything else we know about the reproduction of this species (*Alien 3*). In addition, what happened to Earth (*Alien Resurrection*)? Is there any connection between the species of the space jockey and the predator species (*AvP*)? And so on. The list of questions could be extended indefinitely.

Some friction between storyworlds inevitably arises due to remediation: most *Alien* computer games do not bother with lengthy narrative parts, and graphic novels add visual elements for which there simply is no graphic antecedent in the Giger universe or in the films. In addition, some of the gaps and incongruities are simply the result of flawed storytelling or, for whatever reason, willful omission on the part of the franchise maker(s). Moreover, many of the franchise products are no longer readily available or accessible (e.g. the board game, early PC games), and even if they were, very few people except some aficionados would be likely to be familiar with all of these storyworlds and constituents, and be able to remember them completely whenever they enter a new storyworld contribution to this ever-expanding fictional universe. Furthermore, large parts of the audience simply will not care about illogicalities, inconsistencies, and oversights.

14 For a theoretical discussion of dis- and denarration, see Richardson, *Unnatural Voices*, 87–94.

15 Colin Harvey, *Fantastic Transmedia. Narrative, Play and Memory across Science Fiction and Fantasy Storyworlds* (Hampshire: Palgrave Macmillan, 2015), 2.

My argument builds on the kinds of gaps, incongruities, and indeterminacies – what I will summarily call complications – that inevitably arise not by chance or due to remediation, but due to how storyworlds systemically function and (transmedially) interact.

Radical indeterminacy of fictional worlds and the limits of authorial control

In fact, these complications and their causes and consequences are my key point, and although this point appears to be obvious and has tremendous consequences, I do not think it has been getting enough attention.[16] Let me elaborate. One of the key points of possible worlds theory (as modified for literary studies) is that, as Marie-Laure Ryan summarizes it, no fictional world is or can ever be "complete" or "fully furnished":[17] "because it is impossible for the human mind to imagine an object (much less a world) in all of its properties, every fictional world presents areas of radical indeterminacy."[18] In fact, most fictional worlds are composite and semantically heterogeneous[19] – the complaints in blogs and reviews about *Prometheus* not answering a whole lot of questions are thus beside the point (complaints about logic exempted).

Every new component, every new composite and semantically heterogeneous storyworld or textual contribution might alter the fictional universe and its compossibility.[20] Every recursion, addition, and expansion creates potential discord, divergence, contradiction, and feedback loops; not solely because of what is there, but also because of what is not there. This is also and invariably true for adaptations and remakes, although there are none in the *Alien* franchise so far. Adaptations – here understood in the sense of

16 Wolf, for example, is almost exclusively interested in how transmedia worlds can be constructed (literally: built) and made to cohere.

17 Marie-Laure Ryan, *Possible Worlds, Artificial Intelligence and Narrative Theory* (Bloomington: University of Indiana Press, 1991), 406; Umberto Eco, "'Casablanca': Cult Movies and Intertextual Collage," *SubStance* 14, no. 2 (1985): 3.

18 Marie-Laure Ryan, "Possible Worlds." In *The Living Handbook of Narratology*, ed. Jan-Christoph Meister (Interdisciplinary Center for Narratology, University of Hamburg, 2009–), last modified September 27, 2013, accessed February 15, 2019, www.lhn.uni-hamburg.de/node/54.html.

19 Lubomir Doležel, *Heterocosmica: Fiction and Possible Worlds* (Baltimore: Johns Hopkins University Press, 1998), 23.

20 At this point, there are quite a number of typologies that denominate the different kinds of relation between possible worlds; see, for example, Doležel, *Heterocosmica*, 206–207; Scolari, "Transmedia Storytelling," 598; Wolf, *Building Imaginary Worlds*, 249–264.

remediations or, in Irina Rajewski's terms, medial transpositions[21] – must "add" and "subtract" something from the source(s), most importantly because medium-specific representational techniques differ.[22] In addition, very few if any adaptations do not introduce at least a single new idea or aspect; remakes cannot logically (or ontologically, for that matter) be identical to their premake, else they would not be a remake; with repetition inevitably comes difference.[23]

For example, with the conjoining of the two fictional universes of *Alien* and *Predator*, much information is added, but new gaps and questions appear about this significantly expanded universe. Of course, every new storyworld exploits what is already there in the fictional universe and can alter, revise or rework facts and stories,[24] albeit with an eye on the uncertain and unstable limits of what might be considered acceptable by an imagined audience. At the same time, however, the new storyworld adds new indeterminacies and – although it sounds paradoxical – contributes to what is not there. In fact, I would argue that with every additional storyworld, at least as much of "what is not there" is added as of "what there is."

Let me exemplify this in more detail. In *Alien*, we know next to nothing about the crew, their past, the company that owns the space freighter, Earth, the planet they land on and where they find the alien eggs, the alien creature itself, the vast spaceship, how the company knows about the alien creature, and so on and so forth. The novelization adds the dreams of the crew in their sleeping pods, thereby adding a little bit of character depth, hints about their families and their past, anxieties, etc., but, by way of these minimal hints, also adds further questions about exactly these aspects: their families, their past, their character. The second film, *Aliens*, takes place more than sixty years after the first film, adding information about Ripley's family (she had a daughter who has died in the meantime), about

21 Irina Rajewsky, "Intermediality, Intertextuality, and Remediation: A Literary Perspective on Intermediality." In*termédialités* 6 (Autumn 2005): 51.

22 Wolf stresses the crucial influence of medium as one of the most important factors in determining how a world will grow due to "the medium's unique combination of properties available for the conveyance of the world and its stories." Wolf, *Building Imaginary Worlds*, 248.

23 Rüdiger Heinze and Lucia Krämer, eds., *Remakes and Remaking: Concepts – Media – Practices* (Bielefeld: transcript, 2015), 7–19. Vera Cuntz makes an interesting argument about the repetition of so-called standard situations (birth, joint meal, medical examination, final fight) in all *Alien* movies. Not only do these situations reoccur in all movies, she argues; they always vary slightly, and it is this "repetition with a difference" that contributes to the continuing appeal of the movies. Vera Cuntz, *Kalkulierter Schrecken. Standardsituationen in der* Alien*-Filmreihe* (Remscheid: Gardez, 2007), 13–17.

24 Parody, "Franchising/Adaptation," 215–216.

the Weyland Company (it is powerful, it colonizes planets, and it is just as ruthless as indicated in the first film), and about the universe in general (the unit of colonial marines that accompany Ripley are apparently trained in what they call "bug hunt," indicating that there must be other known species on other planets). At the same time, some questions/gaps become more pertinent: what exactly is the situation on Earth (what kind of society is extant), what exactly is the role and position of the Weyland company, what exactly is Ripley's family background, why, how, and where are other planets colonized, and so on. With the conjoining of the *Alien* and the *Predator* universe, the questions, gaps, and conflicts multiply: is there any relation between the *Predator* and the space jockey species? If, as we learn in *Prometheus*, the space jockey species also colonizes planets (including Earth eons ago) and has created the alien creature as a biological weapon, why does it want to annihilate humanity (as is suggested at the end of the film), and how does it then happen that the *Predator* species has been using the alien creature for millennia as part of an initiation ritual on Earth (*AvP*)?

It becomes obvious that with each new storyworld instalment in a fictional universe (not to mention the joining of entire fictional universes), not only are there added new facts, characters, settings, and storylines, but also new gaps, incongruities, and indeterminacies. All of what is there and not there in the already extant universe then interacts with all of what is there and not there in the new storyworld addition. As consumers of this fictional universe, we consume one storyworld after another, in a particular syntagmatic order (depending on when and to what we have access), and – if we assume that very few people are likely to consume each and every storyworld text for a given fictional universe – paradigmatic selection.[25] As a result, depending on which particular storyworld constellation/selection we are familiar with, a particular set of gaps, incongruities, and indeterminacies arises.[26]

Thus, the legally sanctioned fictional universes of franchises created through franchise storytelling and media convergence already are palimpsestic, "jazzy," and multi-laminated. It is not a prerogative of participatory

25 The particular syntagmatic and paradigmatic order in which we consume the storyworlds of a fictional universe actually depends on a large number of factors, among them our particular predilections (whatever their cause), the canonicity of a given storyworld, but also of a particular medium, and so forth.

26 Another source of complications is the divergence in the quality with and degree to which particular storyworlds in different media are "furnished." Compare, for example, early and more recent computer games, or the board game version of a movie installment. Even the quantitative and qualitative difference in narrative and aesthetic detail/elaboration between the various *Alien* films is a possible source of friction.

contexts or non-sanctioned products; it is not an incidental by-product or solely due to remediation – although this certainly plays an important role. Nevertheless, it is actually a logical and inevitable consequence of fictional storyworlds as possible worlds. Total control, full orchestration, is impossible: neither can we predict or know exactly how an audience will receive a particular storyworld and make sense of it within a particular fictional universe and within their very own constellation and selection of that fictional universe as they have "consumed" it so far. In addition, audiences can be amazingly creative in dealing with differences, divergences, and apparent incompatibilities by coming up with their own explanations, interpretations, complements, and other "sense-making" strategies; in some other cases, they may simply not care.

Consequently, what Linda Hutcheon writes with regard to video games is also true of franchise storytelling: it is "less the story itself than the story world [...] that [is] being adapted."[27] She calls this a heterocosm (but makes no reference to Doležel) that allows for "multiple possible story lines";[28] in the section on transmedia storytelling in his online blog, Henry Jenkins makes a similar point: "[T]ransmedia stories are based not on individual characters or specific plots but rather complex fictional worlds which can sustain multiple interrelated characters and their stories."[29]

Clare Parody is one of the few to elaborate on what this implies, noting that there are "specific dynamics at work when a text adapts a franchise rather than a single source," because in franchises a new text usually engages with "more than one specific text."[30] Within franchises, every new storyworld text is "unavoidably structured in relation to the entire franchise multitext," which is "diffuse and unstable."[31] There is, she writes, a whole "array" (a term she takes from Jim Collins) of "versions, origin points, coexisting, overlapping, and contradictory narrative realities, rather than a master narrative and stable textual corpus."[32] Her conclusion is that there are "cohering principles other than narrative continuity, such as brand identity, adaptations, remakes, and similar re-versionings and re-visionings."[33] I think she is right in that

27 Linda Hutcheon, *A Theory of Adaptation* (New York: Routledge, 2006), xxiv.

28 Ibid.

29 Henry Jenkins, "Transmedia Storytelling 101," *Confessions of an Aca-Fan: The Official Weblog of Henry Jenkins*, last modified March 22, 2007, accessed February 15, 2019, http://henryjenkins.org/2007/03/transmedia_storytelling_101.html.

30 Parody, "Franchising/Adaptation," 212.

31 Ibid.

32 Ibid.

33 Ibid., 215–216.

these are the principles at work; however, I do not think they always and inevitably do a good job at "cohering," because while the "narrative spaces" are indeed "vast in their scope and minute in their detail," they are not, and cannot be, "wholesale envisionings" and "completely imagined worlds."[34] Every storyworld accretion, or initiation, is already incomplete and semantically heterogeneous (with all the complications mentioned above), making the fictional universe they gradually constitute and form part of at least as incomplete and semantically heterogeneous (because the complications compound each other). This is a potentially indefinite process as long as new storyworld texts are added to the fictional universe, not to mention the fact that each "partaker" of this universe assembles his or her very own syntagmatic and paradigmatic constellation of this universe. Admittedly, fans and particular fan cultures are likely to agree on a canon of "must-see" storyworlds within a transmedial universe, so that there may be a shared, intersubjective pattern of assemblage. Nonetheless, fans and fan cultures change (especially over the long time some franchises exist and expand); they often heatedly (and for years) debate which storyworld belongs to the canon for which reasons, and in which order they are best "consumed"; and new storyworld additions to the universe may radically upend large parts of it (consider, for example, the *X-Men* reboot). Overall, given the number of factors that influence both the extension of a transmedial universe and its consumption, I would argue that volatility and coincidence still dominate.

Therefore, when Jenkins writes that "[t]ransmedia storytelling represents a process where integral elements of a fiction get dispersed systematically across multiple delivery channels for the purpose of creating a unified and coordinated entertainment experience,"[35] he is certainly right about the intention, but I am not so sure he is right about its successful implementation resulting in a "systematic," "unified," and "coordinated" fictional universe. In fact, I would argue that while the attempt is certainly made, the intended result is ultimately impossible, simply because of how storyworlds and fictional universes work (and, on a more general level, simply because chance and contingency will always obviate attempts at total control anywhere). As Felan Parker argues using digital games of the *Star Wars* franchise as an example, the dominant discourse of canon and continuity is misleading, not only because "interactive, playable, non-linear [...] digital games [cannot] be rationalized as part of a singular, continuous canon," but "simply [because of] the overwhelming incoherence and complexity of transmedia

34 Ibid., 214.

35 Jenkins, "Transmedia Storytelling 101" (emphasis added).

franchises" – an incoherence and complexity not easily integrated into the critical and corporate rhetoric of controlled world building.[36]

I think there are two other things at stake here beyond possible worlds logic: valorization and control. Parody wryly comments, "franchise adaptation can be exaggeratedly haunted by the specter of the commercial and hegemonic anxieties about the commoditization of art and entertainment."[37] If there is an economic motivation (which of course there is) or if that motivation is too blatant, critics and fans might consider the product as compromised, as "derivative," "imitative," "advertising" rather than "interpretive" or "transformative."[38] This, I believe, shows a naïve notion of purity (not Parody's). It also shows a notion of hegemony and total control by corporations over their franchise, their media products, and the fictional universes these create – and by implication their audiences – which I find problematic and unrealistic. Obviously, participation in and access to the creation, modification, and expansion of a fictional universe is always unequal. But the impossibility of total control over storyworlds, and even more so over entire fictional universes, should provide some solace in that it implies a degree of interpretive freedom and cognitive participation that is not to be underestimated and that has had, time and again, an impressive influence over which storyworlds and universes last, and which do not.

Works Cited

Alien. Directed by Ridley Scott. Brandywine, 1979. DVD.
Aliens. Directed by James Cameron. Twentieth Century Fox, 1986. DVD.
Alien 3. Directed by David Fincher. Twentieth Century Fox, 1992. DVD.
Alien Resurrection. Directed by Jean-Pierre Jeunet. Brandywine, 1997. DVD.
Alien vs. Predator. Directed by Paul W.S. Anderson. Twentieth Century Fox, 2004. DVD.
Alien vs. Predator: Requiem. Directed by Colin Strause and Greg Strause. Twentieth Century Fox, 2007. DVD.
Alien: Covenant. Directed by Ridley Scott. Brandywine, 2017. DVD.
Aliens: Colonial Marines. Produced by Brian Burleson. Gearbox Software. Sega, 2013. Video game.
Alien: Isolation. Directed by Alistair Hope. Creative Assembly. Sega, 2014. Video game.

36 Felan Parker, "Millions of Voices: *Star Wars*, Digital Games, Fictional Worlds and Franchise Canon." In *Game On, Hollywood!: Essays on the Intersection of Video Games and Cinema*, edited Gretchen Papazian and Joseph Michael Sommers (Jefferson: McFarland & Company, 2013), 156; 166.
37 Parody, "Franchising/Adaptation," 216.
38 Ibid.

Boni, Marta. "Introduction." In *World Building. Transmedia, Fans, Industries*, edited by Marta Boni, 9–27. Amsterdam: Amsterdam University Press, 2017.

Cuntz, Vera. *Kalkulierter Schrecken. Standardsituationen in der* Alien*-Filmreihe*. Remscheid: Gardez, 2007.

Doležel, Lubomir. *Heterocosmica: Fiction and Possible Worlds*. Baltimore: Johns Hopkins University Press, 1998.

Eco, Umberto. "'Casablanca': Cult Movies and Intertextual Collage." *SubStance* 14, no. 2 (1985): 3–12.

Foster, Alan Dean. *Alien*. New York: Warner Books, 1979.

—. *Aliens*. New York: Warner Books, 1986.

Harvey, Colin. *Fantastic Transmedia. Narrative, Play and Memory across Science Fiction and Fantasy Storyworlds*. Hampshire: Palgrave Macmillan, 2015.

Heinze, Rüdiger, and Lucia Krämer, eds. *Remakes and Remaking: Concepts – Media – Practices*. Bielefeld: transcript, 2015.

Herman, David. "Regrounding Narratology: The Study of Narratively Organized Systems for Thinking." In *What is Narratology? Questions and Answers Regarding the Status of a Theory*, edited by Tom Kindt and Hans-Harald Müller, 303–332. Berlin: de Gruyter, 2003.

Hills, Matt. "Traversing the 'Whoniverse': Doctor Who's Hyperdiegesis and Transmedia Discontinuity/Diachrony." In *World Building. Transmedia, Fans, Industries*, edited by Marta Boni, 343–361. Amsterdam: Amsterdam University Press, 2017.

—. *Fan Cultures*. London and New York: Routledge, 2002.

Hutcheon, Linda. *A Theory of Adaptation*. New York: Routledge, 2006.

Jenkins, Henry. "Transmedia Storytelling 101." *Confessions of an Aca-Fan: The Official Weblog of Henry Jenkins*. Last modified March 22, 2007. Accessed February 15, 2019. http://henryjenkins.org/2007/03/transmedia_storytelling_101.html.

—. *Convergence Culture: Where Old and New Media Collide*. New York: New York University Press, 2006.

Klastrup, Lisbeth, and Susana Tosca. "Transmedial Worlds – Rethinking Cyberworld Design." In *International Conference on Cyberworlds 2004: Proceedings*, edited by Masayuki Nakajima, Yoshinori Hatori, and Alexei Sourin, 409–416. Los Alamitos, CA: IEEE Computer Society, 2004.

Martinez, Matias, and Michael Scheffel, eds. *Einführung in die Erzähltheorie*. Munich: C.H. Beck, 1999.

Parker, Felan. "Millions of Voices: *Star Wars*, Digital Games, Fictional Worlds and Franchise Canon." In *Game On, Hollywood!: Essays on the Intersection of Video Games and Cinema*, edited by Gretchen Papazian and Joseph Michael Sommers, 156-168. Jefferson: McFarland & Company, 2013.

Parody, Clare. "Franchising/Adaptation." *Adaptation* 4, no. 2 (2011): 210–218.

Predator. Directed by John McTiernan. Amercent Films, 1987. DVD.

Predator 2. Directed by Stephen Hopkins. Davis Entertainment, 1990. DVD.

Predators. Directed by Nimród Antal. Twentieth Century Fox, 2010. DVD.

Prometheus. Directed by Ridley Scott. Twentieth Century Fox, 2012. DVD.

Rajewsky, Irina. "Intermediality, Intertextuality, and Remediation: A Literary Perspective on Intermediality." *Intermédialités* 6 (Autumn 2005): 43–64.

Richardson, Brian. *Unnatural Voices: Extreme Narration in Modern and Contemporary Fiction*. Columbus: Ohio State University Press, 2006.

Ryan, Marie-Laure. "Possible Worlds." In *The Living Handbook of Narratology*, edited by Jan-Christoph Meister. Interdisciplinary Center for Narratology, University of Hamburg, 2009–. Last modified September 27, 2013. Accessed February 15, 2019. www.lhn.uni-hamburg.de/node/54.html.

—. *Possible Worlds, Artificial Intelligence and Narrative Theory*. Bloomington: University of Indiana Press, 1991.

Scolari, Carlos Alberto. "Transmedia Storytelling: Implicit Consumers, Narrative Worlds, and Branding in Contemporary Media Production." *International Journal of Communication* 3 (2009): 586–606.

Scott, Ridley. "Ridley Scott says *Prometheus* is not a prequel to *Alien*." *BBC Radio 5 Live* interview, 2:51. Last modified June 1, 2012. Accessed February 15, 2019. www.bbc.com/news/entertainment-arts-18298709.

Verheiden, Mark, and Mark A. Nelson. *Aliens*. Milwaukie, OR: Dark Horse Comics, 1988–1989.

Wolf, Mark J.P. *Building Imaginary Worlds: The Theory and History of Subcreation*. New York: Routledge, 2012.

About the author

Rüdiger Heinze is Professor for American Studies at the English Seminar of the TU Braunschweig. He is author of a monograph titled *Ethics of Literary Forms* and another one titled *Mosaics & Melting Pots: Children of Immigrants in US-American Literature*. His current research interests are in dystopian & post-apocalyptic literature, multilingual US-American literature, and transmedial narratology.

8. "Everything is Awesome:" Spreadability and *The LEGO Movie*

Joyce Goggin

Abstract

This essay addresses *The LEGO Movie* as a transmedia text that references or includes a remarkable collection of characters and "bits" from other films and TV series. As I argue, the movie is assembled with a kind of cynical humour reminiscent of the exhausted irony described by David Foster Wallace, and effectively short-circuits possible critiques of the LEGO company itself, while presenting a Trumpian dictator who is plotting the end of the minifigures' world. The essay also discusses the economy of transmedia storytelling and its characteristic diversification which mirrors LEGO's own corporate strategy, thus making the LEGO business model cute and entertaining.

Key words: LEGO; money; finance; irony; transmedia storytelling

A Nobel prize, a piece of string
You know what's awesome? Everything
[…]
Rocks, clocks, and socks, they're awesome
Figs, and wigs, and twigs, that's awesome
Everything you see or think or say is awesome

Introduction

The high-spirited affirmation that "everything is awesome" – the hook from the *LEGO Movie*'s (2014) academy-award-winning theme song – is a message that itself could mean just about "everything" and anything. From "rocks, clocks and socks" to "wigs and twigs," the lyrics express not only one minifigure's

Fehrle, J. and W. Schäfke, *Adaptation in the Age of Media Convergence*,
Taylor & Francis Group, 2019
DOI 10.5117/9789462983663_CH08

positive attitude toward work, but also the seemingly random, recombinatory mechanism behind the plot, its construction which relies on intermediality and media convergence, and the narrative's very self-conscious intertextuality. At the same time, the movie offers what I will argue is a complex, self-reflexive view of many of the current global predicaments with which we are confronted on a daily basis. The larger implication is that, while it is goes without saying that *The LEGO Movie* concept derives from various media, including the interlocking bricks, and borrows characters from any number of other narrative franchises, it also foregrounds the kinds of monetary and economic systems through which the film was produced and disseminated.

Importantly, while the film does all of the aforementioned, it also holds up a comedic view of labor and creativity to contemporary Western neoliberalized audiences that remains, as I want to suggest, profitably and productively ambiguous in the film.[1] As I will argue in detail below, then, *The LEGO Movie* promotes the company and its products while at the same time autoreflexively ironizing the various ways in which transmedia storytelling practices, and indeed LEGO bricks, purport to encourage creative freedom while expanding potential markets. In so doing, the film offers numerous points of entry or engagement for a wide range of viewers from children and adults who are already enthusiastic fans, to argumentative academics who might be somewhat skeptical about the film's feel-good message. Therefore, by making fun of LEGO itself, as well as various industries with which the company is complicit in ways that I will elaborate below, the film neatly ensures that consumers and viewers will continue to enjoy LEGO.

The Plot

In order to illustrate how *The LEGO Movie* signifies through the toys and the industry that produces them, as well as through the multi-platform economic

1 The way that the film adapts other narrative franchises and toys while foregrounding the kinds of monetary and economic systems through which it was produced and disseminated, is also discussed in my work on the *Ocean's* film series, finance, and gambling. (Joyce Goggin, "Casinos and Sure Bets: *Ocean's Eleven* and Cinematic Money." In *Money and Culture*, ed. Fiona Cox and Hans-Walter Schmidt-Hannisia (Bern: Peter Lang, 2008), 285–297; "From Remake to Sequel: *Ocean's Eleven* and *Ocean's Twelve*." In *Second Takes: Approaches to the Film Sequel*, ed. Caroline Jess-Cooke and Constantine Verevis (New York: State University of New York Press, 2010), 105–121; "Qu'est qu'on réadapte? *Ocean's Eleven* et l'esthétique de la finance,» in *De la page blanche aux salles obscures: Adaptation et réadaption dans le monde Anglophone*, trans. Ariane Hudelet, ed. Ariane Hudelet ad Shannon Wells-Lassagne (Rennes: Presses Universitaires de Rennes, 2001), 49–59.)

models that subtend it, I need first, briefly, to synopsize the plot. *The LEGO Movie* recounts, in 3D animation, the story of Emmet Brickowski (Chris Pratt), a completely ordinary LEGO minifigure who celebrates his mundane life as a cog in the wheels of industry by singing about the awesomeness of performing repetitive tasks in a faceless workforce. Emmet is, however, unaware of a nasty plan being hatched by the evil, obsessive-compulsive President (aka Lord) Business (Will Ferrell), Tyrant of Bricksburg and the LEGO Universe, as well as Company President of the Octan Corporation. Along with his Micro-Managers, President Business plans to freeze the LEGO universe permanently on a deceptively celebratory day, which he has declared "Taco Tuesday." At that time, all of the figures in Bricksburg will be forever cemented in place with "Kragle," a superweapon that is actually a tube of Krazy Glue on which the "z," the "y," and the "u" have worn off. So, although President Business tells his employees that on Taco Tuesday everyone will get a free snack and his love, the viewer is made privy to the knowledge that Taco is really spelled T.A.K.O.S.; wherein "the 's' is silent"; and wherein the letters stand for "Tentacle Arm Kragle Outside Sprayer," hence what actually awaits the minifigures is being set permanently in place, rather than a Mexican treat.

As the story unfolds, Emmet discovers Wyldstyle (Elizabeth Banks), an appropriately named female minifigure, nosing around on his construction site. Having been instructed by his employer to report "anything weird" immediately, Emmet goes to investigate and falls into a hole where the missing cap to the Kragle is located. This cap, known to freedom fighters as the "Piece of Resistance" and the only thing that can prevent President Business's plan to "end the world on Taco Tuesday," becomes stuck to Emmet's back.[2] His contact with the glue cap causes Emmet to hallucinate and, when he regains consciousness, Emmet finds himself in the custody of President Business' bipolar henchman, Lieutenant Bad Cop/Good Cop (Liam Neeson). Emmet is then rescued by Wyldstyle, who takes him on a journey through various LEGO playsets on the way to meeting Vitruvius (Morgan Freeman), a wizard who has prophesized that a person to be known as "the Special" will find the Piece of Resistance and put an end to President Business' dastardly plot. Therefore, with Vitruvius' recognition of the über-ordinary

2 While the notion of a "Piece of Resistance" might conjure up thoughts of Foucault in the minds of many, it is also one of the clever plays on words and languages in the film. Hence, "Piece of Resistance" is a play on "pièce de résistance," just as "nail pol-EESH" and "Q-TYYPE" – two more of President Business' secret weapons – are Gallicized versions of "nail polish" and "Q-Tip." I read this wordplay in the film as part and parcel of the kind of recombinatory, trans-everything dynamic that informs *The LEGO Movie*, in this case at the level of the signifier.

Emmet's "specialness," the mundane minifigure has greatness thrust upon him along with the missing cap to the Kragle. He is henceforth known as "the most talented, most interesting, and most extraordinary person in the universe," by all of the characters in the film – albeit with some reservations.

Thick as a Brick: Building Storyworlds

There are perhaps few films that self-consciously celebrate the mechanics of transmedial storytelling with as much gusto as *The LEGO Movie*. Quite obviously, the film incorporates characters from other possible worlds and story franchises such as Batman who helps Emmet on his quest, along with a galaxy of other characters including Superman, Wonder Woman, Michelangelo the Teenage Mutant Ninja Turtle, and Millhouse of *The Simpsons* fame. The film also features "real-world" characters like Michelangelo, the Italian renaissance artist, and Shakespeare, the 16th-century English playwright, as well as stock characters such as cops, cowboys, banditos, LEGO's 1980s "retro space guy" minifigure, and so on. By incorporating a colorful cast of real-world and storyworld characters rendered as minifigures, *The LEGO Movie* comes together through the kind of freewheeling, trans-storyworld cherry picking for which Emmet and the other freedom fighters in the film strive to clear the way. Therefore, the implication is that by thwarting Lord Business' plan to glue all of the LEGO minifigures permanently into playsets "the way they're supposed to be," the bricks are set free by the close of the movie to be reconfigured according to the imagination of anyone who plays with them, ensuring maximum creativity.

Having been blithely following the rules and believing that everything is totally awesome with no inkling that Taco (T.A.K.O.S.) Tuesday really spells disaster, Emmet rapidly finds himself in serious need of being brought up to speed on the film's central conflict, and asks Wyldstyle to catch him up. Her reply is understood by Emmet as, "Bla, bla, bla proper name, place name, backstory stuff, I'm so pretty, I like you but I'm angry with you for some reason," indicating that Emmet has stopped listening because he is, predictably enough, attracted to the messenger. At the same time however, this voice-over assumes viewers' familiarity with various mechanisms of storytelling while suggesting that characters ("proper name") are simply interchangeable linguistic markers for what Greimas would have called "actants."[3] This speech also suggests that

3 Algirdas Julien Greimas, *Sémantique structurale: recherche de methode* (Paris: Larousse, 1966). Structural semanticist and semiotician Algirdas Julien Greimas famously synthesized

any setting could be inserted ("place name") from any other story or medium, and indeed the characters move seamlessly from one playset *mise-en-scène* to the next throughout the movie. "Backstory stuff" similarly alerts viewers to the notion that the storyline will contain generic plot elements that can be substituted for one another at will, like so many LEGO bricks. Moreover, Wyldstyle's voiceover (focalized through Emmet), signifies that she is angry with Emmet "for some reason," which is irrelevant because, as viewers will know based on their familiarity with Hollywood conventions, the story will find its resolution in the formation of a heterosexual couple after many misunderstandings and misadventures. Likewise, the inclusion of cues in the form of intertitles with temporal indicators ("10 seconds later") presumes that viewers are knowledgeable about historic cinematic conventions.[4]

As Stephen Keane has noted, albeit in the context of disaster movies, generic story elements such as those just mentioned signal large quantities of information to viewers, making it possible to produce films with minimal backstory, while (partially) eliminating the need to develop characters.[5] Hence, in the present case, much of the Batman humor in the film presupposes previous knowledge of at least one of the many outings of the character across multiple media platforms (the comic books, the 1960s TV show, the movies, and so on). Familiarity with the worlds of Batman is therefore what sparks viewers' knowing chuckles when his alter ego, "Bruce Wayne, CEO of Wayne Enterprises" arrives on the scene and the Caped Crusader

the seven spheres of action and character identified in Vladimir Propp's *Morphologie du conte*, a systematic study of folk tales. Greimas distilled Propp's breakdown into categories of actants, which form what is known as the actantial model. These categories are (1) the subject, (2) the object, (3) the sender or instigator, (4) the receiver, (5) the helper, and (6) the opponent. These are then the basic story actants and may be fleshed out and interchanged as the storyteller chooses.

4 While it is tempting to cite many such moments at which the movie anticipates viewers' familiarity with narrative conventions, and particularly industrialized narrative conventions, the scene in which Wyldstyle concludes the monotonous, formulaic, in-movie TV Series *Where Are My Pants?* is quite remarkable. Here she manages to turn the one gag that informs the entire show into the final episode, by walking onto the set and exclaiming, "Hey! Guess what? Found your pants! Series is over!" which points to viewer fatigue, while foregrounding precisely those conventions that produce jaded viewers. Although there are labels to describe various sorts of irony (i.e. flat hyper-aware irony or de-historicized nostalgic parody or pastiche) my purpose here is not to try to pin down exactly what kind of self-conscious irony is operative in *The LEGO Movie*. While there are indeed many forms of irony in this film, my intention is to discuss how irony works together with transmedial storytelling in this particular case. The irony presented in the film does however have much in common with David Foster Wallace's notion of the debilitating effects of "postmodern irony and cynicism" that typifies TV shows and commercials since the 1980s (171). On this point, more below.

5 Stephen Keane, *Disaster Movies: The cinema of catastrophe* (London: Wallflower, 2001), 5.

casually remarks "Bruce Wayne? Uh... who's that? Sounds like a cool guy." And while this is just one example, it goes without saying that the same applies to virtually all of the other characters in the film, whether borrowed from other story franchises, or pirate lore that dates back to the 17th century and sideways to *Pirates of the Caribbean*.

Clare Parody has proposed a model for thinking about transmedia storytelling that relies both on the convergence of various media, as well as on adaptation. As she argues, adaptation is "fundamentally sympathetic to the aims and protocols of franchise storytelling" as well as an "efficient way of getting maximum use out of a fictional creation" such as a particular character or story franchise.[6] And just as stock characters may migrate freely across storyworlds, Julie Sanders has followed Roland Barthes in arguing for the infinite adaptability of "mythic templates and outlines [for] storytelling purposes," given that the simple elements of myth are constantly (re)appropriated and "persistently relocated in [...] new cultural geograph[ies] at each occasion of adaptation and appropriation".[7] Quite obviously, *The LEGO Movie* exploits several such interchangeable storytelling templates, and Emmet and the other minifigures embark upon their quest precisely to ensure that "templates" – in this case playsets – will once again be as open to reapportion and relocation as they were before President Business "erected walls between [playset] worlds and became obsessed with order and perfection." As Wyldstyle explains, under President Business' reign of surveillance and paranoia the minifigures are compelled to "follow the rules," and to "make everything look like it does in the instructions." Before this oppressive era, the minifigures supposedly enjoyed a golden age in which they were "free to travel and mingle, and build whatever they wanted," in any setting from Outer Space to the Old West. In other words, like myth, or very familiar, simple allegorical stories and plot structures, *The LEGO Movie* seems to permit and even promote endless (re)combinatory possibilities and ludic, narrative freedom to create new stories across platforms. Or, as Jenkins has explained, transmedia stories like the one in *The LEGO Movie* are based on "complex fictional worlds which can sustain multiple interrelated characters and their stories," and should, one might think, be open to infinite disaggregation and reconfiguration.[8]

6 Clare Parody, "Franchising/Adaptation," *Adaptation* 4, no. 2 (2011): 211.

7 Julie Sanders, *Adaptation and Appropriation* (London: Routledge, 2006), 63–64.

8 Henry Jenkins, "Transmedia Storytelling 101," *Confessions of an Aca-Fan. The Official Weblog of Henry Jenkins*, 22 March 2007, accessed February 15, 2019, http://henryjenkins.org/2007/03/transmedia_storytelling_101.html.

Herein however, resides an irony so blatant that I mention it only for the sake of advancing my argument, namely that, beginning as early as 1955 when LEGO released the "Town Plan" marketed as a toy system, the company itself has steadily introduced measures to "Kragle" the bricks into play systems or themed sets. Indeed, it was LEGO that invented the playset and LEGO that began marketing their bricks increasingly in play systems and sets with instructions for structured, correct play from the 1960s onwards. Moreover, it was only in response to customer complaints about not being able to buy spare parts that the company began marketing buckets of bricks on occasion, including "Creative Bucket 10662," advertised as offering "a world of unlimited building fun."[9] Here again, however, the set contains instructions for specific scenarios, guiding child "master builders" in their selection of themes and configurations. So while LEGO constantly promotes itself as encouraging out-of-the-box thinking, it is evidently more cost-efficient and profitable for the company to sell their bricks in boxed sets, so that even the creative bucket is ultimately another building system that invites children to follow instructions, and to produce prefabricated scenarios and constructions.

The implicit self-conscious irony of holding out a kind of prescribed, supposedly unlimited freedom to create anything and everything that actually serves to regulate creative play is staged repeatedly throughout *The LEGO Movie*. Hence, we watch as the characters move fluidly from the generic Bricksburg cityscape, to the Old West, to a nautical setting and so on, which really amounts to moving from one set of rigidly defined parameters and clearly stipulated contents – "Middle Zealand. A wondrous land full of knights, castles, mutton, torture weapons, poverty, leeches, illiteracy, and, um… dragons" – to the next. This answers to Maaike Lauwaert's description of how toy manufacturers like LEGO configure the "user and uses" of toys and set the parameters for user action. Therefore practices – what you can do with a toy like LEGO – are inscribed into its technical make-up, along with "norms and values," and "rules and requirements" that are "embedded into the design and promote specific user behavior."[10] In other words, *The LEGO Movie* trades on what I read as a cynical form of irony that invites

9 On this point, see *CNN*'s coverage of Chinese artist and political activist Ai Weiwei's tussle with LEGO that began in October 24, 2015, when the company refused to sell him a large quantity of bricks without his disclosure of the "thematic purpose" of a project that would require ordering in bulk. LEGO later claimed that they "do not censor or ban creative use of LEGO bricks". "Everything awesome again? LEGO changes guidelines for bulk orders." *CNN*, January 14, 2016, accessed March 1, 2016, http://edition.cnn.com/2015/10/26/arts/gallery/lego-artists/index.html.

10 Maaike Lauwaert, *The Place of Play: Toys and Digital Cultures* (Amsterdam: Amsterdam UP, 2009), 13.

uncomfortable, or perhaps knowing and self-satisfied, smirks aroused by the film's promotion of something like Derridean "free play," while really offering a way to construct yet one more predictable, themed mini-environment.[11]

At the same time, on what one might call the macro-scale of meaning, the film follows the logic of a market in which it is important to hail as many viewers as possible, hence the film's short-circuiting of a number of the most plausible critiques of itself.[12] This is to say that the film seems to criticize and satirize LEGO's own market-driven propensity to claim that the bricks offer children unlimited creative potential and a workout for their young imaginations, while marketing their products in themed sets, with instructions that also act as affective scripts for directing play. Given that modern media companies, like those that produced *The LEGO Movie*, "are horizontally integrated [and] hold interests across a range of what were once distinct media industries," media conglomerates have "an incentive to spread [their] brand[s] or expand [their] franchises across as many different media platforms as possible" (Jenkins 2007, "Transmedia 101").[13] Moreover, this is accomplished, at least in part, by maintaining

11 See Jacques Derrida, *Structure, Sign, and Play in the Discourse of the Human Sciences*, trans. Alan Bass (Chicago: University of Chicago Press, 1978), passim. This contradiction has been commented on in the area of video games by many, including Jenkins, who is cautiously optimistic about the claim to "complete freedom of movement" made by *Die by the Sword* in 1998 (Henry Jenkins, "'Complete Freedom of Movement': Video Games as Gendered Play Spaces" in *From Barbie to Mortal Combat: Gender and Computer Games*, ed. Justine Cassell and Henry Jenkins (Boston: MIT Press, 2000), passim). Martti Lahti ("As We Became Machines: Corporealized Pleasures in Video Games" in *The Video Game Theory Reader*, ed. Mark J.P. Wolf and Bernard Perron (New York and London: Routledge, 2003), 157–171) and James Newman (*Video Games* (London and New York: Routledge, 2004), 120–130) have been much more critical about such radical claims.

12 Much of my argument here resembles "E Unibus Pluram," David Foster Wallace's 1993 critique of television and US fiction, particularly when he writes that "[t]elevision's managed to become its own most profitable critic" (157), or that television "must somehow undercut television-watching in theory [...] while reinforcing television-watching in practice" (164), or again how TV "has become able to capture and neutralize any attempt to change or even protest the attitudes" (171) that it requires to continue passively viewing (David Foster Wallace, "E Unibus Pluram: Television and U.S. Fiction," *Review of Contemporary Fiction*, 13:2 (Summer 1993)). That said, Wallace's essay deals specifically with TV and American fiction of over two decades ago and I believe that *The LEGO Movie* has raised the ante somewhat in the various ways that the present essay seeks to illuminate.

13 On this point see also Parody, who writes that franchise-based storyworlds are "fundamentally driven by corporate desires to colonize and capitalize upon media outlets," and furthermore that "what franchise adaptations adapt can [...] be conceptualized as a brand identity, the intellectual property, advertising language, and presentational devices that cohere, authorize, and market the range of media products that together comprise the franchise experience" (Parody, 213, 214).

a firm grip on the franchise and policing its limits so that everything is *not* possible. Jenkins' observations as to how narrative franchises work through contemporary media companies therefore help to explain the clever irony behind *The LEGO Movie* and how it resides in pointing, in true postmodern, self-conscious fashion, to storyworlds as agglomerated fictional universes, imaginatively extended and developed through transmedia storytelling.

"Arr, thaar be too many micro-managers!!"

As I have been arguing, *The LEGO Movie* both exemplifies and autoreflexively ironizes the various ways in which transmedia storytelling practices seem to promote creative freedom, while expanding potential markets for their properties by offering different points of entry for various audience segments. In this case, those market segments include children who play with LEGO bricks and playsets, and who will enjoy watching their favorite toy through an alternative media platform, AFOLs (Adult Fans of LEGO), viewers familiar with the storyworlds like *Batman* and *Star Wars* that the film incorporates, and so on. At the same time, I would argue, the film makes an effort to entertain viewers like myself who are skeptical about the industrial creativity-and-freedom message that the movie potentially communicates, and this, I believe, is done by means of the kind of self-conscious humor that I have just outlined. *The LEGO Movie*, then, is a slick, slyly self-conscious film, based on an enormously popular toy and the industry that produces it, as well as the multi-platform economic models that subtend it, featuring figures such as the neoliberal, paranoid, obsessive-compulsive Lord Business and his micro-managing henchmen. And what's wrong with that?

To begin answering this question I refer to Octan, the supposedly fictional company at the center of *The LEGO Movie* run by Lord Business, that "make[s] good stuff: dairy products, TV shows, coffee, surveillance cameras, all history books, [and] voting machines." This description, of course, loosely describes many of the "big ten" multinationals, and enormous, highly diversified corporations like LEGO, so it is not without significance that Octan is lampooned in the film as a patently evil, despotic corporate dictatorship. Importantly, moreover, Octan made its first appearance in various LEGO sets beginning in 1992, whereas before 1992, LEGO used the logos of real-world oil companies Esso, Shell, and Exxon in their boxed playsets. While LEGO dropped the Esso and Exxon logos sometime thereafter due to negative associations that consumers might have with these companies, it continued to use the Shell logo until 2014, when the company announced that it would not renew its marketing agreement with Shell under pressure from Greenpeace.[14]

It seems safe to conclude, then, that LEGO is well aware that many potential customers freely and eagerly consume fossil fuel in multitudinous forms including LEGO bricks, yet they might see the companies that extract and distribute it as being evil.[15] In other words, by making fun of an industry with which LEGO is complicit, the film offers a thinly veiled attempt to ensure that consumers and viewers who are concerned about the environment will continue to enjoy LEGO toys, the movie, and possibly the video games or a trip to a LEGO Land.

This same in-film criticism is also applied to the neoliberal, highly diversified corporate model represented in *The LEGO Movie*, run by President Business and his Micro-Managers. Key to President Business' approach to management is the constant use of Octan's surveillance cameras to ensure that everything be rigid and proceed according to the rules, hence Emmet's frequent objections that he cannot do anything that is "against the instructions." Yet while foregrounding corporate business models and the kinds of generic, interchangeable worker subjectivities it shapes, the film also features a hero whose very conformity ironically helps him to subvert the oppressive order. Likewise, in spite of having a face that is so generic that it matches every other face in the database and cannot be identified by President Business' surveillance cameras, Emmet nonetheless becomes attached to the "Piece of Resistance" and is henceforth known as The Special. Here again, by holding a business model very similar to that of LEGO up to ridicule, along with the conventions of transmedial storytelling as a cynical means of extending popular brands and storytelling franchises, LEGO and the companies that produced the film have short-circuited a number of possible critiques while increasing their viewer and fan base.[16] This layer of irony makes it possible for viewers who might be critical of neoliberal

14 Alanna Petroff, "Lego ditches Shell after Arctic oil protests." *CNN*. October 9, 2014: 8:07. Accessed March 1, 2016, http://money.cnn.com/2014/10/09/news/companies/lego-shell-greenpeace/index.html.

15 It is perhaps worthy of note here that the LEGO Group is one of the world's leading tire manufacturers. "7 things you might not know about Lego," CNN, accessed March 6, 2016, http://edition.cnn.com/videos/showbiz/2014/02/17/orig-7-cool-things-about-lego-npr.cnn.

16 LEGO's business model is a frequent topic of CNN feature stories, such as "Lego boss reads *The Opposable Mind*" in which LEGO's CEO, Jorgen Vig Knudstorp, explains how the company attempts to incorporate or co-opt a variety of points of view and connect them, much as LEGO bricks can potentially be combined in various configurations, to produce winning concepts. "Lego posts 25% revenue jump, profits up 31%," CNN, accessed March 1, 2016, http://edition.cnn.com/search/?text=lego.

management schemes to sit back and enjoy the film, just as feminists who might be irritated by the dearth of female characters in the movie may be assuaged by the inclusion of Wyldstyle as a "liberated," albeit post-feminist, action figure.

Goldbricking

I believe that there is a deeper argument to be made here, which I would like to begin to unfold that argument by concurring with Fredric Jameson that there is a cultural logic to late capitalism, and with David Harvey who argued that it "should be possible to consider how [...] the changing experience of space, time and money has formed a distinctive material basis for the rise of distinctive systems of interpretation and representation" just as "money and commodities are themselves the primary bearers of cultural codes".[17] So if money – and the ways in which it circulates in capitalist systems – both bears and lends its logic to culture, I think it is instructive as well to revisit Georg Simmel's work on the role of money as the great leveler, based on the observation that it creates commensurability between widely dissimilar commodities. Writing at a key juncture in economic modernity late in the 19th century, Simmel theorized money as the autonomous manifestation of the relationship of exchange that transforms "desired objects into economic objects and establishes the *substitutability* of objects."[18] As an agreed-upon signifier of value, money provides "the means to be exchangeable for something else [...] by sublimating the relativity of things," which makes money "similar to the forms of logic which lend themselves equally to any particular content, regardless of that content's development or combination."[19] For Simmel, then, money is a sort of ur-LEGO form, which serves an equivalency, uniformity, and exchangeability function just like the bricks, which no doubt also "bear" the cultural logic of money.

More recently, and in the context of full-blown late capitalism and postmodern finance, Mark C. Taylor has synthesized the work of various thinkers on the topic of money, from Aristotle to Marx, in writing that

17 David Harvey, "Time Space Compression and the Postmodern Condition." *The Condition of Postmodernity*, 284–308 (Oxford: Blackwell, 1991), 299.

18 Simmel, *The Philosophy of Money*, trans. David Fisby (London and New York: Routledge, 2004), 119 (emphasis added).

19 Ibid., 121, 441.

"[s]tandardization allows money to be a unit of account and durability" which makes it particularly amenable to use as a medium of exchange.[20] Moreover, quoting Simmel, Taylor concludes that money is "the condition of possibility of a structure" and therefore "must retain a certain neutrality that, in Shimmel's [sic] terms, is "completely adaptable to any use. As a result of this neutrality money can take many forms; it is, in other words, polymorphous, polyvalent, and, some would insist, perverse."[21] In other words, if I may gloss both Simmel and Taylor, money "legofies" our life-worlds by collapsing difference and rendering all things commensurate and exchangeable, just as a building, scene, or person may be rendered in identical, interchangeable LEGO bricks.[22]

In the current, neoliberal capitalist paradigm, money shapes our lifeworlds perhaps somewhat more openly and profoundly than it has at any juncture in the past. While there are many reasons as to why this might be the case, probably the most salient is the progressive deregulation of the market over the past several decades, which has entailed the lifting of restrictions concerning what constitutes ethical trading practice and what banks are able to do. One of the consequences of banks and lending institutions becoming ever freer to self-regulate is a tremendous shift from the backing of solid assets in favor of using money to create more money through the development of various instruments of credit, exposure to risk and numerous trade mechanisms, all of which have led to what Randy Martin famously called the financialization of daily life. Moreover, with the growing importance of finance capitalism and the economic developments that I just noted, the role of large corporations has also changed so that, where they were once "chartered to serve both their *shareholders and society as a whole*" including employees

20 Mark C. Taylor, *Confidence Games: Money and Markets in a World without Redemption* (Chicago and London: The University of Chicago Press, 2004), 59.

21 Taylor, 60; Simmel, 441.

22 It would be interesting to connect LEGO, which got its start in 1932, to many cultural and economic developments typical of "modernism" and "structuralism," of which Simmel's thought is representative. Such a study would take into account the early days of the science of management and Max Weber's notions concerning "the administered" world, Saussure's model of the signifier, and architectural modernism of which Frank Lloyd Wright, who played with an early German construction toy called Froebel Blocks, is the vanguard. His mother purchased the bricks at the Centennial Exposition in Philadelphia 1876, and Wright wrote in his autobiography "the maple wood blocks [...] are in my fingers to this day. These primary forms and figures were the secret of all effects [...], which were ever got into the architecture of the world" (J. Froebel-Parker "The Influence of Friedrich Froebel on Frank Lloyd Wright," Froebel Web: An Online Resource, accessed March 4, 2016, www.froebelweb.org/web2000.html).

and customers, the Business Roundtable of the United States officially changed its mandate in 1997, stating that "the notion that the board must somehow balance the interests of other stakeholders [than shareholders] *fundamentally misconstrues the role of directors.*"[23] While this trend was already developing in the 1980s, it led to massive downsizing and staffing/cost reductions, which were put in force as a way to boost share prices, based on the assumption that layoffs would increase shareholder confidence, in turn having a positive impact on prices. So, as shareholders' profits have come to "trump all other considerations" including any concern for "society as a whole," managers have found that the easiest way to increase profits in the short term is through constant restructuring, which invariably results in mass layoffs and, ultimately, the end of the ideal of lifelong careers and all of the psychological and social stability that goes with such a concept.[24]

Furthermore, while market deregulation has often led to massive downsizing, deregulation has also produced a pronounced market dependence on derivatives. Briefly, derivatives amount to a disaggregation of assets to be reassembled in (partially) new configurations so that, whereas in the past industry and the market attempted to build,

> tightly integrated commodit[ies] that [were] more than the sum of [their] parts, financial engineering play[s] this process in reverse, disassembling a commodity [or company] into its consistent and variable elements and dispersing these attributes to be bundled together with elements of other commodities of interest to a globally oriented market for risk-managed exchange. Each of these moveable parts is reassembled by risk attribute so that they become worth more as derivatives than their individual commodities, leveraged as they are for the further purchase of credit instruments.[25]

This model, according to Martin, is structured by the logic of the derivative, and it works in much the same way as LEGO's bricks, the company's business model, and its many transmedial outputs. As one business-blogger wrote under the heading of "The Legofication of Business," "the key to [the] LEGO block is the simple and consistent interface. Doesn't matter what the shape

23 Barbara Ehrenreich, *Smile or Die: How Positive Thinking Fooled America & The World* (Croydon: Granata, 2009), 109 (emphasis added).

24 Ibid.

25 Martin, 89.

of the block is, the fact that every block has the same interface allows them to be connected" and disconnected in profit-generating ways (ObjectSharp Blog).[26] Moreover, derivatives' supposed purpose, namely to distribute risk as a means of hedging against failure, equally applies to *The LEGO Movie*. This is to say that little imagination is required to see how this kind of derivative, recombinatory logic applies to an inherently complex film like this one, put together through the decentralized dynamics of culture that operate along the lines of shifting connections between various storyworlds and, significantly, I would add, between human and non-human actors.

What kind of Minifigure am I? Subjectivity, Affect, Cuteness

The Daily Mash recently published a piece entitled "LEGO 'promoting unrealistic body image'" in which Julian Cook, a father of three, reportedly complained, "LEGO is promoting an aesthetic standard that is simply not achievable for human beings." He went on to explain that his "12-year-old daughter spends all her time trying to make her body shorter and stockier, and her nose disappear completely."[27] While this is obviously a fictional spoof on very legitimate concerns surrounding Barbie, appropriate body shape, and the ostensibly negative influence that such dolls have on girls' self-images, the piece is not without significance in the present context. Indeed, if Henry Jenkins is correct in arguing that transmedia texts do "not simply disperse information" but rather provide sets of "roles and goals which readers [and viewers] can assume as they enact aspects of the story through their everyday life,"[28] and if, according to Randy Martin,

26 "The Legofication of Business", Object Sharp Blog, posted August 13, 2012, accessed February 15, 2019, http://blogs.objectsharp.com/post/2012/08/13/The-Legofication-Of-Business.aspx. Here one might argue that the term "legofication" as it appears in this title to the blog entry I am quoting fails to take into account how LEGO, as a cultural form, is itself an epiphenomenon of an economic base. Were this the case, the suggestion would be that legofication is simply a reverse logic whereby commoditized culture informs economic structures and practices. That said, however, I use the term "legofication" as more than simply a metaphor based on similarities between capital and LEGO, and intend it to refer to the logic of the neoliberal practices that I have been at pains to bring to light in this essay. My goal is to look at the cultural and economic significance of LEGO in order to illustrate how a brand can become an underlying phenomenon, or at least partially inform the underlying systems of management and production which in turn inform and rely on culture, while also taking their cue from cultural production.

27 "Lego 'Promoting Unrealistic Body Image'," *The Daily Mash*, posted June 18, 2015, accessed March 2, 2016 and February 15, 2019, www.thedailymash.co.uk/news/society/lego-promoting-unrealistic-body-image-2015061899397.

28 Jenkins, "Transmedia Storytelling 101."

"derivatives are not essentially economic but feature in all manner of social relations, sites and forms," then the legofication of industry, the market, and entertainment commodities may have a serious impact on us as subjects.[29] In other words, as lightly as one would like to take this fictional account of parental heartbreak over the need to explain to children that their "hands will never come to resemble half-eaten Hula Hoops, nor will [their] head[s] develop a circular growth onto which various hats and hairstyles can be clicked," it is nonetheless true that children's stories, games, and toys mold us as children in ways that stay with us into adulthood.

As I have been arguing, the current economic order favors the progressive legofication of businesses, corporations, and public institutions and deals in mass layoffs, constant restructuring, and the loss of job security. This model both requires and shapes a specific kind of legofied subjectivity; that is, people who are separate yet interchangeable and perform much like minifigures who can figuratively click on whatever hat or hairstyle they need to move from job to job, or contract to contract, having given up on the notion of a professional calling or lifelong career. This kind of postmodern subject was first referred to by Deleuze as a "dividual" – that is, constituted from a mixed bag of "sub- and trans-individual arrangements of intensities at the level of bodies-in-formation."[30] According to Appadurai, this kind of subjectivity comes into sharp focus in what he refers to as our current "predatory" capitalist mode, wherein,

> [n]umbers are attached to consumer purchases, discrete interactions, credit, life-changes, health profiles, educational test results and a whole battery of related life events, so as to make these parts of the individual combinable and customizable in such ways as to render moot or irrelevant the idea of the "whole," the classic individual.[31]

The upshot is a world of "dividuals" whose information, the substance of who we are, can then be "further searched, combined and re-aggregated" to increase profits, and thoroughly legofied worker subjects capable of snapping on a different hat as they move from one temporary contract to the next, taking on legofied work-packages that amount to a parcel – a brick – of

29 Randy Martin, "After Economy? Social Logics of the Derivative." *Social Text 114*. 31.1 (Spring 2013): 83–106, 85.

30 Anderson, 165.

31 Ibid., 109–110.

what would formerly have been an entire job, performed by an *in*dividual. And this constant precarity, this failure to achieve what only a few decades ago was considered the norm, is what we are constantly enlisted, through various media in various places, to understand as freedom, recasting upsets as success. In short, we are invited to believe that disappointment, or what may be construed as failure (i.e. the failure to achieve what was formerly the mark of even a moderately successful career such as tenure or a permanent contract) should be reframed as an opportunity to succeed. Hence, by never "letting a good crisis go to waste," by never giving in to low-grade depression and anxiety that might affect our performance at work, we are constantly incited to tell ourselves "everything is awesome!"[32]

Seen in this light, the opening sequences of *The LEGO Movie*, in which we watch Emmet as he goes about his morning ablutions, are particularly revealing. Upon waking, Emmet immediately consults his copy of *Instructions on How to Fit in, Have Everybody Like You, and Always Be Happy!*, a twenty-one-step program that includes:

> Step 1: Breathe, Step 2: Greet the day, smile and say: Good morning city! [...] Step 11: Obey traffic signs and regulations, [...] Step 13: Park between the lines, [...] Step 15: Always root for the local sports team (Go sports team!), Step 16: Always return a compliment, Step 17: Drink overpriced coffee, Step 18: If you see anything weird report it immediately [...], Step 20: Always obey President Business, Step 21: Go to sleep, wake up in the morning and repeat the instructions.

Quite obviously, this is a mock-up of the multibillion-dollar motivational products industry that has informed American culture at least since Ben Franklin published his pithy advice manuals in the 18th century, and since the publishers of Norman Vincent Peale's *Power of Positive Thinking*

32 One of the best examples of what I am describing may be observed in the progressively privatized contemporary university, wherein entire programs are now regularly disaggregated, merged and course offerings recombined, often seemingly randomly, producing bizarre interdisciplinary grab-bags aimed at reducing teaching staff. Such management practices supposedly allow students greater interdisciplinary freedom, while euphemisms such as "reducing tenure density" or "career-change opportunities" have been coined to describe the practice of rendering the lion's share of faculty "adjunct," "independent," "freelance contractors," who receive no benefits or research time. In this model, the elimination of tenure is held out as offering teachers and researchers the "freedom" to chase part-time, legofied contracts, composed of disaggregated courses for which adjunct faculty are paid low, flat rates, from one university to the next. On this point, see also Randy Martin's rather more hopeful "Taking an Administrative Turn: Derivative Logics for a Recharged Humanities," (*Resources*, Vol. 116, no. 1 (Fall 2011): 156–176), passim.

urged executives to "give the book to employees. It pays dividends!"[33] So while the opening scene of *The LEGO Movie* is an excellent portrayal of the transparent monetization of the human psyche that drives the self-help and motivational industries, it is clear that Emmet is being coached to fit in, like a faceless cog in the wheel who obeys the rules and contributes to maximum productivity, while performing surveillance for the company on the side (Step 18), and consuming the overpriced products of other large corporations while smiling (Step 17).[34]

This last point is, at least tangentially, connected to developments such as those noted by Barbara Ehrenreich that involve "about thirty million full-time American workers [who] lost their jobs in corporate downsizings" between 1981 and 2003.[35] One particularly disturbing result of this trend of downsizing as a means of increasing share prices has been the growth of the self-help industries who dole out advice to the newly unemployed, and those (still) employed who suffer from ever-greater intensification of work. Likewise, these developments have also spawned a massive team-building industry as the answer to deteriorating employment conditions. The irony is of course that, "just as layoffs were making a mockery of the team concept, employees were urged to find camaraderie and a sense of collective purpose at the micro level of the 'team'".[36] And these industrial developments are all, of course, reflected in Emmet's careful and enthusiastic adherence to the instructions for everything from work to personal hygiene (Step 4: Take a shower, Step 5: Brush your teeth [...], Step 7: Comb your hair, Step 8: Wear clothes), and yet more volubly in the movie's theme song "Everything is Awesome." This is Emmet's favorite song which he "loves listening to over and over again" while becoming indoctrinated into the notion that "everything is cool when you're part of a team!" In other words, the film cynically follows management trends aimed at "helping" workers to accept greater job precarity and shrinking opportunity with a smile, rather than actually doing anything about the larger, macroeconomic problems that give rise to worker precarity in the first place.

33 Ehrenreich, 100. Various aspects of the happiness industries and happiness culture are increasingly the target of criticism by authors like Sara Ahmed, Lauren Berlant, and William Davies. Sara Ahmed, *The Promise of Happiness* (Durham and London: Duke UP, 2010); Lauren Berlant, *Cruel Optimism* (Durham and London: Duke UP, 2010); William Davies, *The Happiness Industry: How the Government and Big Business Sold Us Well-Being* (London and New York: Verso, 2015).

34 While the overpriced coffee moment in the film is quite clearly a poke at Starbucks, it equally advertises the franchise, however implicitly.

35 Ibid., 114.

36 Ibid., 120.

Such strategies and models were first referred to by Hardt and Negri as "affective labour," that is, labor that is immaterial "even if it is corporeal and affective, in the sense that its products are intangible: a feeling of ease, well-being, satisfaction, excitement, passion – even a sense of connectedness or community."[37] Affective labor feeds into "affective capitalism," through which sensational and sensorial products and services are produced that distract us from the real, serious problems entailed in the neoliberal economic order in which we must now operate. Affective practices (including everything from cute company mascots to wellness initiatives and office fun, to various kinds of commercial coping strategies for customers of various services and venues such as comfort animals) embrace subjects who have been rendered precarious through operations such as downsizing or generalized economic attrition, with manufactured warmth and care in order to extract more labor and mental resources from an increasingly exhausted work force. One excellent example of this kind of affective strategy is President Business' Taco Tuesday. As he tells the multitudes of LEGO workers, "don't forget Taco Tuesday's coming next week! That's the day every rule-following citizen gets a free taco and my love! Have a great day everybody!" Indeed, affective strategies including Emmet's company-supplied, self-help manual are presented throughout *The LEGO Movie* with such overwhelming cynicism that even Vitruvius blithely admits that the film's central, heart-warming message was just made up, "because the only thing anyone needs to be special is to believe that you can be." This is immediately followed by the wizard's admission that he knows "that sounds like a cat poster," at which moment we see just such a motivational poster in the background featuring a kitten and a single word: "Believe."[38]

The LEGO Movie's motivational cat poster brings me to one last aspect of the current economic paradigm that I have been endeavoring to sketch out, and which is a key feature of the film, namely the enormous role that cuteness has come to play in our daily lives, particularly in the form of cute cats, from the endless cute cat videos that infest our waking lives as we tap into social media, to Princess Unikitty of the film, who recalls Kitty White of Hello Kitty fame. As recent work on cuteness invariably

37 Hardt, 96.

38 Note that *The LEGO Movie* "Commitment Hanging Kitten Motivational Poster" is also available for purchase at many outlets, including amazon.com. While the film's cat poster may be a parody of Fox Mulder's famous, "I Want to Believe" poster, it also reiterates the cynically fake moral of this story, namely that even an ordinary person like Emmet can be a hero if only he believes in himself.

points out,[39] there has been an astonishing proliferation of cute aesthetics over the last few decades; an aesthetic and affective agent that was first taken seriously by ethologist Konrad Lorenz in his 1943 study, "The Innate Forms of Possible Experience" [*Die angeborenen Formen möglicher Erfahrung*] (1943). Here Lorenz advanced the Darwinian notion that, as a result of natural selection, most infants have an innate quality that prompts caring in adults. Lorenz then broke this quality down into an "inborn schema of the infant [*das Kindchenschema*]," with which he mapped out a number of cute [*herzig*] characteristics that act as innate releasing mechanisms in adults, including smallness as well as a "large head, predominance of the brain capsule, large and low-lying eyes, bulging cheek region, short, thick extremities, a springy elastic consistency, and clumsy movements".[40]

While quite obviously not all LEGO products tick all of these boxes, it is equally evident that the company has both promoted and profited from cuteness since its beginnings, trading on cute aesthetics and affects, just as cuteness has come to sugarcoat increasingly vast expanses of our daily lives.[41] Cute aesthetics are then supposed to induce profitably cuddly affects from emotionally and psychically self-regulating subjects always caught in the labor of self-improvement like Emmet, beginning every morning with the 21 steps to happiness. Cuteness aids in co-opting resistance by rebranding various forms of disappointment (i.e. loss of employment and opportunity) as success, and then acts as an affective veneer that insulates us as precarious, financialized subjects with puppies, kittens, and emoji as emotional anchors. In other words, we are invited to "amuse ourselves to death," to borrow Neil Postman's felicitous phrase, and to consume cute products as we witness the constant erosion of social safety nets, shrinking opportunities for youth, increased precarity in the work place, and so on.

Importantly, all the fun and cuteness of LEGO also inspires or encourages "playbor," a term coined to describe the increasing trend to "gamify" labor with the goal of fooling workers (as in "Taco Tuesday") into believing that they are having fun. The term playbor refers to labor performed, most often free of charge, by fans, bloggers, and other interactive media users who

39 Examples include Sianne Ngai's *Our Aesthetic Categories: Zany, Cute,* Interesting (Harvard: Cambridge University Press, 2012) and Christine Yano's *Pink Globalization: Hello Kitty's Trek across the Pacific* (Durham: Duke University Press, 2013).

40 Lorenz, 276–277.

41 Many of these problematics are explored in Joshua Paul Dale, Joyce Goggin, Julia Leyda, Anthony P. McIntire, and Diane Negra, *The Aesthetics and Affects of Cuteness* (New York and London: Routledge, 2016).

generate content for companies like LEGO.[42] Hence, as the wiki *TV Tropes* points out, "a lot of the film's humor comes from jokes that can be done with LEGO Toys, like the similar *LEGO Adaptation Game* series (which even has a game based on this film)" ("Western Animation"). Therefore, as Maaike Lauwaert has explained, "[b]y incorporating peripheral, many-to-many activities and practices within new products, these activities and practices are commodified [...] [and] work penetrates play. The result is a partly commodified geography of play in which certain divergent user practices are 'harvested' and commercially used".[43] True to Lauwaert's description, this same blogger goes on to explain that the

> "LEGO Adaptation Game" has become a catch-all term for a loosely-connected series of Multi-Platform VideoGames made by Travellers' Tales, based on combining the license for LEGO with that of another work, generally a film, as tie-ins to licensed toy lines based on the same films LEGO is producing and selling around the same time. These games [...] consist of LEGO interpretations of previously licensed work, with tongue-in-cheek, often parodical [sic] cut-scenes poking fun at both those works and the fact that they are made out of LEGO bricks.[44]

In other words, the labor of fans who have long produced "jokes that can be done with LEGO Toys" and short films on YouTube become both consumers of the bricks and producers of content based on the bricks. A portion of that content is then appropriated by LEGO and ultimately feeds an organizational form that rehashes "previously licensed work," and maintains control over storyworlds for the corporate generation of enormous profits.

But again, what is the big deal if everyone is having a good time? How seriously should one take a light-hearted toy and film that, we are told, is all about people being "inspired by each other, people taking something you made and making something new out of it," or making "whatever weird thing that comes into your head and building things only you can build"? First, as

42 For a detailed discussion of playbor in various media, see Julian Kücklich, "FCJ-025 Precarious Playbour: Modders and the Digital Gaming Industry," The Fibreculture Journal, Vol. 5 (2005), and Joyce Goggin "Playbour, Farming and Leisure," Ephemera: Theory and Politics in Organziation, Vol. 11, no. 4 (2011): 357–368. See also S.C. Bolton and M. Houlihan "Are we having fun yet? A consideration of workplace fun and engagement." In *Employee Relations*, Vol. 31, no. 6 (2009): 556–568, on employee "fun."

43 Lauwaert, 69.

44 "The Lego Movie" on TV Tropes, accessed February 15, 2019, http://tvtropes.org/pmwiki/pmwiki.php/WesternAnimation/TheLEGOMovie.

I intimated above, toys mold us as children into the adults we become – as the existence of the term AFOL would imply. In a related essay on *World of Warcraft*, Scott Rettberg has commented on how toys and games prepare us as adults for the labor market and how the game

> serves as a tool to educate its players in a range of behaviors and skills specific to the situation of conducting business in an economy controlled by corporations. The game is training a generation of good corporate citizens not only to consume well and to pay their dues, but also to climb the corporate ladder, to lead projects, to achieve sales goals, to earn and save, to work hard for better possessions, to play the markets, to win respect from their peers and their customers, to direct and encourage and cajole their underlings to outperform, to become better employees and perhaps, eventually, effective future CEOs.[45]

While this is the view of an academic, it is important to note that it is shared by IBM who published a report on games and entrepreneurship in 2007, in which we read, "[i]f you want to see what business leadership may look like in three to five years, look at what's happening in online games," claiming that video games, of which LEGO has produced many, train leaders to deftly navigate the motivational, emotional and social needs [...] in a highly competitive, distributed, virtual environment."[46]

Perhaps it is equally important to view the transmedial spread of narrative as an industrialized process "where integral elements of a fiction get dispersed systematically across multiple delivery channels for the purpose of creating a unified and coordinated entertainment experience" while generating profits.[47] If we connect this thought to Thomas Elsaesser's observation that narratives and games "'rehearse' life at the same time as they replay it" and that narratives and storytelling serve as "collective memory, as problem-solving mechanism, as imaginary resolution to real contradictions, as ordering principle of contingent events, as therapy for life's traumata, as consolation and agent of redemption," then the implications are vast.[48] To point to just

45 Rettberg, 33. It is something of a truism that play shapes us as children; hence Wallis Simons' piece entitled "Why Lego is ruining our kids' imaginations" for CNN news (CNN, accessed March 2, 2016, http://edition.cnn.com/2014/12/01/opinion/lego-imagination-opinion/index.html) in which he argues that "play is a vitally important part of a child's development, and toy manufactures are uniquely placed to influence their lives – for the better or for the worse."

46 "Virtual Worlds, Real Leaders."

47 Jenkins, "Transmedia Storytelling 101."

48 Elsaesser, 309.

one example, consider the contemporary role of authors and how they are now required to tell and sell their stories in a market hungry for transmedial spreadability. In Simone Murray's work on *The Adaptation Industry*, she explains how the ways in which storytelling has become part of the "creative industries" make it desirable for authors to engage in "twin-track writing," simultaneously producing novels and screenplays, and eventually game scenarios, while they "acknowledge that content proliferates across multiple platforms, often simultaneously and frequently with print its subsequent not its initial incarnation".[49] This is just one of the many ways that transmedia storytelling reflects the economics of media consolidation and convergence, or what industry observers call "synergy," rather than the free play of the signifier, the random combination of story elements, or the potential products of just anyone's imagination – unless these can be co-opted as playbor.

Conclusion: Freedom Friday or T.A.K.O.S. Tuesday?

In Mark Wolf's essay on *Star Wars* and LEGO, he explains that the adaptation of a film "into a physical playset is qualitatively different from narrative adaptation between audiovisual media," at least in part because "[t]he design [of LEGO playsets] has a way of compartmentalizing the film's action, even though [...] a number of locations are adjacent" as they were in the film, and then rendered in brick sets.[50] These observations capture the double message of *The LEGO Movie* and indeed, of the LEGO enterprise more generally, namely its acknowledgement, use, and self-conscious critique of the constant oscillation between the poles of free play and corporatized fun. LEGO negotiates inherent contradictions such as those entailed in promoting the creation of random "weird dorky stuff," as the characters in the movie call it, in playworlds in which "everything is thought out," or in following "the rules [to an] inter-locking brick thing" and "embrac[ing] what is special about you." So, as Lauwaert pointed out, there are rules and requirements that

49 Simone Murray, *The Adaptation Industry: The Cultural Economy of Contemporary Literary Adaptation* (New York and London: Routledge, 2012), 93, 95. Note that, at the time of writing, a quick trip to amazon.com will yield any number of spin-off products and titles from *The LEGO Movie*, including children's books and novelizations of the film with titles such as *The LEGO Movie: Junior Novel* by Kate Howard, *The LEGO Movie: Calling All Master Builders!* by Helen Murray, *The LEGO Movie: Meet Unikitty!* by Shari Last and *The LEGO Movie: Emmet's Awesome Day*, by Anna Holmes.
50 Mark J.P. Wolf, "Adapting the Death Star into LEGO: The Case of LEGO Set #10188." in *LEGO Studies: Examining the Building Blocks of a Transmedial Phenomenon*, edited by Mark J.P. Wolf, 15–40 (New York and Oxon: Routledge, 2014), 15, 28.

are "embedded into the design and promote specific user behaviour," hence claims made by toys and games companies about offering complete freedom of movement can only ever be partially true.[51] As Clare Parody has likewise suggested, "convergence culture may even be conditioning consumers to actively want to see" particular characters and storyworlds in various media.[52] Given that we all know that narrative and game worlds are structured by rules and delimited by specific parameters, it would appear that we are destined to repeat Hamlet's lament: "Oh God, I could be bounded in a nutshell and count myself a king of infinite space, were it not that I have bad dreams".[53]

Moreover, because totally "free play" is both a heuristic and a utopian notion, the issues I have just mentioned have plagued thought on play for centuries; at least since Kant and Schiller were writing about play in the 18th century. So how is the current paradigm any different and how does transmedia storytelling bring such irksome issues more sharply into focus? In part, the answer resides in the increasing complicity between play and industrialization at a historical juncture and in an economic paradigm in which notions such as the "creative industries" have become thoroughly naturalized. If this is coupled with Jenkins' argument that "the encyclopedic ambitions of transmedia texts often results [sic] in what might be seen as gaps or excesses in the unfolding of the story [...] so that readers [...] have a strong incentive to continue to elaborate on these story elements, working them over through their speculations, until they take on a life of their own," the implications are many and serious.[54] But here again, as anyone who works in the area of literary hermeneutics and gives much thought to how readers are interpolated when a text is activated will tell you, this is nothing new. What is different is the injection of technology and the immediacy that the internet affords fan culture to participate in storyworlds while also having considerable parts of their own worlds reciprocally shaped by narrative franchises. Coupled with the economic developments I have been at pains to sketch out here, the idea of spending time in LEGO Land takes on new resonance.

Likewise, I would concur with those scholars who argue that "there is one characteristic of modernity [...] emphasised by intellectuals since the eighteenth century: modernity is 'disenchanted'," while also considering that, in the present era of financialization, what mystifies and enchants is

51 Lauwaert, 25.

52 Parody, 216.

53 *Hamlet* 2:2.

54 Jenkins, "Transmedia Storytelling 101."

finance itself.[55] As Appadurai has argued "even a simple housing mortgage is a mysterious thing," structured as mortgages are on "immeasurably complex" derivative packages whereby "unlimited distances" separate "the instrument [of credit] and underlying commodity," such that they become "opaque quantitative forms that are illegible to the average citizen."[56] In other words, as Mark Hanna (Matthew McConaughey) so aptly explains to Jordan Belfort (Leonardo DiCaprio) in *The Wolf of Wall Street*, finance is a "fugazi, a fugazi. It's a wazy. It's a woozie. It's fairy dust." And this is where we now find our enchantment – and perhaps excitement, horror, and entertainment – namely, in the vicissitudes and functioning of the market, upon which the story at the heart of *The LEGO Movie* is built, and of which the film and the company provide such excellent, animated, toy illustrations. If we then connect this with recent work on myth and the market, along with my earlier observations about myth and simple story templates, and view both through the notions of narrative spreadability and transmedial profitability, then we finally begin to get a fuller picture of where contemporary enchantment comes from, namely the financial market and the way it structures imagination and creativity, and disseminates narrative today.[57]

And, given all of this, I feel compelled to conclude that one can only look on in awe at the cheeky corporate cleverness of a film that closes by suggesting that T.A.K.O.S. Tuesday will be superseded by "Freedom Friday." This, once again, ties into the larger argument of this essay about how laying open and poking fun at the very mechanisms that structure our capitalist realities and the LEGO franchise's increasing spread across media in a world-weary defeatist "amusing ourselves to death" fashion manages to boost the very sale of the movie and the larger franchise. One shudders to think what form of Kragle will be created to cement such a motivational tradition in place.

Works Cited

Ahmed, Sara. *The Promise of Happiness*. Durham and London: Duke UP, 2010.

Anderson, Ben. "Modulating the Excess of Affect." *The Affect Theory Reader*, edited by Melissa Gregg and Gregory J. Seigworth, 161–168. Durham and London: Duke UP.

55 Michael Saler, *As If: Modern Enchantment and the Literary Prehistory of Virtual Reality*. (New York: Oxford University Press, 2012), 8.

56 Saler, 101, 107.

57 On myth and the market, see the introduction to Miriam Meissner, *Narrating the Global Financial Crisis* (London and New York: Palgrave MacMillan, 2017), 1–20.

Appadurai, Arjun. *Banking on Words: The Failure of Language in the Age of Derivative Finance*. Chicago and London: The University of Chicago Press, 2016.

Berlant, Lauren. *Cruel Optimism*. Durham and London: Duke UP, 2010.

Bolton, S.C., and M. Houlihan. "Are we having fun yet? A consideration of workplace fun and engagement." *Employee Relations* 31, no. 6 (2009): 556–568.

Davies, William. *The Happiness Industry: How the Government and Big Business Sold Us Well-Being*. London and New York: Verso, 2015.

Derrida, Jacques. "Structure, Sign, and Play in the Discourse of the Human Sciences." In *Writing and Difference*, translated by Alan Bass, 278–295. Chicago: University of Chicago Press, 1978.

Ehrenreich, Barbara. *Smile or Die: How Positive Thinking Fooled America & The World*. Croydon: Granata, 2009.

Elsaesser, Thomas. "Pushing the Contradictions of the Digital: 'Virtual Reality' and 'Interactive Narrative' as Oxymorons between Narrative and Gaming." *New Review of Film and Television Studies* 12, no. 3 (2014): 295–311.

Froebel-Parker, J. "The Influence of Friedrich Froebel on Frank Lloyd Wright." *Froebel Web: An Online Resource*. Accessed March 4, 2016. www.froebelweb.org/web2000.html.

Goggin, Joyce. "Casinos and Sure Bets: *Ocean's Eleven* and Cinematic Money." *Money and Culture*, edited by Fiona Cox and Hans-Walter Schmidt-Hannisa, 285–297. Bern: Peter Lang, 2008.

—. "Playbour, Farming and Leisure." *Ephemera: Theory and Politics in Organization* 11, no. 4 (2011): 357–368. Accessed March 2, 2016. www.ephemerajournal.org/sites/default/files/11-4goggin.pdf.

—. "From Remake to Sequel: *Ocean's Eleven* and *Ocean's Twelve*." *Second Takes: Approaches to the Film Sequel*, edited by Caroline Jess-Cooke and Constantine Verevis, 105–121. New York: State University of New York Press, 2010.

—. "Qu'est qu'on réadapte? *Ocean's Eleven* et l'esthétique de la finance." In *De la page blanche aux salles obscures: Adaptation et réadaption dans le monde Anglophone*, translated by Ariane Hudelet, edited by Ariane Hudelet and Shannon Wells-Lassagne, 49–59. Rennes: Presses Universitaires de Rennes, 2011.

—. "Regulating Virtual Subjects: Finance, Fun and Games." Special issue *Financial Subjects: Culture and Materiality*, edited by Paul Langley and Andrew Leyshon. *Journal of Cultural Economy* 5, no. 4 (2012): 441–456. Accessed March 2, 2016. www.tandfonline.com/doi/pdf/10.1080/17530350.2012.702121.

Gray, Jonathan. *Show Sold Separately: Promos, Spoilers, and Other Media Paratexts*. New York: New York University Press, 2010.

Greimas, Algirdas Julien. *Sémantique structurale: recherche de méthode*. Paris: Larousse, 1966.

Hardt, Michael. "Affective Labor." *Boundary 2* 26.2 (1999): 89–100.

Harvey, David. "Time Space Compression and the Postmodern Condition." In *The Condition of Postmodernity*, 284–308. Oxford: Blackwell, 1991.

Huizinga, Johan. *Homo ludens: A Study of the Play Element in Culture*. 1938. Boston: The Beacon Press, 1955.

Jameson, Fredric. *Postmodernism or, The Cultural Logic of Late Capitalism*. Raleigh: Duke UP, 1991.

Jenkins, Henry. "Complete Freedom of Movement: Video Games as Gendered Play Spaces." In *From Barbie to Mortal Kombat: Gender and Computer Games*, edited by Justine Cassell and Henry Jenkins, 262–298. Boston: MIT Press, 2000.

—. "Transmedia Storytelling" 101. *Confessions of an Aca-Fan*, posted March 22, 2007. Accessed February 15, 2019. http://henryjenkins.org/2007/03/transmedia_storytelling_101.html.

Jenkins, Henry, Sam Ford, and Joshua Green. *Spreadable Media: Creating Value and Meaning in a Networked Culture*. New York and London: New York UP, 2013.

Keane, Stephen. *Disaster Movies: The Cinema of Catastrophe*. London and New York: Wallflower, 2006.

Kücklich, Julian. "FCJ-025 Precarious Playbour: Modders and the Digital Games Industry." *The Fibreculture Journal* 5 (2005), accessed March 2, 2016. http://five.fibreculturejournal.org/fcj-025-precarious-playbour-modders-and-the-digital-games-industry/.

Lahti, Martti. "As We Become Machines: Corporealized Pleasures in Video Games." In *The Video Game Theory Reader*, edited by Mark J.P. Wolf and Bernard Perron, 157–171. New York and London: Routledge, 2003.

Lauwaert, Maaike. *The Place of Play: Toys and Digital Cultures*. Amsterdam: Amsterdam UP, 2009.

LEGO Movie, The. Dir. Phil Lord and Christopher Miller. Warner Bros. 2014.

"LEGO 'promoting unrealistic body image'." *The Daily Mash*. June 18, 2015. Accessed March 2, 2016. www.thedailymash.co.uk/news/society/lego-promoting-unrealistic-body-image-2015061899397.

Lorenz, Konrad. "Die angeborenen Formen möglicher Erfahrung." *Zeitschrift für Tierpsychologie* 5, no. 2 (1943): 245–409.

Martin, Randy. "After Economy? Social Logics of the Derivative." *Social Text* 114, 31, no. 1 (Spring 2013): 83–106.

—. *The Financialization of Daily Live*. Philadelphia: Temple University Press, 2002.

—. "Taking an Administrative Turn: Derivative Logics for a Recharged Humanities." *Representations* 116, no. 1 (Fall 2011): 156–176.

Meissner, Miriam. *Narrating the Global Financial Crisis: Urban Imaginaries and the Politics of Myth*. London and New York: Palgrave Macmillan, 2017.

Murray, Simone. *The Adaptation Industry: The Cultural Economy of Contemporary Literary Adaptation*. New York and London: Routledge, 2012.

Newman, James. *Video Games*. London and New York: Routledge, 2004.

Ngai, Sianne. *Our Aesthetic Categories: Zany, Cute, Interesting*. Cambridge: Harvard UP, 2012.

Outbrain.com. "Everything awesome again? LEGO changes guidelines for bulk orders." *CNN*, January 14, 2016. Accessed March 1, 2016. http://edition.cnn.com/2015/10/26/arts/gallery/lego-artists/index.html.

Parody, Clare. "Franchising/Adaptation." *Adaptation* 4, no. 2 (2011): 210–218.

Petroff, Alanna. "Lego ditches Shell after Arctic oil protests." *CNN*. October 9, 2014: 8:07. Accessed March 1, 2016. http://money.cnn.com/2014/10/09/news/companies/lego-shell-greenpeace/index.html.

Postman, Neil. *Amusing Ourselves to Death*. London: Methuen, 1984.

Propp, Vladimir. *Morphologie du conte*. Paris: Éditions du Seuil, 1970.

Quest, Richard. "LEGO boss reads *The Opposable Mind*." *CNN*. Accessed March 1, 2016. http://edition.cnn.com/search/?text=lego.

—. "LEGO posts 25% revenue jump, profits up 31%." *CNN*. Accessed March 1, 2016. http://edition.cnn.com/search/?text=lego.

Rettberg, Scott. "Corporate Ideology in *World of Warcraft*," in *Digital Culture, Play, and Identity: A* World of Warcraft *Reader*, edited by Hilde Corneliussen and Jill Walker Rettberg, 19–39. Boston: MIT Press, 2008.

Saler, Michael. *As If: Modern Enchantment and the Literary Prehistory of Virtual Reality*. Oxford: Oxford UP, 2012.

Sanders, Julie. *Adaptation and Appropriation* (*The New Critical Idiom*). New York: Routledge, 2006.

Simmel, Georg. *The Philosophy of Money*, edited by David Fisby, translated by Tom Bottomore and David Fisby. London and New York: Routledge, 2004.

Taylor, Mark C. *Confidence Games: Money and Markets in a World without Redemption*. Chicago and London: The University of Chicago Press, 2004.

Torres, César Albarràn. "Gambling Machines and the Automation of Desire." *PLATFORM: Journal of Media and Communication* 5, no. 1 (October 2013): 34–51.

"Virtual Worlds, Real Leaders: On-line games put the future of business leadership on display" (2007). Accessed March 2, 2016. http://domino.watson.ibm.com/comm/www_innovate.nsf/images
/gio-gaming/$FILE/ibm_gio_gaming_report.pdf.

Wallace, David Foster. "E Unibus Pluram: Television and U.S. Fiction." *Review of Contemporary Fiction* 13, no. 2 (Summer 1993): 151–194.

Wallis Simons, Jake. "Opinion: Why LEGO is ruining our kids' imaginations." *CNN*. Accessed March 2, 2016. http://edition.cnn.com/2014/12/01/opinion/lego-imagination-opinion/index.html.

"Western Animation/*The Lego Movie*." *TV Tropes*. Accessed September 13, 2017. http://tvtropes.org/pmwiki/pmwiki.php/WesternAnimation/TheLEGOMovie.

Wolf, Mark. "Adapting the Death Star into LEGO: The Case of LEGO Set #10188." in *LEGO Studies: Examining the Building Blocks of a Transmedial Phenomenon,* edited by Mark J.P. Wolf, 15–40. New York and Oxon: Routledge, 2014.

Wolf of Wall Street, The. Dir. Martin Scorsese. Paramount Pictures, 2013.

Yano, Christine R. *Pink Globalization: Hello Kitty's Trek across the Pacific.* Durham: Duke University Press, 2013.

"7 things you might not know about LEGO." *CNN.* Accessed March 2, 2016. http://edition.cnn.com/videos/showbiz/2014/02/17/orig-7-cool-things-about-lego-npr.cnn.

About the author

Joyce Goggin is a senior lecturer at the University of Amsterdam, where she teaches literature, film, and media studies. She has published on gambling and finance in various media and is currently writing on casino culture, gamification, and the entertainment industries. Her recent publications include "'How do those Danish bastards sleep at night?': Fan Labour and the Power of Cuteness" in *The Games and Culture Journal* (2018) and "The Pro Wrestling Audience as Imagined Community," forthcoming in *Convergent Wrestling.*

9. Localization as Adaptation in the *Wolfenstein* Franchise

Werner Schäfke-Zell

Abstract
In a globalized market, media products are adapted to fit the constraints of specific markets and appeal to their preferred tastes. As the *Wolfenstein* franchise is set against the backdrop of the Second World War, it has to address cultural memory in a preferred way. The franchise constructs cultural memory of the Second World War and the holocaust differently, depending on the intended audience. "Family friendly" versions exist, tailored for branded platforms such as NES and iOS, as well as "sanitized" versions for the German market, where legal provisions pose constraints on depictions of Nazism. The resulting corporate adaptations of *Wolfenstein* games are shown to contradict the intention of legal statutes regarding cultural memory, and lead to further mythologization of Nazism.

Key words: Localization; video games; cultural memory; National Socialism in popular media; Wolfenstein; law and humanities

Introduction

Cinema, video games, comics, and novels continue to deal with the Second World War, National Socialism (NS), and the Holocaust. The foci of these media products range widely from historical documentation aimed at enlightening the audience about the inhumanity of the Holocaust (e.g. *Maus*; *Schindler's List*), to films spicing their plot with Nazi antagonists (e.g. *Raiders of the Lost Ark*; *Captain America*), to mere "Nazisploitation" that

Fehrle, J. and W. Schäfke, *Adaptation in the Age of Media Convergence*, Taylor & Francis Group, 2019
DOI 10.5117/9789462983663_CH09

amplifies exploitation and splatter with "factual horror" (e.g. *Ilsa: She-Wolf of the SS*; *Inglourious Basterds*).[1]

Regardless of exploitative characteristics, any such media products offer an interpretation of the past. Due to their distinctive influence on popular culture, the *Wolfenstein* video games have been argued to be a "site of mass-schooling" about the Second World War.[2] Despite their use of retro science fiction elements, the games also feature many historically accurate elements and a meticulously designed Second World War backdrop. The games' production company filters these factuality signals in two ways. Firstly, when games are designed or redesigned for a broader audience (in the case of the *Wolfenstein 3D* SNES version and *Wolfenstein RPG*), and secondly when they are localized for the German market, where legal restrictions exist regarding the display of NS symbols and NS rule.[3] This process can be called institutional filtering, meaning that production companies and social institutions set constraints on media content.

The changes to the *Wolfenstein* games go beyond simple filtering of forbidden symbols like the swastika, and affect the ideological interpretations of the past such games offer. The result is a superficially "sanitized" media product that camouflages WWII references. This camouflaging of the war backdrop intensifies its function as a factuality signal. The camouflaging grants NS rule an aura of taboo, further adding to the mythologization of Nazi Germany in the *Wolfenstein* series. Furthermore, the interpretations of the past that the *Wolfenstein* games offer become more selective when they are adapted to the German market.

By examining the legal background for the filtering of *Wolfenstein* games, and how it amplifies the WWII mythologization in the filtered version, this chapter provides an exemplary look at adaptations of a global transmedial franchise in the course of transculturation processes. The chapter furthermore shows the interplay of various contextual domains in shaping discourse. The following section introduces the ways in which the *Wolfenstein* series follows popular media strategies for remembering the Holocaust. Then, the processes of institutional filtering that the *Wolfenstein* games undergo are highlighted, before discussing the German

1 Steven Spielberg, *Raiders of the Lost Ark* (1981); Joe Johnston, *Captain America* (2011); Don Edmonds, *Ilsa: She-Wolf of the SS* (1974); Quentin Tarantino, *Inglourious Basterds* (2009).

2 Jeff Hayton, "Digital Nazis: Genre, History and the Displacement of Evil in First-Person Shooters." In *Nazisploitation!: The Nazi Image in Low-Brow Cinema and Culture*, ed. Daniel H. Magilow, Elizabeth Bridges and Vander Lugt, Kristin T. (New York: Continuum, 2012), 200.

3 Inc. id Software, *Wolfenstein 3D* (Imagineer Co., Limited, 1993); id Mobile, *Wolfenstein RPG* (Apple, Inc., 2009).

legal background for these filtering processes regarding the *Wolfenstein* series' German market. The German legal background is then compared to the actual filtering that happened in the *Wolfenstein* games. This allows for an evaluation of the results of institutional filtering. The final section shows how the narrative strategy of mythologization is amplified in the filtered *Wolfenstein* games, and why this seems to be a paradoxical result of the intentions behind the legal restrictions against depicting (symbols of) the Nazi regime.

Mythologization of the Holocaust in Popular Media

What are the views of the past in popular media, and how do they conceptualize history? Florian Evers examines popular media strategies for narrating the Holocaust and the depiction of Nazi Germany. One of the strategies he reconstructs can be found in the *Wolfenstein* games. It is the narrative strategy of mythologization (*Mythisierung*).[4] The tabooed cultural trauma of a Western society committing genocide is transformed into a modern myth by amalgamating fact with fantastic fiction. In mythicized narratives, the world can function according to dichotomies of good and evil.[5] What cannot be explained in a factual discourse is explained by an irrational, mythical discourse. Mythologization enables explanations of the irrationality of a modern, "rational" society committing genocide:

> For what is most scary about Nazism is that it could happen again. That the murder of millions could take place at the center of Western civilization is frightening, as is the understanding that it was not sadists who were the perpetrators of genocide as Nazisploitation films would have you believe.[6]

Due to the genre's specific narrative possibilities, first-person shooters narrate stories as shaped by individual actions. Set during the Second World War, *Wolfenstein* consists of missions whose goals are to hinder Nazi Germany's

4 Florian Evers, *Vexierbilder des Holocaust: Ein Versuch zum historischen Trauma in der Populärkultur*, Populäre Kultur und Medien 4 (Berlin: Lit, 2011), 60–65; cf. Hayton, "Digital Nazis," 208, who argues the Second World War to be "mythologized" in the *Wolfenstein* games.

5 Eva Kingsepp, "Hitler as Our Devil? Nazi Germany in Mainstream Media." In *Monsters in the Mirror: Representations of Nazism in Post-War Popular Culture*, ed. Sara Buttsworth and Maartje M. Abbenhuis (Santa Barbara, CA: Praeger, 2010), 37.

6 Hayton, "Digital Nazis," 210.

victory. Staying with the genre conventions, they therefore display history as shaped by the individual acts of the player.[7]

Combining Evers' and Hayton's findings, the appeal of the *Wolfenstein* video game series becomes explainable: within the fictional but semi-historical scenario of the *Wolfenstein* games, the player can seemingly fight against engaging with the irrationality of Nazism and the Holocaust by playing the game. The player as an individual can play through the etiological mythos of the birth of the post-war world by purging it of National Socialism.

Apart from the etiological narrative structure, the mythologization of National Socialism is achieved by depicting National Socialism as something supernatural and demonic; an evil the player can destroy by aiming for its corrupted leaders. This demonization is facilitated by the narrative conventions of first-person shooters, which model dichotomous worlds of good vs. evil, in which National Socialism can take the place of transcendental evil. This is a rather extreme example of mythologization as one of the general principles of making a historical event palatable for cultural memory.[8]

By only drawing on parts of historical National Socialism "the Holocaust remains unspoken and Jews intriguingly absent" in the game.[9] This highly selective historical accuracy prevents a connection of the game's storyworld to traumatic elements of the actual historical past. National Socialism is thus conceptualized in the *Wolfenstein* games as partly detached from history's burden. Instead, National Socialism becomes a modern myth detached from the all too concrete and ghastly aspects of 20th-century history. The myth narrates a transcendental struggle between good and evil. In this form of mythicized historical fiction, fictional and counterfactual narratives become acceptable, appealing to the taste of a wider public. This mythical narrative character not only detaches the game from the historical burden of its setting, it also makes the inclusion of contrafactual fictional events, conspiracy theories, and the fantastic acceptable, as these are often elements of mythical genres.

The *Wolfenstein* series' constructions of the past aim for acceptability by larger/mass audiences. These constructions thus need to conform to their audiences' cultural memories. The *Wolfenstein* games are part of an international franchise, which aims to sell its products to various groups with differing cultural memories. It is therefore interesting to see what changes to products of this franchise are entailed by the process of localization

7 ibid., 202–206.

8 Aleida Assmann, *Der lange Schatten der Vergangenheit: Erinnerungskultur und Geschichtspolitik* (München: Beck, 2006), 40.

9 Hayton, "Digital Nazis," 210–211.

for the German market. The localization process is best understood as an adaptation process, as described by Regina Schober in her article in this volume. Adaptation, then, is not merely the appropriation of the "original" for a new medium. Rather, speaking in a biological metaphor, media adaptation can be understood as the changes to a media product (i.e. the "mutation" of the media product) in order to make it "fit" into a new environment with its specific constraints and possibilities.

Looking at the adaptation of the *Wolfenstein* games for the German market, the process goes beyond the filtering of forbidden symbols. Instead, the changes, ostensibly brought about by legal restrictions, amount to an amplification of the mythologization process of the Second World War as described above. Due to the series' sensationalist use of a delicate theme, extra-medial factors demand the games' adaptation in order to be sold on the German market. In popular discussions of this process, German legislature prohibiting the use of Nazi symbols is usually named, but as I will argue, the changes in fact go beyond reasons commensurable with the law. As I will show, the adaptation processes that the *Wolfenstein* games underwent in order to become saleable on the German market are partly inconsistent with the restrictions that can be derived from applicable law on this topic. The camouflaging of references to Nazi Germany, deriving from political decisions and broader societal efforts to control the rise of Neo-Nazism in Germany, render National Socialism as taboo, and as a result give it the appeal or lure of the forbidden. This is a filtering process that is upheld in the German version of the most recent installment of the *Wolfenstein* series, *Wolfenstein: The New Order*, whose removal of references to the Holocaust conserves the "sanitized" and mythicized concepts of Nazism that have marked these games' German editions from the franchise's first installment.[10]

The *Wolfenstein* video game series and its institutional narrative filtering

Since 1981, eleven *Wolfenstein* video games have been released. The following list gives an overview of the games as well as those variant versions that are discussed in this chapter (passing reference to other *Wolfenstein* games is made in footnotes):

- *Castle Wolfenstein* (1981; not discussed in this chapter),
- *Beyond Castle Wolfenstein* (1984; not discussed in this chapter),

10 Bethesda Game Studios et al., *Wolfenstein: The New Order* (Bethesda Softworks, L.L.C., 2014).

- *Wolfenstein 3D* (1992;[11] discussed in this chapter including its 1993 SNES version),[12]
- *Spear of Destiny* (1992;[13] discussed in this chapter),
- *Return to Castle Wolfenstein* (2001;[14] discussed in this chapter including its 2001 German version),[15]
- *Wolfenstein: Enemy Territory* (2003; not discussed in this chapter),
- *Wolfenstein RPG* (2008; discussed in this chapter) for smartphones,[16]
- *Wolfenstein* (2009; discussed in this chapter),[17]
- *Wolfenstein: The New Order* (2014; discussed in this chapter),[18]
- *Wolfenstein: The Old Blood* (2015; discussed in this chapter),[19] and
- *Wolfenstein II: The New Colossus* (2017; not discussed in this chapter).[20]

Different types of media products can be subject to different laws or rating systems, limiting their permitted content or constraining their availability to audiences below a certain age. Trade associations such as the Motion Picture Association of America's film rating system and other limited companies established by the relevant trade associations conduct such self-regulation. An example of this is the rating system of the Entertainment Software Self-Regulation Body (*Unterhaltungssoftware Selbstkontrolle* GmbH, hereafter USK), which is applied to video games. In addition to a certain medium's aesthetic possibilities and boundaries, internationally distributed media products face further constraints. In this case, institutions such as self-regulation bodies function as gatekeepers for the distribution of media products.

Media companies consider such constraints when designing their products with certain target audiences in mind and when localizing their products to

11 Inc. id Software, *Wolfenstein 3D* (Apogee Software, Limited, 1992).

12 Inc. id Software, *Wolfenstein 3D* (Imagineer Co., Limited, 1993).

13 Inc. id Software, *Spear of Destiny* (FormGen Corp., 1992).

14 Gray Matter Interactive Studios, Inc. et al., *Return to Castle Wolfenstein* (Activision UK, Limited, 2001)

15 Gray Matter Interactive Studios, Inc. et al., *Return to Castle Wolfenstein* (Activision Deutschland GmbH, 2001).

16 id Mobile, *Wolfenstein RPG* (Apple, Inc., 2009).

17 Inc. Raven Software et al., *Wolfenstein* (Activision Publishing, Inc., 2009).

18 Bethesda Game Studios et al., *Wolfenstein: The New Order* (Bethesda Softworks, L.L.C., 2014).

19 MachineGames et al., *Wolfenstein: The Old Blood* (Bethesda Softworks, L.L.C., 2015).

20 Bethesda Game Studios et al., *Wolfenstein II: The New Colossus* (Bethesda Softworks, L.L.C., 2017).

markets with specific constraints.[21] Such local constraints can often be cast into law, prescribing self-regulation procedures and delineating forbidden content. An example of the redesign of a product for a certain target audience is the 1993 SNES version of *Wolfenstein 3D*.[22] In the process of porting the game from computer to console, many violent elements as well as references to Nazi Germany were removed from its gameplay. The changes to the storyworld thus reached beyond what was technically necessary to adapt the game to the new platform in order to meet the constraints of the SNES's "family friendly" branding.[23] In contrast, the localization of *Return to Castle Wolfenstein* (2001) for the German market reflects German legal constraints.[24] These constraints made it necessary for the producers to remove certain references to Nazi Germany. A reduction of violent gameplay features, in contrast, was only necessary for a number of instances of ultra-violence.

Media companies themselves conducted these changes, functioning as "narrative filters in the same way as material or technical media do."[25] As this example shows, the narrative filtering of the *Wolfenstein* series is an interesting case, since it is not solely motivated in relation to a target audience, but by the target market's legislation. It is also noteworthy that the video games in question are treated differently in legal terms from comparable movies or books. This shows how local constraints can preserve clear-cut distinctions between media types, based on lawmakers' cultural biases against newer media.[26]

21 E.g. Dennis Kogel, "Wolfenstein: The New Order – Interview mit Bethesda: Warum die deutsche Version anders ist," *GameStar*, May 10, 2014, accessed January 20, 2017, www.gamestar.de/spiele/wolfenstein-the-new-order/artikel/wolfenstein_the_new_order,49503,3055635.html%20viewed%202015-04-29.

22 Inc. id Software, *Wolfenstein 3D* (Imagineer Co., Limited, 1993).

23 Cf. "Nintendo of America's video game content guidelines and an assessment of their policy" by Steven A. Schwartz and Janet Schwartz, *Parent's Guide to Video Games* (Rocklin, CA: Prima, 1994), 21–24.

24 Gray Matter Interactive Studios, Inc. et al., *Return to Castle Wolfenstein* (Activision Deutschland GmbH, 2001).

25 Karl N. Renner, "Erzählen im Zeitalter der Medienkonvergenz." In *Medien – Erzählen – Gesellschaft: Transmediales Erzählen im Zeitalter der Medienkonvergenz*, ed. Karl N. Renner, Dagmar von Hoff and Matthias Krings, Media Convergence/Medienkonvergenz 2 (Berlin: de Gruyter, 2013), 4, my translation.

26 The frequently criticized fact that video games face more restrictions than movies in Germany (Michael Kauert, "Computerrecht – Computerspiele." In *Medienrecht: Praxishandbuch*, Vol. 2, ed. Artur-Axel Wandtke and Claudia Ohst, 3rd ed., 5 vols. (Berlin, Boston: de Gruyter, 2014), 2:522, paragraph 177) is easily demonstrated when looking at the first official *Wolfenstein* movie, released in 2009 (Lasse Nolte, *Der Goldene Nazivampir von Absam 2. Das Geheimnis von Schloß Kottlitz* (2007)). Unlike the *Wolfenstein* video games, it was neither indexed nor confiscated in Germany. The movie is a German production and its title translates literally to "The Golden

The legal basis for institutional narrative filtering of video games in Germany lies in limitations to the right to freedom of expression granted by article 5 of the Basic Law (*Grundgesetz*) provided by, among others, the Criminal Code (*Strafgesetzbuch*, hereafter StGB), as well as the Protection of Young Persons Act (*Jugendschutzgesetz*, hereafter JuSchG).[27] All data

Nazi Vampire of Absam 2." The holder of the rights of the *Wolfenstein* franchise, id Software, approved the movie's use of elements of the franchise.

27 Basic Law, GG, Federal Ministry of Justice (2014), accessed March 25, 2015, www.gesetze-im-internet.de/englisch_gg/; German Criminal Code, StGB, Federal Ministry of Justice (2013), accessed July 11, 2013, www.gesetze-im-internet.de/englisch_stgb/; Protection of Young Persons Act, JuSchG, Federal Ministry of Family Affairs, Senior Citizens, Women and Youth, accessed July 11, 2013, www.bmfsfj.de/RedaktionBMFSFJ/Abteilung5/Pdf-Anlagen/juSchGenglisch,property=pdf,bereich=bmfsfj,rwb=true.pdf. Article 5, paragraph 1 of the Basic Law describes the right to freedom of expression, forbidding censorship (my emphases): "*Every person shall have the right freely to express and disseminate his opinions in speech, writing, and pictures* and to inform himself without hindrance from generally accessible sources. Freedom of the press and freedom of reporting by means of broadcasts and films shall be guaranteed. *There shall be no censorship.*" The "censorship" precluded here means censorship of products before their publication and distribution, i.e. pre-censorship. Content control after a medium's publication (i.e. post-censorship) is made possible by article 5, paragraph 2, which states the limitation of the freedom of expression by provisions of further laws. Art, however, is attributed especially high value in this context: "Art and scholarship, research, and teaching shall be free" (paragraph 3). The conclusion might lie close at hand that, if video games were considered pieces of art in judicature, they would be granted special protection under German basic law (Michael Köhne, "Kennzeichen verfassungswidriger Organisationen in Computerspielen," *Deutsche Richterzeitung* 81 (2003)). Subsequently, Nazi Symbols forbidden in Germany would be no issue for selling *Wolfenstein* games in Germany. However, judicature applies an "open" or "formalistic concept of art" instead of a "material concept of art" (Thomas Fischer et al., *Strafgesetzbuch und Nebengesetze*, 58th ed., Beck'sche Kurz-Kommentare 10 (München: Beck, 2011), 775, § 86, no. 21). In order to delimit what is considered art in terms of Article 5, paragraph 3 of the Basic Law, the formalistic concept of art examines the production process, the design and the composition of the media product in question. Legal studies explicitly note that it is hardly possible to differentiate between movies and video games based on the formalistic legal concept of art due to media convergence (*Medienkonvergenz*; Marc Liesching, "Hakenkreuze in Film, Fernsehen und Computerspielen: Verwendung verfassungsfeindlicher Kennzeichen in Unterhaltungsmedien," *Multimedia und Recht* 13, no. 5 (2010): 311; Kauert, "Computerrecht – Computerspiele," 2:572, paragraph 177). Media convergence in the formalistic understanding pertains to the production process of the media product in question. There is no difference between movies and video games when comparing investment sums, the number of workers, and the professions involved in the production of these media types (Liesching, 311; Köhne, 211–212). More importantly, the individual assessment of media products following the formalistic concept of art entails the legal rationale that the freedom of art according to article 5 of the Basic Law does not take precedence over the art's content being punishable (Fischer et al., *Strafgesetzbuch und Nebengesetze*, 1235, § 184, no. 8). Instead, a holistic assessment (*Gesamtabwägung*) of the individual media product in question is conducted (ibid., 775, § 86, no. 21). It is noteworthy that an inflationary use of forbidden symbols, as can be found in most of the *Wolfenstein* games, might be considered as not being "in

media to be electronically or physically distributed in Germany have to be examined for content harmful to young persons.[28] No data media may be distributed to young persons in Germany before this examination is completed.[29] The Supreme Youth Protection Authorities of the Federal States (*Oberste Landesjugendbehörden*, hereafter OLJB) authorize the Entertainment Software Self-Regulation Body (USK) to rate video games[30] against a rating system established by the OLJB.[31]

The rating procedure of the USK and its following steps can have one of three results, which impose restrictions on the sale and marketing of video games:

1. Mild restrictions, being rated "not released for young people" by the USK;
2. Severe restrictions, not being rated by the USK and optionally subsequently indexed by the Federal Department for Media Harmful to Young Persons (*Bundesprüfstelle für jugendgefährdende Medien*, BPjM);
3. Confiscation, i.e. the criminalization of sale and marketing by court order.

If the USK considers a video game to be "harmful to young people," then the mildest restrictions will apply. The video game is then labeled by the USK as "not released for young people," i.e. persons under the age of 18. The criteria relate to instigation of violence, crime, and racism as well as denial of the rule of law.[32]

Severe restrictions apply to video games that do not receive a label from the USK because they are considered "*severely* harmful to young people." If a video game is considered to be in that category the USK informs the OLJB. Consequently, a video game can be indexed by the BPjM.[33] The same restrictions apply if a video game remains unrated.[34] The criteria relevant to the *Wolfenstein* series are glorification of war, ultra-violence, and especially displaying "in a disgraceful manner people who are dying or are exposed to

the service of art" in general, and thus might still be punishable by criminal law (Liesching, 310). The different treatment of different media product types however, is considered problematic in legal studies (Köhne, 211; Liesching, 309–310). Nonetheless, the use of forbidden symbols in video games is scarcely treated by research and in judicature (ibid., 309–310).

28 JuSchG, §§ 12 and 14; Kauert, 2:572, paragraph 178.

29 JuSchG, § 12, paragraph 3; Kauert, 2:572, paragraph 178.

30 JuSchG, § 14, paragraph 6.

31 Described in ibid., § 14, paragraph 2.

32 According to ibid., § 18, paragraph 1.

33 The BPjM is established by ibid., §§ 19–25.

34 Ibid., § 18, paragraph 1.

severe physical or psychic suffering."[35] Another criterion in this paragraph is that the video game in question violates certain paragraphs in the StGB, which deal with similar issues.[36]

The most severe restriction, illegalization of sale and marketing of a video game, results in confiscation (*Einziehung*).[37] Confiscations are issued by court order. The first instance in these cases is a Local Court (*Amtsgericht*, AG). A confiscation order requires that the video game violates criminal law, usually in relation to the same paragraphs of the StGB listed in the JuSchG.[38]

The restrictions to sales and marketing that are imposed by indexing mean significant economic damage for the publishing companies of the video games in question.[39] In order to avoid indexing and any subsequent economic damage, there is an existing practice of exploratory talks between the publishing companies and the USK. This practice is both recommended by and criticized in the legal literature.[40] Such exploratory talks, as well as implicit or explicit anticipation based on the publishing companies' interpretations of relevant legislation, can be assumed to form the basis for self-censorship of video games by their respective makers or adapters.

Only the German versions of the two recent *Wolfenstein* video games were rated "not released for young people" by the USK, i.e. the localized German versions of *Wolfenstein: The New Order*, and *Wolfenstein: The Old Blood*.[41] All other German and non-German versions of *Wolfenstein* games were not rated by the USK and subsequently indexed by the BPjM. In individual cases, indexed games were also confiscated (*Wolfenstein 3D* and *Wolfenstein*) or never even released in Germany (*Wolfenstein RPG*).[42] A closer description

35 Ibid., § 15, paragraph 2.

36 Ibid.

37 StGB, §§ 74 and 74d.

38 JuSchG, § 15, paragraph 2.

39 Kauert, "Computerrecht – Computerspiele," 2:573, paragraph 180.

40 A recommendation can be found in ibid.; A critique can be found in: Theresia Höynck and Christian Pfeiffer, "Verbot von "Killerspielen"? Thesen und Vorschläge zur Verbesserung des Jugendmedienschutzes," *Zeitschrift für Rechtspolitik* 40, no. 3 (2007): 93–94.

41 Bethesda Game Studios et al., *Wolfenstein: The New Order* (Bethesda Softworks, L.L.C., 2014); MachineGames et al., *Wolfenstein: The Old Blood* (Bethesda Softworks, L.L.C., 2015).

42 Muse Software, *Castle Wolfenstein* (Muse Software, 1981): indexed (*Bundesanzeiger*, no. 97 (1987)); Muse Software, *Beyond Castle Wolfenstein* (Muse Software, 1984): the game has apparently not been rated, which gives it the same legal status as an indexed game; Inc. id Software, *Wolfenstein 3D* (Apogee Software, Limited, 1992): indexed (*Bundesanzeiger*, no. 20 (1994)), and confiscated (AG München January 25, 1994); Inc. id Software, *Wolfenstein 3d* (Atari Corp., 1994): apparently not rated, and confiscated (AG Berlin Tiergarten December 07, 1994); Inc. id Software, *Wolfenstein 3D* (Imagineer Co., Limited, 1993): indexed (*Bundesanzeiger*, no. 20 (1994)); Inc. id Software and Stalker Entertainment, *Wolfenstein 3D* (BAM! Entertainment, Inc., 2002):

of video games' legal treatment illustrates the pitfalls which the production companies behind the *Wolfenstein* games aimed to avoid when adjusting their games to the German market.

Legal reasons for the narrative filtering of *Wolfenstein* games in Germany

Two reasons for the indexing and confiscation of *Wolfenstein* games are recognized in legal literature.[43] The criteria for indexing pertain to depictions of ultra-violence.[44] The criteria for confiscation, meanwhile, regard the display of violence and of unconstitutional symbols, e.g. swastikas,[45]

indexed (*Bundesanzeiger*, no. 224 (2003)); Inc. id Software, *Spear of Destiny* (FormGen Corp., 1992): indexed (*Bundesanzeiger*, no. 62 (1999)); Gray Matter Interactive Studios, Inc. et al., *Return to Castle Wolfenstein* (Activision UK, Limited, 2001): indexed (*Bundesanzeiger*, no. 41 (2002)); *Return to Castle Wolfenstein* (DE version): indexed (BAnz. 81, 2002); L.L.C. Raster Productions, *Return to Castle Wolfenstein: Operation Resurrection* (Activision Publishing, Inc., 2003): indexed (*Bundesanzeiger*, no. 227 (2004)); L.L.C. Nerve Software et al., *Return to Castle Wolfenstein: Tides of War* (Activision Publishing, Inc.): indexed (*Bundesanzeiger*, no. 99 (2007)); Inc. Raven Software et al., *Wolfenstein* (Activision UK, Limited, 2009): indexed (*Bundesanzeiger*, no. 164 (2009)); Inc. Raven Software et al., *Wolfenstein* (Activision Pty., Limited, 2009): indexed (*Bundesanzeiger*, no. 198 (2009)), and confiscated (JurionRS 45327 (AG Detmold January 19, 2010); Inc. Raven Software et al., *Wolfenstein* (Activision UK, Limited, 2009): indexed (*Bundesanzeiger*, no. 10 (2013)); Inc. Raven Software et al., *Wolfenstein* (Activision Blizzard Deutschland GmbH, 2014): distribution in Germany stopped and all media withdrawn by publisher; Inc. Raven Software et al., *Wolfenstein* (Activision Korea, 2009): indexed (*Bundesanzeiger*, no. 60 (2010)); Inc. Raven Software et al., *Wolfenstein* (Activision Publishing, Inc., 2009): indexed (*Bundesanzeiger*, no. 66 (2010)); id Mobile, *Wolfenstein RPG* (Apple, Inc., 2009): no distribution in Germany by publisher; Bethesda Game Studios et al., *Wolfenstein: The New Order* (Bethesda Softworks, L.L.C., 2014): Non-German versions are not distributed in Germany, as they cannot be downloaded after purchase from their online distribution platform due to geo-lock; the localized German version is rated "18" by the USK; MachineGames et al., *Wolfenstein: The Old Blood* (Bethesda Softworks, L.L.C., 2015): Non-German versions are not distributed in Germany due to geo-lock; the localized German version is rated "18" by the USK.

43 Liesching, "Hakenkreuze in Film, Fernsehen und Computerspielen"; Antje Schumann, "Ist die Ausfuhr von Computerspielen mit NS-Symbolen strafbar? Bemerkungen zu § 86a Abs. 1 Nr. 2 StGB," *Multimedia und Recht* 14, no. 7 (2011).

44 JuSchG, § 18, paragraph 1.

45 StGB, §§ 131 and 86a, respectively; *id.*, § 86a, paragraph 1 on the "Use of Symbols of Unconstitutional Organizations" punishes, among other things, production, import, stock (no. 2) and domestic distribution (no. 1) of certain symbols (no. 2). The law pertains to symbols used as "means of propaganda, the contents of which are intended to further the aims of a former National Socialist organization" (no. 4) with "imprisonment for not more than three years or a fine." Paragraph 2 further specifies the type of symbols in question: "in particular, flags, insignia, uniforms, slogans and forms of greeting." There are three goods, this law aims to protect: 1) the

without educational intent.[46] Legal studies reconstruct the intentions behind the prohibition of the display of unconstitutional symbols to achieve the "banishment" (*Verbannung*) of the forbidden symbols from public view.[47] A ruling of the Federal Constitutional Court (*Bundesverfassungsgericht*) explicitly speaks of the prohibition serving a "tabooing function" (*Tabusierungsfunktion*).[48] The judicial aim of setting up a "communicative taboo" (*kommunikatives Tabu*)[49] has been criticized, however. Firstly, a

constitutional order, 2) political peace, 3) Germany's international reputation (Schumann, "Ist die Ausfuhr von Computerspielen mit NS-Symbolen strafbar?" 440–441). While the last good pertains to the export of objects containing or displaying forbidden symbols (ibid.), the first good especially seems to find application in judicature on the *Wolfenstein* games (cf. Liesching, "Hakenkreuze in Film, Fernsehen und Computerspielen").

46 There are exceptions to the media content that falls under this law, depending on the assumed communicative intention of the media product. Media products intended for political and historical education in agreement with constitutional values do not fall under this law due to the so-called provision of social adequacy (*Sozialadäquanzklausel*; StGB, § 86, paragraph; cf. Liesching, 309, footnote 3). This provision exempts media products "if the means of propaganda or the act serves to further civil enlightenment, to avert unconstitutional aims, to promote art or science, research or teaching, reporting about current historical events or similar purposes." The application of law subsumes historical drama movies such as Steven Spielberg, *Schindler's List* (1993) under this provision. However, it appears difficult to subsume movies such as Spielberg, *Raiders of the Lost Ark*, Spielberg, *Indiana Jones and the Last Crusade* (1989), or the counterfactual Quentin Tarantino movie *Inglourious Basterds* (2009) under this provision as well (Liesching, "Hakenkreuze in Film, Fernsehen und Computerspielen," 309–310). The divergent treatment of similar plots in different media is exemplified when comparing the indexed *Wolfenstein* game *Spear of Destiny* with the *Indiana Jones* movies (Inc. id Software, *Spear of Destiny* (FormGen Corp., 1992)). In *Spear of Destiny* the protagonist controlled by the player (the player avatar) is an allied agent. This agents' mission is to capture the Spear of Destiny from the Nazis. The context of the appearance of forbidden symbols in the two *Indiana Jones* movies and the game *Spear of Destiny* is congruent with regard to Nazi characters functioning as antagonists and the genre of fantastic historical fiction. The culpability of displaying NS symbols in video games when assigned to the game's enemies is addressed by a judgment of the Higher Regional Court in Frankfurt am Main (19 Neue Zeitschrift für Strafrecht 356 (OLG Frankfurt am Main, March 18, 1998)). The Court ruled that StGB, § 86a, paragraph 1, no. 1 applies, even if the forbidden Nazi symbols are assigned to video game characters functioning as enemies in the respective game, superseding a regional court's previous ruling (cf. Schumann, 440). If judgments regarding the culpability of the distribution of *Wolfenstein* games would consider the provision of social adequacy in their examination of these games, the games' use of forbidden symbols might be considered legal. As noted above, however, the economic damage for the *Wolfenstein* publishers already arises from their products being indexed based on regulations found in the JuSchG.

47 Schumann, 442.

48 59 Neue Juristische Wochenschrift 3052 (Bundesverfassungsgericht March 23, 2006).

49 Tatjana Hörnle, "Verwendung von NS-Symbolen in offenkundig-eindeutig ablehnender Tendenz: StGB § 86a I," *Neue Zeitschrift für Strafrecht* 27, no. 12 (2007): 698–699 with reference to 59 Neue Juristische Wochenschrift 3052 (Bundesverfassungsgericht March 23, 2006); 55 Neue Juristische Wochenschrift 3186 (Bundesgerichtshof July 31, 2002); 28 Entscheidungen des

communicative taboo could make these symbols more powerful.[50] Secondly, a taboo at the same time could hinder political enlightenment, as the public may assume that the respective anti-constitutional movements would not exist if they were rendered invisible.[51]

In non-confiscated versions of *Wolfenstein* games, unconstitutional symbols were removed (e.g. the English language SNES version of *Wolfenstein 3D*, or the German language version of *Return to Castle Wolfenstein*).[52] Nonetheless, most of these versions were indexed. The main remaining reason for their indexing was apparently an excessive display of violence. Considering that a large part of the *Wolfenstein* games' appeal to their audiences involves occupying the "exploitation" genre, violence has only been reduced in a single instalment of the series, the SNES version of *Wolfenstein 3D*. This version does not show any blood. Skeletons of dead prisoners visible in the original PC version were removed from the SNES version. However, the SNES version was indexed in Germany through the same legal announcement as the original version of *Wolfenstein 3D*.[53] As the SNES version is a global, English language version, and not a localized German version, it can be assumed that the producers aimed to create a version fitting to the more family-friendly branding of Nintendo.[54] The filtering in the SNES version also goes far beyond removing NS symbols whose display is forbidden under German law. All references to the Second World War are likewise removed or veiled through wordplay.

This raises the question of whether publishers are solely motivated by avoiding indexing or confiscation when filtering *Wolfenstein* video games. Considering the filtering of *Wolfenstein* video games as motivated by German legislation, this leaves in play only those laws of the criminal code that pertain to media content, in this case two legal provisions on depictions of

Bundesgerichtshofes in Strafsachen 394 (Bundesgerichtshof April 25, 1979); cf. Tatjana Hörnle, *Grob anstößiges Verhalten: Strafrechtlicher Schutz von Moral, Gefühlen und Tabus*, Juristische Abhandlungen 46 (Frankfurt am Main: Klostermann, 2005), 276–281.

50 Hörnle, "Verwendung von NS-Symbolen," 698–699; Fischer et al., *Strafgesetzbuch und Nebengesetze*, 779, § 86a, no. 2 b.

51 Hörnle, "Verwendung von NS-Symbolen," 698–699. In August 2018, the USK however changed its legal opinion and takes the provision of social adequacy into account when rating the use of unconstitutional symbols in video games.

52 Inc. id Software, *Wolfenstein 3D* (Imagineer Co., Limited, 1993); Gray Matter Interactive Studios, Inc. et al., *Return to Castle Wolfenstein* (Activision Deutschland GmbH, 2001).

53 *Bundesanzeiger*, no. 20 (1994).

54 For a reproduction of the guidelines, see Schwartz and Schwartz, *Parent's Guide to Video Games*, 21–24.

violence and on NS propaganda.[55] Only *Wolfenstein* (2009) was confiscated on the grounds of depictions of violence,[56] and no attempts at reducing violence for German versions were made.[57] While none of the games were prosecuted on the grounds of NS propaganda,[58] the following analysis of the content of "sanitized" *Wolfenstein* games intended for the German market indicates that it is, nonetheless, this prosecution on the grounds of NS propaganda that the video game publishers tried to avoid.[59]

The Second World War in non-filtered *Wolfenstein* versions

In order to better illustrate the impact of filtering on the image of the Second World War and National Socialism that the *Wolfenstein* series conveys, this section presents an overview of the unfiltered versions, and their mythologization of Nazi Germany and National Socialist rule.

In the *Wolfenstein* games examined here, a morbid fascination with occultism in German National Socialism is amalgamated in the plot with known conspiracy theories. Through a supposedly strong sense of occult influences on political leaders, Nazi Germany is mystified and indirectly glorified.[60] The video games' plots are loosely connected to historiographical discourses about the Second World War. Only *Wolfenstein: The New Order* directly references the Holocaust, but in an alternate-history context.[61] The narrative horizon of the *Wolfenstein* series – except for *Wolfenstein: The New Order* – thus only encompasses elements that can readily be used for entertainment purposes.

The combination of historical and counterfactual references has a dissimulating effect, blurring out the worst crimes against humanity committed by Nazi Germany. The first-person shooter genre's concept of individual

55 *German Criminal Code*, §§ 131 and 130, respectively.

56 Ibid., § 131.

57 The German version of *Return to Castle Wolfenstein* is unfiltered in its display of violence and was originally rated "16" by the USK, but afterwards indexed by the BPjM regardless ("Return to Castle Wolfenstein," accessed January 2, 2017, www.schnittberichte.com/schnittbericht.php?ID=4120).

58 *German Criminal Code*, 130.

59 Ibid., § 86a; E.g. Kogel, "Wolfenstein: The New Order – Interview mit Bethesda"; Schumann, "Ist die Ausfuhr von Computerspielen mit NS-Symbolen strafbar?"; Hörnle, "Verwendung von NS-Symbolen."

60 Cf. René Freund, *Braune Magie? Okkultismus, New Age und Nationalsozialismus*, 2nd ed. (Wien: Picus, 1995), 87 and 10.

61 Bethesda Game Studios et al., *Wolfenstein: The New Order* (Bethesda Softworks, L.L.C., 2014).

historical agency combined with many fantastic, occult, and counterfactual elements furthermore leads to a mythologization of Nazi Germany and the Holocaust detached from factual history.

This mythologization enables the player to fight for transcendent good against a fantastic, nearly almighty evil. The game thus casts the Second World War as "a romantic throwback to the days when good triumphed over evil,"[62] an evil that does not lie in the cultural "We," but rather in the fantastic "Other." Nazism is thus understood as something transcendent and external that cannot be rooted in a Western society, but instead takes a sort of demonic possession of it.[63]

The depictions of Nazi Germany in the *Wolfenstein* games are meaningful, since they result from a constructive selection process regarding the knowledge of Nazi Germany and the Second World War available to developers. In this construction process, the ontological status of historical facts and conspiracy theories is not relevant in itself. It is the resulting construction of the past that the *Wolfenstein* games as media carriers offer that is relevant.[64] These constructions are a part of popular culture which constitutes "a site of mass schooling."[65] This "mass schooling" probably reaches further than the official construction of the past usually analyzed in cultural memory studies.

But what is this past that the *Wolfenstein* games construct? In *Wolfenstein 3D*, only allusions to Nazi Germany's war crimes and crimes against humanity can be found.[66] Most levels feature skeletons hanging from the ceilings in some of the game rooms, which might allude to the starvation or general fate of concentration camp prisoners. In episode 2 of the game, the player has to eliminate Dr. Schabbs, who creates undead Nazi warriors wearing guns in their chests. This mission might refer to the pseudo-scientific medical experiments performed on humans in Nazi Germany's concentration camps with Dr. Schabbs perhaps alluding to Dr. Mengele. Further examples of occultism and counterfactual history abound in the *Wolfenstein* games.

While the SS stands as representative of the Nazis' evil works in *Return to Castle Wolfenstein*, it is the first *Wolfenstein* game to make a clear distinction between "Nazis" and "Germans" by introducing the historical resistance

62 cf. Hayton, "Digital Nazis," 208: "The defining aspect of FPS gameplay (history) is the narration of war as Manichean confrontation between a moral order of good threatened by evil."

63 Kingsepp, "Hitler as Our Devil?" 37; cf. Hayton, "Digital Nazis," 208.

64 cf. Assmann, *Der lange Schatten der Vergangenheit*, 40.

65 Hayton, "Digital Nazis," 200.

66 Inc. id Software, *Wolfenstein 3D* (Apogee Software, Limited, 1992).

group of the Kreisau Circle to the game. Hayton argues that this constellation resembles the historical and apologetic self-image of Germany as having been a victim of Nazi rule, rather than the broader German population having supported or acquiesced to National Socialism.[67] However, one would need to assume that the resistance group represents the broader German population in this game in order to affirm a Nazis/Germans binary. Since the game also features neutral civilian characters, the constellation "Nazis" vs. "German resistance" is not absolute, and symbolic room is left for "acquiescing Germans." In *Wolfenstein* (2009),[68] however, the Kreisau Circle becomes a popular mass movement,[69] something which more clearly transports an idea similar to the historical, apologetic self-image of Germany as having been a victim of Nazi rule.[70]

The connection of Nazi Germany with occult and fictional science is again the driving force of the plot in *Wolfenstein* (2009).[71] As a new element of the narrated world, the historical Thule society is introduced. The video game's Thule society is on a quest for a mystic, Aryan controlled energy source, the "Black Sun," which they find in a parallel dimension. This energy source is reminiscent of the historical occultist belief in a "Black Sun" as a source of occult power and "Vril" as a conceptualization of this occult power. While these beliefs existed in minor occult groups in 1930s Germany,[72] they have only been popularized in conspiracy theory and Neo-Nazi esotericism since the 1960s.[73] This popularization started in 1960 with the book *Le matin des magiciens* by Louis Pauwels and Jacques Bergier, in which they claimed that the NS elite had tried to ally itself with supernatural forces.[74] Neo-Nazi groups in Europe still draw on these phantasms in justifying Nazism as an occult battle of the forces of good (here: the Nazis) against evil. This conspiracy theory is a key feature of the *Wolfenstein* games from *Wolfenstein 3D* to *Wolfenstein* (2009), with the only alteration being that Nazis are the elemental evil and the Allies an elemental good.

67 Hayton, "Digital Nazis," 209.

68 Inc. Raven Software et al., *Wolfenstein* (Activision Publishing, Inc., 2009).

69 Hayton, "Digital Nazis," 209.

70 Robert Moeller, "Germans as Victims? Thoughts on a Post-Cold War History of World war II's Legacies," *History and Memory* 17, no. 1 (2005): 161.

71 Raven Software et al., *Wolfenstein*.

72 Nicholas Goodrick-Clarke, *Black Sun: Aryan Cults, Esoteric Nazism and the Politics of Identity* (New York: New York University Press, 2001), 166.

73 Julian Strube, "Die Erfindung des esoterischen Nationalsozialismus im Zeichen der Schwarzen Sonne," *Zeitschrift für Religionswissenschaft* 20, no. 2 (2012): 224.

74 Pauwels, Louis and Jacques Bergier, *Le matin des magiciens: Introduction au réalisme fantastique* (Paris: Gallimard, 1960).

As a further development, the plot of *Wolfenstein: The New Order* clearly enters the realm of alternate history.[75] The first part of the game is set in 1946 where the allied forces are fighting a losing battle against Nazi Germany. The main, second part of the game is set in 1960, where Nazis have taken over the world, and even *The Beatles* are forced to translate their name and lyrics into German, performing as *Die Käfer*. The game can be seen as part of the recent Nazisploitation trend, similar to the crowd-funded Finnish movie *Iron Sky* (2012), in which Nazis hide on the moon after fleeing Earth on the (fictional) *Reichsflugscheiben*.

Wolfenstein: The New Order is the first *Wolfenstein* game to explicitly reference the Holocaust. In Chapter 8 of the game, the player's avatar awakens in the incinerator of an extermination camp named "Camp Belica." This camp is considered to refer to the historical extermination camp Jasenovac by the online community.[76] The game is also the first in the series to mention Jews as part of its narrated world, in the form of a secret society of scientists, Da'at Yichud, whose work has been stolen by Nazis, enabling the Nazis to win the war.[77] In contrast to earlier installments, *Wolfenstein: The New Order* hardly draws on magic in a strict sense, although an occult feature is present in the shape of said secret society. These aspects do return, however, in its prequel *Wolfenstein: The Old Blood*.[78]

Narrative filtering of *Wolfenstein* Games in Germany

Only a part of the filtering of the German versions of the *Wolfenstein* games, as well as the games intended for broader audiences (i.e. the *Wolfenstein 3D* SNES version and the *Wolfenstein RPG*), pertains to NS symbols forbidden in Germany.[79] The filtering process that the *Wolfenstein* games undergo concentrates on camouflaging references to Nazi Germany and the Holocaust,

75 Bethesda Game Studios et al., *Wolfenstein: The New Order*.

76 "Camp Belica." In *Wolfenstein Wiki*, accessed January 2, 2017, wolfenstein.wikia.com/wiki/Camp_Belica.

77 cf. Hayton, "Digital Nazis," 207.

78 MachineGames, Kjell, L.L.C. Brandracket, A.B. Doctor Entertainment, Dynamedion Sounddesign, Game Audio Australia, Inc. id Software, Motion Grinder, and Soundworks. *Wolfenstein: The Old Blood*. Bethesda Softworks, L.L.C., 2015.

79 The Austrian website *Schnittberichte.com* ("reports on editing") includes an extensive documentation of all the edits done in the *Wolfenstein* series, "Wolfenstein 3D," accessed January 2, 2017, www.schnittberichte.com/schnittbericht.php?ID=3597; Wurm, "Return to Castle Wolfenstein"; see "Wolfenstein," accessed January 2, 2017, www.schnittberichte.com/schnittbericht.php?ID=5982811; "Wolfenstein: The New Order," accessed January 2, 2017, www.

although German legislation of course does not prohibit references to the Holocaust, only its belittlement.[80] In the filtered versions, all references to Nazi Germany are obfuscated, but remain easily decodable by the average player. These thinly veiled references grant Nazism the aura of a taboo, and amplify the mythologization of Nazism and the Second World War.

In the SNES version of *Wolfenstein 3D*, for example, references to the Second World War are camouflaged by translations into English or are rephrased in non-idiomatic German.[81] For example, "Hitler" in the original is replaced by "Staatmeister," which should read "Staatsmeister" in Standard German and translates into "master of state." The term "Master State" replaces the "The Third Reich" in the original version of *Wolfenstein 3D*, and the original version's "The Reichstag" is consequently changed to "The legendary Master State Keep Wolfenstein." The term obviously refers to the Nazi master race ideology. The same strategy can be found in the German versions of *Return to Castle Wolfenstein* and *Wolfenstein* (2009).[82] In the *Wolfenstein RPG*, anything that could be read as a vague reference to Nazi crimes has been removed, although the game was not released in Germany. This hints at the felt necessity for a filtering process that is not necessarily limited to the German market's restrictions. It shows the selectivity in the process of constructing "sanitized" pictures of Nazis as an abstract, elemental Evil fit for a global entertainment market.

In the German version of *Wolfenstein: The New Order*, references to historical extermination camps have been removed, as are references to Jews (see Table 9.1). Instead, Jews are referred to as "persecuted citizens." Explicit references to Adolf Hitler or his wife Eva Braun are likewise filtered. "The Reich" is changed to "Germania," which, interestingly, allows for a direct connection between the filtered version's "Regime" and historical Nazi Germany. The filtering process in this installment results in the most direct tabooing of National Socialism and the war crimes committed by

schnittberichte.com/schnittbericht.php?ID=363269; "Wolfenstein: The Old Blood," accessed January 2, 2017, www.schnittberichte.com/schnittbericht.php?ID=309507.

80 StGB, § 130.

81 Cf. Wurm, "Wolfenstein 3D."

82 Gray Matter Interactive Studios, Inc. et al., *Return to Castle Wolfenstein*; Inc. Raven Software et al., *Wolfenstein* (Activision Blizzard Deutschland GmbH, 2009). References to Nazi Germany in the filtered versions are superficially camouflaged, e.g. by calling Nazis "the Wolves." The Kreisau circle is not camouflaged in the German version of *Return to Castle Wolfenstein*. The dichotomy between "Allies" (*Alliierte*) and "the Axis (*die Achsenmächte*) in the translation is in itself sufficient to identify the enemy characters as Nazis – especially since the architecture, civilian clothing, and even the enemy characters' uniforms remain unchanged apart from the removal of forbidden symbols.

Nazi Germany, countering the broader and more serious handling of the matter in the video game, which is given a darker mood than previous installments.

Table 9.1 Changes to appellations from the US version to the German version of *Wolfenstein: The New Order*[83]

US Version	German Version	Translation of the German Term
The Nazis	Das Regime	"The Regime"
Nazis	Feinde, Schergen des Regimes etc.	"Enemies," "henchmen of the regime," etc.
Kreisau	Wiesenau	Proper noun
Jewish citizens	Verfolgte Bürger	"Persecuted citizens"
Hitler	Das Staatsoberhaupt	"The head of state"
Eva's hammer	Hammerfaust	"Hammerfist"
The Reich	Germanien	"Germania"
Belica	Selo	Proper noun
Auschwitz	[missing]	
Buchenwald	[missing]	

Consequences of narrative filtering

The many fantastic and counterfactual elements of the *Wolfenstein* games construct a fictional image of Nazi Germany as ruled by supernatural forces rooted in the occult (*Wolfenstein 3D, Spear of Destiny, Return to Castle Wolfenstein*) and biblical mythology (*Spear of Destiny*), combining these with references to conspiracy theories such as Hitler doppelgangers (*Wolfenstein 3D, Spear of Destiny, Wolfenstein* [2009]). The amalgamation of the counterfactual with the fantastic and an etiological narrative structure that individualizes historical agency results in a problematic mythologization of National Socialism in the *Wolfenstein* series.

The series' historically accurate elements and the meticulous design of its Second World War backdrop serve as factuality signals for the plot's legitimacy. The narrative filtering of forbidden symbols results in camouflage through the self-filtering process of "sanitization." This camouflage adds to the already extant mythologization of Nazi Germany in the *Wolfenstein* series by turning the signification process surrounding Nazi Germany into

83 Cf. Wurm, "Wolfenstein: The New Order."

an easily solved riddle. This camouflage, coupled with the above-named dissimulation through selective references to Nazi crimes and the Holocaust, results in a product centered on entertainment rather than education. Perhaps surprisingly, only the unfiltered version of *Wolfenstein: The New Order* could be regarded as an exception to this trend. In general, however, camouflage and dissimulation amplify the mythologization of Nazi Germany.

This camouflaging and dissimulation of references to National Socialism in the filtered versions have been triggered by a restrictive application of the law prohibiting the use of forbidden symbols in Germany.[84] Paradoxically, this result can be argued not to serve the law's intention by granting National Socialism the aura of something obscure and tabooed, rather than by preventing NS propaganda.[85]

However, the resulting amplified mythologization is closely related to a punishable communicative intention in media products containing references to Nazi Germany, captioned "Incitement to hatred" in the *German Criminal Code*:

> Whosoever publicly or in a meeting *disturbs the public peace in a manner that violates the dignity of the victims by* approving of, *glorifying*, or justifying *National Socialist rule of arbitrary force* shall be liable to imprisonment not exceeding three years or a fine.[86]

Legal commentary further characterizes what is meant by glorification of Nazi rule: "glorification" in the legal sense is, among other things, understood as depicting Nazi rule "as something great, impressive, or heroic," or as "highly valuing principal actors or symbolic figures of the NS regime by emphasizing them in a special way."[87] *Wolfenstein: The New Order* depicts Nazi world domination, including hallmarks such as the establishment of a permanent lunar base. This depiction of Nazism might fall under this prohibition. Indeed, this could explain the very thorough filtering process

84 Cf. Schumann, "Ist die Ausfuhr von Computerspielen mit NS-Symbolen strafbar?."

85 Cf. Hörnle, "Verwendung von NS-Symbolen," 698–699; Hörnle, *Grob anstößiges Verhalten*, 276–281; Fischer et al., *Strafgesetzbuch und Nebengesetze*, 779, § 86a, no. 2b.

86 *German Criminal Code*, § 130, paragraph 4, own emphases.

87 "[…] als etwas Großartiges, Imponierendes oder Heldenhaftes […] oder in der Schilderung der Unrechtshandlungen und ihrer Verantwortungsträger entsprechende positive Wertakzente setzt […] z.B. dadurch […], dass ein Verantwortungsträger oder eine Symbolfigur des NS-Regimes angepriesen oder in besonderer Weise hervorgehoben wird" (Georg Bauer et al., eds., *Strafgesetzbuch: Leipziger Kommentar*, 12., neubearbeitete Auflage, 14 vols. (Berlin: de Gruyter, 2007), 503, paragraph 116, my translation). While paragraph 6 of this article introduces the provision of social adequacy to this law, this provision has not yet been applied to video games.

that this game underwent, even if the reference to "Germania" remains a critical lapse in this context that can only be accredited to a mistake on the makers' part. In the other installments of the *Wolfenstein* series, heroicization can only be traced in the mythologizing depiction of the Nazis and the function of computer game characters depicted as Nazi leaders. These especially powerful "bosses" are hard to overcome. As a result, it is justified to state that the *Wolfenstein* games emphasize "principal actors" (i.e. historical and fictitious Nazi leaders) by depicting them as antagonists that are more powerful than "regular" game characters.

The provision "incitement to hatred" might constitute the legal reason for the "sanitization" of the *Wolfenstein* games beyond the removal of symbols forbidden in Germany. That the legal framework is highly relevant for the production company is often stated in interviews with the gaming press.[88] This is also underlined by a disclaimer shown on one of the start screens of *Wolfenstein: The New Order* that states:

> *Wolfenstein®: The New Order* is a fictional story set in an alternate universe in the 1960s. Names, characters, organizations, locations and events are either imaginary or depicted in a fictionalized manner. The story and contents of this game are not intended to and should not be construed in any way to condone, glorify or endorse the beliefs, ideologies, events, actions, persons or behavior of the Nazi regime or to trivialize its war crimes, genocide and other crimes against humanity.[89]

That the camouflage resulting from "sanitization" might amplify mythologization is also implied in the developer's statement. This statement can be read as demonstrating awareness of the complex and often-unforeseen effects of legal regulation, underlining the argument that Fischer et al. make about the tabooing of forbidden symbols. They argue that such tabooing hinders a rational argument against NS ideology:

> A tabooing of symbols – abstracted from the communicative and performative context of their use – can hardly be considered legitimate in a society whose legitimacy derives from the *formal openness* of its communication. Such a tabooing carries the threat that a *demonization* of the totalitarian regime's symbols would mirror the regime's absurd

88 E.g. Kogel, "Wolfenstein: The New Order – Interview mit Bethesda."
89 The disclaimer is shown on the screen in several languages. The German version is not sanitized of direct references to the Nazi regime, and is faithful to the disclaimer's English text.

> overestimation of its symbols without allowing for a debate of its content other than in the form of a prescribed disgust. A substantial debate is thus prevented rather than facilitated. Since tabooed symbols do not become obsolete, their provocative power is preserved permanently by being pushed away into the realm of secret rituals. In reality, this problem is solely relevant with regard to *symbols of National Socialism*.[90]

Admittedly, the *Wolfenstein* games partially draw their success from sensational references to Nazi Germany. As I have shown, the "sanitization" of forbidden symbols used in the filtered versions, however, only amplifies this sensationalism, and will not keep any significant portion of *Wolfenstein* players from recognizing the original references. As legal commentary has underlined, it is precisely this content that needs to be further debated and discussed educationally. In this case, German legislation lags behind the challenges of transculturation in the shape of media's abilities to adapt to environmental constraints (as discussed in Regina Schober's article in this volume), such as the situation of the German market.

Works Cited

Bundesanzeiger, no. 10 (2013).
Bundesanzeiger, no. 20 (1994).
Bundesanzeiger, no. 41 (2002).
Bundesanzeiger, no. 60 (2010).
Bundesanzeiger, no. 62 (1999).
Bundesanzeiger, no. 66 (2010).
Bundesanzeiger, no. 97 (1987).
Bundesanzeiger, no. 99 (2007).
Bundesanzeiger, no. 164 (2009).

90 "Eine vom Äußerungs- und Handlungskontext abstrahierende Tabuisierung von Zeichen oder Worten kann unter den Bedingungen einer Gesellschaft kaum als legitim gelten, die Legitimität gerade auch aus der *formalen Offenheit* der Kommunikation gewinnt. Sie begründet die Gefahr, dass eine *Dämonisierung* von Symbolen des Totalitarismus dessen absurde Überbewertung solcher Zeichen gleichsam spiegelt, ohne eine inhaltliche Auseinandersetzung anders als in vorgegebenen Formen des Abscheus zuzulassen. Dadurch wird eine inhaltliche Auseinandersetzung eher verhindert als erleichtert, da sich tabuisierte Symbole nicht kommunikativ abnutzen, ihre Provokationskraft wird dauerhaft erhalten, indem sie in einen irrationalen Bereich geheimer Rituale abgedrängt wird. In der Praxis bedeutsam ist diese Problematik allein im Hinblick auf *NS-Kennzeichen*" (Fischer et al., *Strafgesetzbuch und Nebengesetze*, 779, § 86a, no. 2b, emphases in original, my translation).

Bundesanzeiger, no. 198 (2009).

Bundesanzeiger, no. 224 (2003).

Bundesanzeiger, no. 227 (2004).

AG Berlin Tiergarten, December 7, 1994.

JurionRS 45327. AG Detmold, January 19, 2010.

AG München, January 25, 1994.

Assmann, Aleida. *Der lange Schatten der Vergangenheit: Erinnerungskultur und Geschichtspolitik*. München: Beck, 2006.

Bauer, Georg, Duscha Gmel, Annette Kuschel, Heinrich W. Laufhütte, Wilhelm Schmidt, and Friedrich-Christian Schroeder, eds. *Strafgesetzbuch: Leipziger Kommentar*. 12th ed. 14 vols. Berlin: de Gruyter, 2007.

Bethesda Game Studios, Dynamedion Sounddesign, Game Audio Australia, id Software, Inc., Just Cause Productions, Inc., RAD Game Tools, Inc., and Torus GmbH. *Wolfenstein: The New Order*. Bethesda Softworks, L.L.C., 2014.

28 Entscheidungen des Bundesgerichtshofes in Strafsachen 394. *Bundesgerichtshof*, April 25, 1979.

55 Neue Juristische Wochenschrift 3186. *Bundesgerichtshof*, July 31, 2002.

59 Neue Juristische Wochenschrift 3052. *Bundesverfassungsgericht*, March 23, 2006.

"Camp Belica." In *Wolfenstein Wiki*. Accessed January 2, 2017. wolfenstein.wikia.com/wiki/Camp_Belica.

Edmonds, Don. *Ilsa: She-Wolf of the SS*. 1974.

Evers, Florian. *Vexierbilder des Holocaust: Ein Versuch zum historischen Trauma in der Populärkultur*. Populäre Kultur und Medien 4. Berlin: Lit, 2011.

Protection of Young Persons Act. JuSchG. Federal Ministry of Family Affairs, Senior Citizens, Women and Youth. Accessed July 11, 2013. www.bmfsfj.de/RedaktionBMFSFJ/Abteilung5/Pdf-Anlagen/juSchGenglisch,property=pdf,bereich=bmfsfj,rwb=true.pdf.

German Criminal Code. StGB. Federal Ministry of Justice. 2013. Accessed July 11, 2013. www.gesetze-im-internet.de/englisch_stgb/.

Basic Law. GG. Federal Ministry of Justice. 2014. Accessed March 25, 2015. www.gesetze-im-internet.de/englisch_gg/.

Fischer, Thomas, Herbert Tröndle, Eduard Dreher, and Otto G. Schwarz. *Strafgesetzbuch und Nebengesetze*. 58th ed. Beck'sche Kurz-Kommentare 10. München: Beck, 2011.

Freund, René. *Braune Magie? Okkultismus, New Age und Nationalsozialismus*. 2nd ed. Wien: Picus, 1995.

Goodrick-Clarke, Nicholas. *Black Sun: Aryan Cults, Esoteric Nazism and the Politics of Identity*. New York: New York University Press, 2001.

Gray Matter Interactive Studios, Inc., Atlantis Group, Blur Studio, Inc., Even Balance, Inc., id Software, Inc., Nerve Software, L.L.C., and Soundelux Design Music Group. *Return to Castle Wolfenstein*. Activision UK, Limited, 2001.

—. *Return to Castle Wolfenstein*. Activision Deutschland GmbH, 2001.

Hayton, Jeff. "Digital Nazis: Genre, History and the Displacement of Evil in First-Person Shooters." In *Nazisploitation!: The Nazi Image in Low-Brow Cinema and Culture*, edited by Daniel H. Magilow, Elizabeth Bridges, and Vander Lugt, Kristin T., 199–218. New York: Continuum, 2012.

Hörnle, Tatjana. *Grob anstößiges Verhalten: Strafrechtlicher Schutz von Moral, Gefühlen und Tabus*. Juristische Abhandlungen 46. Frankfurt am Main: Klostermann, 2005.

—. "Verwendung von NS-Symbolen in offenkundig-eindeutig ablehnender Tendenz: StGB § 86a I." *Neue Zeitschrift für Strafrecht* 27, no. 12 (2007): 698–699.

Höynck, Theresia, and Christian Pfeiffer. "Verbot von 'Killerspielen'? Thesen und Vorschläge zur Verbesserung des Jugendmedienschutzes." *Zeitschrift für Rechtspolitik* 40, no. 3 (2007): 91–94.

id Mobile. *Wolfenstein RPG*. Apple, Inc., 2009.

id Software, Inc. *Spear of Destiny*. FormGen Corp., 1992.

—. *Wolfenstein 3D*. Apogee Software, Limited, 1992.

—. *Wolfenstein 3D*. Imagineer Co., Limited, 1993.

—. *Wolfenstein 3d*. Atari Corp., 1994.

id Software, Inc., and Stalker Entertainment. *Wolfenstein 3D*. BAM! Entertainment, Inc., 2002.

Johnston, Joe. *Captain America*. 2011.

Kauert, Michael. "Computerrecht – Computerspiele." In *Medienrecht: Praxishandbuch*. Vol. 2, edited by Artur-Axel Wandtke and Claudia Ohst. 3rd ed. 5 vols., 521–573. Berlin, Boston: de Gruyter, 2014.

Kingsepp, Eva. "Hitler as Our Devil? Nazi Germany in Mainstream Media." In *Monsters in the Mirror: Representations of Nazism in Post-War Popular Culture*, edited by Sara Buttsworth and Maartje M. Abbenhuis, 29–52. Santa Barbara, CA: Praeger, 2010.

Kogel, Dennis. "Wolfenstein: The New Order – Interview mit Bethesda: Warum die deutsche Version anders ist." *GameStar*, May 10, 2014. Accessed January 20, 2017. www.gamestar.de/spiele/wolfenstein-the-new-order/artikel/wolfenstein_the_new_order,49503,3055635.html%20viewed%202015-04-29.

Köhne, Michael. "Kennzeichen verfassungswidriger Organisationen in Computerspielen." *Deutsche Richterzeitung* 81 (2003): 210–213.

Liesching, Marc. "Hakenkreuze in Film, Fernsehen und Computerspielen: Verwendung verfassungsfeindlicher Kennzeichen in Unterhaltungsmedien." *Multimedia und Recht* 13, no. 5 (2010): 309–313.

MachineGames, Kjell, Brandracket, L.L.C., Doctor Entertainment, A.B., Dynamedion Sounddesign, Game Audio Australia, id Software, Inc., Motion Grinder, and Soundworks. *Wolfenstein: The Old Blood.* Bethesda Softworks, L.L.C., 2015.

Moeller, Robert. "Germans as Victims? Thoughts on a Post-Cold War History of World war II's Legacies." *History and Memory* 17, no. 1 (2005): 147–194.

Muse Software. *Castle Wolfenstein.* Muse Software, 1981.

—. *Beyond Castle Wolfenstein.* Muse Software, 1984.

Nerve Software, L.L.C., Atlantis Group, Blur Studio, Inc., id Software, Inc., Mad Doc Software, L.L.C., Mondo Media, Inc., RAD Game Tools, Inc., Soundelux Design Music Group, Splash Damage, Ltd., andThreewave Software, Inc.. *Return to Castle Wolfenstein: Tides of War.* Activision Publishing, Inc.

Nolte, Lasse. *Der Goldene Nazivampir von Absam 2. Das Geheimnis von Schloß Kottlitz.* 2007.

19 Neue Zeitschrift für Strafrecht 356. OLG Frankfurt am Main, March 18, 1998.

Pauwels, Louis, and Jacques Bergier. *Le matin des magiciens: Introduction au réalisme fantastique.* Paris: Gallimard, 1960.

Raster Productions, L.L.C. *Return to Castle Wolfenstein: Operation Resurrection.* Activision Publishing, Inc., 2003.

Raven Software, Inc., Activision Publishing, Blur Studio, Inc., DemonWare, Ltd., Endrant Studios, Ltd., Even Balance, Inc., Havok Physics, Inc. et al. *Wolfenstein.* Activision Pty., Limited, 2009.

—. *Wolfenstein.* Activision Publishing, Inc., 2009.

—. *Wolfenstein.* Activision Blizzard Deutschland GmbH, 2009.

—. *Wolfenstein.* Activision Korea, 2009.

—. *Wolfenstein.* Activision UK, Limited, 2009.

—. *Wolfenstein.* Activision Blizzard Deutschland GmbH, 2014.

Renner, Karl N. "Erzählen im Zeitalter der Medienkonvergenz." In *Medien – Erzählen – Gesellschaft: Transmediales Erzählen im Zeitalter der Medienkonvergenz,* edited by Karl N. Renner, Dagmar von Hoff and Matthias Krings, 1–16. Media Convergence/Medienkonvergenz 2. Berlin: de Gruyter, 2013.

Schumann, Antje. "Ist die Ausfuhr von Computerspielen mit NS-Symbolen strafbar? Bemerkungen zu § 86a Abs. 1 Nr. 2 StGB." *Multimedia und Recht* 14, no. 7 (2011): 440–443.

Schwartz, Steven A., and Janet Schwartz. *Parent's Guide to Video Games.* Rocklin, CA: Prima, 1994.

Spielberg, Steven. *Raiders of the Lost Ark.* 1981.

—. *Indiana Jones and the Last Crusade.* 1989.

—. *Schindler's List.* 1993.

Strube, Julian. "Die Erfindung des esoterischen Nationalsozialismus im Zeichen der Schwarzen Sonne." *Zeitschrift für Religionswissenschaft* 20, no. 2 (2012): 223–268.

Inglourious Basterds. Dir. Quentin Tarantino. The Weinstein Company, 2009.
Wurm, Gerald. "Return to Castle Wolfenstein." Accessed January 2, 2017. www.schnittberichte.com/schnittbericht.php?ID=4120.
—. "Wolfenstein." Accessed January 2, 2017. www.schnittberichte.com/schnittbericht.php?ID=5982811.
—. "Wolfenstein 3D." Accessed January 2, 2017. www.schnittberichte.com/schnittbericht.php?ID=3597.
—. "Wolfenstein: The New Order." Accessed January 2, 2017. www.schnittberichte.com/schnittbericht.php?ID=363269.
—. "Wolfenstein: The Old Blood." Accessed January 2, 2017. www.schnittberichte.com/schnittbericht.php?ID=309507.

About the author

Werner Schäfke-Zell is Assistant Professor at the Faculty of Law, University of Copenhagen. He has published on law and literature, including a chapter on the influence of legal systems on the mediality of medieval Icelandic law books, to be published in 2019 in *Distributed Cognition in Medieval and Renaissance Culture*, eds. Miranda Anderson and Michael Wheeler.

Index

For Product Safety Concerns and Information please contact our
EU representative GPSR@taylorandfrancis.com Taylor & Francis
Verlag GmbH, Kaufingerstraße 24, 80331 München, Germany